THE POETICS OF EARLY CHINESE THOUGHT

The Poetics of Early Chinese Thought

HOW THE *SHIJING* SHAPED THE CHINESE
PHILOSOPHICAL TRADITION

Michael Hunter

Columbia University Press
New York

Columbia University Press wishes to express its appreciation for
assistance given by the Chiang Ching-kuo Foundation for International
Scholarly Exchange and Council for Cultural
Affairs in the publication of this book.

Columbia University Press
Publishers Since 1893
New York   Chichester, West Sussex

Copyright © 2021 Columbia University Press
All rights reserved

Library of Congress Cataloging-in-Publication Data
Names: Hunter, Michael, Ph.D., author.
Title: The poetics of early Chinese thought : how the Shijing shaped the Chinese
philosophical tradition / Michael Hunter.
Description: New York : Columbia University Press, [2021] | Includes bibliographical
references and index.
Identifiers: LCCN 2020051488 (print) | LCCN 2020051489 (ebook) | ISBN 9780231201223
(hardback ; acid-free paper) | ISBN 9780231201230 (paperback ; acid-free paper) |
ISBN 9780231553995 (ebook)
Subjects: LCSH: Shi jing. | Chinese poetry—To 221 B.C.—History and criticism. | Poetics.
Classification: LCC PL2466.Z7 H86 2021 (print) | LCC PL2466.Z7 (ebook) | DDC 181/.11–dc23

Cover image: Bi Disk, 206 BCE–220 CE, Minneapolis Institute of Art,
Bequest of Alfred E. Pillsbury. Public domain image.

For James and Kieran

CONTENTS

ACKNOWLEDGMENTS   ix

Introduction   1

Chapter One
Reading the *Shi*   17

Chapter Two
A Poetry of Return   35

Chapter Three
Shi Poetics Beyond the *Shi*   83

Chapter Four
The *Shi* and the *Verses of Chu* (*Chuci* 楚辭)   139

Chapter Five
Comparing Canons: The *Shi* Versus the Masters   168

Conclusion
A Classic of N/Odes   189

NOTES   193

BIBLIOGRAPHY   213

INDEX   225

ACKNOWLEDGMENTS

My sincerest thanks to Tina Lu for steering this project in the right direction; to Luke Bender for his critical feedback at every step in its evolution; to Paul North for keeping me (mostly) sane; to Aaron Gerow for his advocacy when it mattered most; to Ed Kamens and Kang-i Sun Chang for their mentorship; to Nick Admussen for being such a dependable sounding board; to Christine Dunbar at Columbia University Press for her enthusiastic and unwavering support; to the team at KnowledgeWorks Global Ltd. for their editing prowess; to the anonymous reviewers who rescued me from many embarrassing mistakes; to Fritz-Heiner Mutschler for inviting me to the Homer's Epics and the Book of Songs conference at Beijing University in 2014, which prompted my reengagement with the *Shijing*; and to the East Asian Studies communities at Princeton, UC Berkeley, UCLA, Vanderbilt, Cornell and the University of British Columbia for their invaluable feedback.

Special thanks to my Princeton advisers Willard Peterson and Martin Kern, whose work on early intellectual typologies and the *Shijing*, respectively, were the dual inspirations for this book.

Finally, thank you to Catherine for making all of this possible and worthwhile.

THE POETICS OF EARLY CHINESE THOUGHT

Introduction

This book argues that *Shi* 詩 poetry, a tradition known primarily through the *Shijing* 詩經 (*Classic of Poetry*), was the most foundational corpus of early Chinese thought. As the most widely learned, memorized, and quoted canonical tradition, the *Shi* (pronounced in Mandarin Chinese like the "shr" of "shrug" but with a high-level tone) was a sine qua non of elite education in the Warring States period (fifth century BCE–221 BCE), that so-called Golden Age of Chinese thought. The *Shi* immersed elites in a world of movement and flow and showed them that wisdom lay in understanding its currents. They cemented the conceit that "virtue" is "power" (*de* 德) and that a good king radiates an inexorable gravity. Without *Shi*, there might not have been a Kongzi 孔子 (Confucius), a Laozi 老子, or a Qu Yuan 屈原. The *Shi* established "The Way" (*dao* 道) as the most emblematic concept in East Asian history. In these and other respects, *Shi* poetry inculcated certain basic patterns of thought and expression in the classical period.

From an ancient perspective, the idea that poetry conveys essential wisdom is unremarkable.[1] However, that isn't the impression one has from the standard model and canon of early Chinese thought in the modern era, which treats the *Shi* as background to a roster of singular thinkers. To the extent that the *Shi* figure in intellectual histories of the period, it's less because of their intrinsic interest than because of the approving statements of Kongzi 孔子 (Confucius; trad. 551–479 BCE) et al. Taking the *Shi* as seriously as early thinkers did isn't simply a matter of expanding or rearranging that canon. It also prompts us to ask why the *Shi* were marginalized in the first place and how the study of Chinese thought might change to accommodate them.

By the word *thought*, I mean human beings' efforts to make sense of the world and their place within it; by *thinkers*, I mean those human beings whose sense-making efforts remain accessible today; by *ideology*, I mean a highly selective vision of the world intended to condition the sense-making of others.[2] These definitions are expansive for a reason. Modern academic institutions carve up human sense-making by medium (e.g., art history), mode (e.g., literature or philosophy), and content (e.g., religion). These categories aren't just anachronistic when applied to peoples who lacked such institutions. For those of us seeking to understand premodern modes of sense-making and thereby expand our own sense of the possibilities of human imagination and culture, they can be actively misleading.

The pigeonholing of the *Shi* as literature but not philosophy is a case in point. In modern disciplinary terms, my argument is that the foundations of one of the world's great philosophical traditions are to be found in a work of literature; put bluntly, students of philosophy should be reading more poetry. A better, less anachronistic description is that the *Shi*, by virtue of their cultural authority, established a common worldview and conceptual vocabulary that conditioned early thinkers' sense-making efforts more than other extant ideologies and systems of thought. If we are to make sense of their efforts, then it behooves us to think about and through the *Shi* as much as they did.

THE *CLASSIC OF POETRY*

What are the *Shi*? The answers are complicated.[3]

In their most canonical form, the *Shi* are the 305 poems of the *Shijing*, an anthology in four divisions and just under 30,000 characters. The first 160 pieces belong to the "Airs of the States" (Guo feng 國風) and are grouped into fifteen subsections named for specific regions in and around the Yellow River Valley and North China Plain. Taken together, these subsections map the domain of the Western Zhou 西周 dynasty (ca. 1045–771 BCE) at its apex. The "Airs" appear to depict life on the lowest rungs of Zhou society. There are songs of love and courtship, happy depictions of various communal activities, and laments of homesick soldiers. The seventy-four poems of the "Lesser Court Songs" (Xiao ya 小雅) take us into the world of Zhou dynasty elites with their banquets, military campaigns, songs of praise for virtuous leaders, and admonishments by (would-be) advisers. The focus of the thirty-one "Greater Court Songs" (Da ya 大雅) is the Zhou royal house and its triumph over the Shang 商 dynasty. Finally, the forty "Ritual Hymns" (Song 頌) are the liturgical relics of sacrificial rites to ancestor spirits and other divinities. Internal references to the fall of the Western Zhou capital in 771 BCE indicate that the collection couldn't have reached its final form before the early part of the Eastern Zhou 東周 period (770–256 BCE) at the earliest.[4]

The *Shijing* is one of the Five Classics (*wu jing* 五經) of ancient China. Along with the *Changes* (*Yi* 易), *Documents* (*Shu* 書), *Annals* (*Chunqiu* 春秋), and *Ritual* (*Li* 禮) classics, it was an integral part of the official, state-sponsored curriculum from the Western Han 西漢 dynasty (202 BCE–9 CE) onward. As the most authoritative repositories of knowledge about the ancient sage-kings, the Five Classics were roadmaps that ruling elites had to master as part of the ongoing quest to bring contemporary governance in line with ancient ideals.

However, answering a question about the *Shi* by talking about the *Shijing* is misleading because the *Shijing* is just one instantiation of an older *Shi* tradition. Also called the *Mao Shi* 毛詩 after the scholar(s) credited with introducing it to the Han dynasty,[5] the received *Shijing* was one of four officially recognized recensions circulating in the early imperial period, and the last to receive imperial sanction. Moreover, the *Mao Shi* is more than an anthology. It includes line-by-line commentary and brief encapsulating prefaces for each poem as well as a "Great Preface" (*Da xu* 大序) to the collection as a whole.

Before its canonization in written form, the *Shi* tradition was a fluid oral repertoire that "didn't depend solely on bamboo and silk" 不獨在竹帛.[6] Sources from the Warring States onward show elites deploying *Shi* in various performative contexts, peppering their speech with *Shi* quotations and allusions, and even using the *Shi* to code and decode messages on diplomatic occasions. *Shi* material in transmitted and excavated sources also reveal a high degree of variability at every level of that repertoire, from individual words and characters to lines, couplets, stanzas, titles, and the organization of entire poems.

If the *Shi* were a fluid repertoire in the preimperial context, then what was *a Shi*? *Shi* quotation practice obscures more than it clarifies on this point. Sometimes *Shi* were cited by title or even stanza. But the most common quotation formula—*Shi yue* 詩曰 or *Shi yun* 詩云—can be translated as "The *Shi* [in the aggregate] say," "A [particular] *Shi* says," or even "[Someone once] uttered a *Shi* [and] said." Did early quoters think of these quotations as loose snippets of *Shi* stuff or as parts of discrete poems? It's hard to say. In any event, the tremendous variability of the *Shi* suggests that we might think of a single poem not as a stable, independently circulating work but as a localized instantiation of the repertoire.[7]

Complicating matters further, the word *shi* 詩 was also a generic label for classical poetry from the early period onward.[8] In early sources, too, we encounter *shi* poems outside the *Shi*. According to legend, it was Kongzi who first selected the 305 canonical *Shi* from a corpus of more than three thousand.[9]

The *Shi* were more than poetry. As Mozi 墨子 (fifth century BCE?) says to one ritually minded interlocutor in a dialogue from the *Mozi* 墨子, "You recite the three-hundred *Shi*, you strum the three-hundred *Shi*, you sing the three-hundred *Shi*, and you dance the three-hundred *Shi*" 誦詩三百, 弦詩三百, 歌詩三百, 舞詩三百 (48.458). In their most fully realized form, the *Shi* were fully embodied, multimedia performances. Text is just the tip of the *Shi* iceberg.

The word *Shi* is hard to translate. "Songs" helpfully emphasizes their performative dimension, except that *Shi* is often contrasted with the usual word for songs (*ge* 歌) in classical Chinese. *Odes* implies a comparison with a particular genre of Western praise poetry and so doesn't capture the heterogeneity of the *Shi* tradition. I refer to *Shi* as poetry or poems throughout this book, but the word *poetry* isn't the best fit either, etymologically speaking. Early Chinese commentators tend to gloss *shi* as *zhi* 志, meaning "intention" or "what is on the mind"; thus, a *Shi* is an expression of a person's inner thoughts and feelings, not something made. English (and Greek and Latin) morphology makes the leap from *poetry* to *poem* to *poet* seem trivial. Not so with *Shi*, which refers either to the act of reciting a *Shi* or to the recited text itself. A *Shi ren* 詩人 (literally *Shi* + "person") isn't a "poet" but "the person or people of the *Shi*," that is, the people who first uttered them and whose thoughts are disclosed therein. "The Verses" isn't a bad choice (so long as we forget that *versus* in Latin is the "turning" of a line of written text): as with *Shi*, one can "versify" and create "verses" without being a "versifier."

Finally, the *Shi* were *the* preeminent canonical tradition of ancient China.[10] As seen in the wealth of quotations, commentaries, and other *Shi*-centric material in both transmitted and excavated sources, they were the one set of texts that educated elites throughout the Central States probably knew in one form or another. They were the literary linchpin of a Zhou ritual system that endured long after the Zhou dynasty's fall from power, and they were the centerpiece of the elite Panhuaxia culture (to borrow Alexander Beecroft's term) of the pre- and early imperial period.[11] The *Shi* tradition was "the common coin of official discourse and the supreme distillation of the very highest expressions of culture," "one of the few available sources upon which elites could build a shared lingua franca accepted across the entire Central States cultural horizon."[12] "It was not merely a particular text used by the classicist tradition; it was the text around which the tradition arranged itself."[13]

If the *Shi* were so important, then we should expect them to have shaped the development of Chinese thought as much as they shaped the literary tradition. However, that isn't how most readers approach the *Shi* today. That is because some of the most prominent answers to the "What are the *Shi*?" question over the last two and half millennia discourage us from taking the *Shi* seriously as artifacts of thought. Their exclusion from the modern canon of classical Chinese philosophy in the early twentieth century is the biggest factor. But even within literary and classical studies (*jing xue* 經學), the ways in which scholars frame the *Shi* sustain an impression that they lack intellectual content, or that we have no way of accessing it. There is a sense in which the thought of the *Shi* has fallen through the cracks of the study of literature and philosophy in at least four respects, as described below.

A Poetry of Disclosure

The most canonical statement on the origins of the *Shi* belongs to the legendary sage-king Shun 舜: "*Shi* tell what is on the mind; singing prolongs the telling" 詩言志，歌永言.[14] Stephen Owen elaborates:

> [I]f we take a text to be a "poem," a "made" text, then it is the object of its maker's will; it is not the person himself but rather something he has

"made" ... If, on the other hand, we take a text to be *shi*, the author's crafting of the text is not essential to what a *shi* "is" ... The writer of *shi* cannot claim the same quality of control over his text that a poet does. As a result the *shi* is not the "object" of its writer; it *is* the writer, the outside of an inside ... In short, this canonical statement on *shi*, an assumption that remained with the form for two and half millenia, assures us that the *shi* is, in some way, what was in the mind of the person.[15]

This is the conceit of immediacy or transparency, the notion of *shi* as crystallized moments of unmediated expression. To quote Michael Fuller, "In the classical Chinese tradition, all poems are true by their very existence; the only questions are *how* they are true and if their truth is of any significance"—hence the prioritization of *Shi* hermeneutics over *Shi* poetics in that tradition.[16]

Why should a king like Shun care about poetry? The answer is that a literature of disclosure served the ancient Chinese state's domestic intelligence-gathering apparatus:

> Feelings of sorrow and joy stir in the heart and are given voice in song. Recited as words, they are called *shi*; drawn out by the voice, they are called "song." Thus, in ancient times there was an office for collecting *shi* for the king to contemplate the prevailing customs, to recognize successes and failures, and to examine and correct himself.
>
> 哀樂之心感，而（哥）〔歌〕詠之聲發。誦其言謂之詩，詠其聲謂之（哥）〔歌〕。故古有采詩之官，王者所以觀風俗，知得失，自考正也。(*Hanshu* 30.1709)

Collecting *shi* allowed rulers to take the temperature of their people, to diagnose what ailed them, and to change their policies accordingly. Their use as a tool of sociopolitical critique is reflected in the prefaces of the Mao commentary, which present *Shi* as artifacts of the moral order at particular moments in the rise and fall of the Zhou 周 dynasty. This framework fit some pieces better than others. The overt panegyrics of the "Greater Court Songs" only had to be summarized, whereas the less overtly political or didactic pieces of the "Airs" had to be allegorized (or, following Pauline Yu, "contextualized").[17] For our purposes, the key point is that this view locates any and all intellectual work outside the poetry within the mind of a "contemplating" (*guan* 觀) and "recognizing" (*zhi* 知) interpreter.

A Poetry of the Folk

The dream of an artifice-free poetry reemerged in the early twentieth century under the influence of Romanticism and modern folklore studies, which sought "the localization of national essence in the poetic language of the folk."[18] In China, the classic at the forefront of that project was the *Shijing*, and the "Airs of the States" in particular, which Gu Jiegang 顧頡剛 (1893–1954) and other advocates of the New Culture Movement (*xin wenhua yundong* 新文化運動) claimed as precedent for a newly revitalized popular culture (*minsu wenhua* 民俗文化).[19] In the words of one scholar, "Our only glimpse of society at the bottom is afforded by the 'Airs of the States,' wherein we find many beautiful, spontaneous, and folksy poems . . . It is our only bible for exploring ancient literature and social problems, particularly women's problems."[20] Before it could fulfill that promise, however, the *Shi* had to be rescued from the excrescent artificialities of traditional elite culture, beginning with the politicized readings of the *Mao Shi* and its successors.[21]

A number of Western sinologists were enthusiastic participants in that project, including Herbert Giles in his 1901 *A History of Chinese Literature*:

> Early commentators, incapable of seeing the simple natural beauties of the poems, . . . and at the same time unable to ignore the deliberate judgment of the Master [=Kongzi], set to work to read into countryside ditties deep moral and political significations . . . Possibly the very introduction of these absurdities may have helped to preserve to our day a work which would otherwise have been considered too trivial to merit the attention of scholars.[22]

Marcel Granet went so far as to banish "[a]ll symbolic interpretations, and likewise any interpretation that supposes a refined technique on the part of the poets."[23] For him, its art was "entirely primitive":

> The odes reveal none of those literary processes which mark the art of the author. Their art is entirely spontaneous. No tricks of language are employed. Metaphor and simile are, one may say, almost entirely wanting. Without

doubt the charm of the poems is due to the combining of simple pictures and of feelings ingenuously expressed, in which there is no suggestion of art; they are apparently not intentional but are the outcome of the facts themselves. *The correspondences between things reappear in the poems* [emphasis in the original].[24]

To quote Haun Saussy, Granet's *Shi* are a "poetry without poems or poets," "a poetry of and for all, executed in preset formulas by speakers who do not know themselves as individuals but only as voices of a collectivity, accurately enacting their predetermined roles."[25] Arthur Waley, whose 1937 *Shijing* translation features prominently in this study, also "discovered [in the *Shijing*] a folk poetry that confirmed modern Western notions of archaic society."[26] Waley's translation is dotted with references to folk literature and the rituals of "contemporary primitives."[27] He also refrained from translating a number of pieces whose overtly elite, didactic tenor didn't fit that framework.[28]

The problem with the folklorists' approach, as Bernhard Karlgren and Gu Jiegang saw, is that "the stanzas in the *Odes* anthology are unquestionably too polished, their rhymes too regular, and their choice of language too elegant and too uniform to represent unedited folk poetry gathered from different dialect regions."[29] Scholars working in the wake of the folklorists have been much more willing to read *Shi* as the products of elite interests.[30] Nevertheless, entwined as it is with the origins of modern academic sinology, and abetted by an implicit contrast with modernist Western poetry and its rejection of "just about everything that makes naïve reading possible," the framing of the *Shi* as simple folk songs persists.[31] When Owen opens his forward to Waley's (reissued) translation with observations on the "direct and honest world [of the *Shi*, which] could probably never have existed in a real human society, but somehow it did exist in poetry," the possibility of reading *Shi* as ideological constructs feels remote.[32]

An Endlessly Mediated Poetry

More recent scholarship has questioned the possibility of reading the *Shi* at all. In a series of studies of *Shi* material in Warring States and Western Han manuscript finds, Martin Kern has argued that reading the "Airs of the States" independently of the Mao commentary or some other frame of reference is impossible because the *Shi* are so profoundly underdetermined from an orthographic and hermeneutic perspective:

> The language of the ["Airs of the States"] is frequently discontinuous, and their capacity to become applied to a wide range of historical situations or philosophical arguments is based on their very nature of being indeterminate, ambiguous, and therefore fundamentally contingent texts that embodied a wide range of latent meanings. By definition, such texts can never be explained out of their own words but only through external reference; in fact, from the mere textual surface, they cannot even be confidently established on the level of the individual word.³³

The variability of the written language was such that a given word in the *Shi* could be written with any number of homophonic characters, as when the character for *island*—州 or *tu in Old Chinese—was used to write the word for *boat* 舟, also pronounced *tu. One implication of this problem is that, prior to the standardization of particular transcriptions and commentaries under the Han, knowing what the sounds of the *Shi* meant—or, for readers, knowing which words the characters actually referred to—likely depended on complementary oral instruction.³⁴ A second consequence is a brutally vicious hermeneutic circle. As Kern shows through a comparative analysis of the base text and commentaries of the *Mao Shi*, the choice of characters was dictated by the transcriber's understanding of the poem as a whole, which was then enshrined in the Mao prefaces and further reinforced by the Mao character glosses:

> While we know that the *Odes* as they circulated in 300 BC were composed of the same—or at least homophonous—words as those of the received Mao tradition, once we eliminate their Mao graphic choices and glosses, we no longer know what these characters and words actually are . . . We cannot reject the [allegorical readings of the] Mao "minor prefaces" while at the same time accepting the words of the Mao text, because this text is not at all in any way "original" or prior to the Mao glosses . . . There are no original *Odes* available to us; all we have are the *Mao Odes*—that is, a text constructed through a particular interpretation.³⁵

Like turtles, interpretations of the *Shi* go all the way down. For Kern, such are the "Socratic pleasures" of studying the *Shi*.[36] So, too, for Haun Saussy, "the *Odes* shorn of their commentaries (the form in which they're usually taught today) make up a 'classic' whose very presence in many centuries of Chinese history is disputable."[37] "[W]e have to be sure of knowing 'what the texts literally mean' apart from the allegorical interpretation. And the difficulty of knowing that (other than by intimate conviction) may be what gives *Odes* scholarship its special charm."[38]

Charming or *pleasurable* is one way to put it; *dispiriting* is another.[39] Before we can read the *Shi* for its ideas, we have to figure out whether we can read "the *Shi*" (as opposed to the *Mao Shi* or another instantiation) at all. That problem is the subject of chapter 1.

Not Philosophy

The main reason why the thought of the *Shi* hasn't been taken seriously has to do with its exclusion from the modern canon of Chinese philosophy. For several decades now, most surveys of the subject have followed a common template:[40] a series of chapters or lesson plans organized around the most important "Masters" (*zhuzi* 諸子) of the Warring States period, typically with Kongzi 孔子 (Confucius; trad. 551–479 BCE) toward the beginning followed by Mozi 墨子, Mengzi 孟子 (Mencius), Xunzi 荀子, Han Feizi 韓非子, Laozi 老子, Zhuangzi 莊子, and so on, in some order. Early Chinese thought is represented as an evolving conversation or debate among thinkers who responded to their predecessors and argued with their contemporaries against the backdrop of the collapse of the Bronze-age aristocratic order of the Zhou dynasty.[41] That story generally ends with the advent of the Qin 秦 (221–206 BCE) and Han 漢 (202 BCE–220 CE) empires, which supposedly stifled the "radiant originality and variety" of the preimperial "Golden" or "Axial Age."[42] I refer to this model as the *Masters Narrative*.

The focus on the Masters as the protagonists of early Chinese thought is a relatively recent historical development—the emergence of Chinese philosophy (*zhexue* 哲學) as a modern academic discipline in the late nineteenth and early twentieth centuries. Faced with an influx of new ideas and technologies from the West, Chinese scholars turned to "Masters studies" (*zhuzi xue* 諸子學) as "a field of learning . . . with the potential to engage and accommodate the new systems of knowledge" while simultaneously "resist[ing] . . . the perceived hegemonic potential of Western philosophy to deprive Chinese philosophy of its emerging self-identity," to quote John Makeham.[43] Those interested in agriculture; astronomy; commerce; diplomacy; engineering; geography; law; mathematics; military studies; optics; and especially logic, that sina qua non of philosophy, all found useful precedents in the Masters. Also fueling this interest was a desire for native antecedents that predated the moribund imperial system.[44] Advocates of the "national learning" (*guoxue* 國學) movement, like Liang Qichao 梁啟超 (1873–1929), upheld the Warring States period as a golden age of intellectual freedom against the "ruler learning" (*junxue* 君學) of empire, thus equating political decentralization with philosophical dynamism.[45] (Karl Jasper's oft-cited "Axial Age" theory promotes the same association.[46]) These currents helped to push the supposedly pre-philosophical, pre–Warring States *Shijing* out of the domain of philosophy and into that of literary studies.

How do the *Shi* figure into the Masters Narrative? Barely. When the *Shi* are discussed, they're typically introduced via the Masters as if Kongzi and friends were responsible for activating their philosophical potential.[47] The value of the *Shi* is often of the pre- or proto- variety. For Benjamin Schwartz, the *Shijing* and *Exalted Documents* (*Shangshu* 尚書) are "limited in scope and content. We might say that they reflect a 'proto-Confucian' outlook, or perhaps more accurately, that they reflect earlier attitudes with which Confucius and his disciples strongly identified."[48] Edward Slingerland prefaces an illuminating discussion of the notion of "non-action" or "effortless efficacy" (*wu wei* 無為) in the *Shijing* and *Exalted Documents* by labeling them sources of the "religious thought" of the "pre-Confucian tradition": "These texts are relatively vague and not nearly as conceptually developed as 'writings of the masters.' "[49]

At its core, the Masters Narrative is a historical argument about the thinkers and ideas that mattered in ancient China and a disciplinary argument about what should matter to us. On both counts, the *Shi* fall short. If *philosophy* is defined as "self-conscious reflection upon, modification, and defense of one's views," and if philosophy in China "begins with the debate between Kongzi and Mozi" in the early Warring States period, then the *Shi* are pre-philosophical texts; in other words, their authors didn't contribute to the debates that made the Warring States scene so vibrant.[50] Hu Shih

胡適 (1891–1962) was at least willing to contemplate the possibility that "it was the poets [of the *Shi*] who had produced the philosophers."[51] Even Plato did poets the favor of taking them seriously when he banished them from his ideal polity and poured gasoline on the "ancient quarrel" between poetry and philosophy.[52] But most versions of the Masters Narrative leave little room for the minds behind the *Shi*.

THE THOUGHT OF THE *SHI*

How do we start taking the thought of the *Shi* seriously? We have already taken step one of the argument: the *Shi* tradition is prima facie the most influential corpus from preimperial China because it was the one most likely to have been in the heads of the people whose texts survive today.

A Readable Repertoire

Step two is my answer to the methodological conundrum posed by Kern. In brief, Kern's characterization of the *Shi* as "fundamentally contingent texts that embodied a wide range of latent meanings" hinges on the "texts" and "meanings" at issue. For the *Mao Shi* and thus for its many critics, the controlling unit of meaning is (usually) the poem. When grappling with the interpretation of a discrete poem, discarding a counterintuitive *Mao Shi* preface while retaining the *Mao Shi* text and character glosses is methodologically problematic. However, we aren't obligated to engage the *Shi* on that same level. We can read across individual poems for wider themes. We can identify patterns at the level of stanzas or couplets without worrying overmuch about the interpretation of the poems in which they appear. We can manage character variants by availing ourselves of reconstructed Old Chinese pronunciations and aggregating glosses across and beyond the *Mao Shi*. And we can read the *Mao Shi* alongside other instantiations of the early *Shi* tradition, including *Shi* quotations, "lost *Shi*" (*yi Shi* 逸詩), and even noncanonical *shi* or "songs" (*ge* 歌) that reflect the same poetics. In short, we can try to read the *Shi* as a fluid repertoire—which is precisely what they were prior to their crystallization under the Han.[53] In chapter 1, I characterize this approach as "reading from the midrange" to position it between the closer, poem-centric readings problematized by Kern and the "distant reading" of digital humanists.[54]

INTRODUCTION

An Ideological Construct

Step three is my theory of *Shi* poetics and the ideology advanced therein, which is the subject of chapter 2. It begins with a characterization of the *Shi* as a profoundly kinetic poetry. There are flowing rivers, blowing winds, busy peasants, revolving seasons, marching soldiers, the descents and ascents of ancestor spirits in and out of the ancestral temple, and so on. The world of the *Shi* is in a perpetual state of flow; to live in such a world is to be subject to its currents.

The ideology of the *Shi* is manifest in the obsession with a particular movement amid the symphony of motion: *gui* 歸, literally "to return" or "to go/come home." The significance of *gui* is a function both of the power of home and of the range of homes human beings return to. In the *Shi*, the object of *gui* is the center of one's existence, be it a mate, one's parents, the wider community or homeland, or a virtuous ruler, and its gravity is inexorable. The tragedy of human existence is that we can't always be at home—or if we are at home, we don't always feel at home. And so the movement of *gui* has aspect, grammatically speaking: it's either perfective or imperfective. On the one hand, there are *Shi* whose personas are at home and thus physically and emotionally centered; on the other hand, there are personas who long to return home but can't for one reason or another. The hallmark of the former is that they're voiced by the happy "we," the latter by the "anxious" (*you* 憂) "I." This "I" gives the *Shi* their occasionally heartbreaking pathos.

The value of such a worldview as a legitimating ideology is clear. Depicting the movements of *gui* alongside the rhythms of nature creates the impression that its version of sociopolitical belonging is normal and inevitable. Treating virtuous rulers as objects of *gui* makes political submission seem as natural as familial or romantic love. A more insidious consequence concerns the fate of individuals within this worldview. The "I" of the *Shi* isn't the more stable "individual and highly self-reflexive subjective consciousness" associated with lyric poetry.[55] Individuation in the *Shi* is a fallen state, a side effect of being cut off from one's home or alienated from one's family. This is another respect in which the *Shi* subordinate individuals to the collective and, by extension, to the ruler at its center.

At the same time, the presentation of this ideology isn't monolithic. At the heart of the *Shi* genre is a fascination with personas who are caught between conflicting modes of *gui* and for whom a true homecoming is impossible. A few voices at the margins even expose that ideology's dehumanizing tendencies, thus showing that the imperative to belong could be wielded against those who made belonging impossible.

The Foundational Corpus of Early Chinese Thought

Step four of the argument (chapter 3) is to trace the influence of *Shi* poetics through several case studies:

- The "Way" (*dao* 道) as the most emblematic concept in the Chinese intellectual tradition. *Dao* in the *Shi* and elsewhere isn't simply "The [Abstract Proper] Way [One Has to Follow]," it is "The Way Home," the path back to the center and a state of fulfilled belonging.
- "Happy prince / Father and mother to the people" 豈弟君子，民之父母, which was among the most cited *Shi* couplets and thus the most widely attested ideas from ancient China.
- "Water" (*shui* 水) as the most powerful metaphor in early Chinese thought. The *Shi* taught early Chinese thinkers that being wise was a matter of understanding the often metaphorical, but sometimes literal, "flows" (*liu* 流) of the world.
- Kongzi as the most quoted individual from early China and a figure whose legend was woven out of the *Shi* tradition. Although the *Shi* are often introduced through the sayings of Kongzi, it makes more sense to introduce Kongzi through the *Shi*.
- The *Laozi* 老子, which I read as the product of a counterdependent poetics.
- *Shi*-style "anxiety" (*you* 憂) as a foundational problem in early Chinese thought.
- Sima Qian's 司馬遷 (ca. 87 BCE) autobiographical postface to the *Grand Scribe's Records* (*Shiji* 史記). Against the backdrop of a textual milieu in which authors didn't name themselves or explain the genesis of their texts, the anxious "I" of the *Shi* was a key precedent for the first true authors in the Western Han.

Chapter 4 extends this argument to the other great verse anthology from the classical period, the *Verses of Chu* (*Chuci* 楚辭), which in literary histories is typically presented as an artifact of southern literary culture against the northern culture of the *Shi*. In contrast, I read the anthology and its flagship poem—"Parting's Sorrow" (Li sao 離騷)—as explorations of the limits of *Shi* poetics. When the most noble men suffer the most ignoble treatment at the hands of their sovereigns, what then? Are such men obligated to cling to the center, as they do in the *Shi*? Or can they choose not to belong, to leave and to search for happiness elsewhere? Such questions were the ethical fuel for a poetic genre whose participants included some of the most influential thinkers of the Han era.

EARLY CHINESE THOUGHT VIA THE *SHI*

The final step in the argument is to explore the consequences of locating the foundations of Chinese thought in *Shi* poetics. The most obvious takeaway is that there's a very large *Shi*-sized gap in most histories and surveys of the subject. If nothing else, I hope to motivate others to read and study the *Shi* in the hopes of retracing the mental pathways of ancient Chinese learners.

Another set of implications concerns the standard model of early Chinese thought in the modern era—the Masters Narrative. If that model leaves too little room for the thought of the *Shi*, then perhaps it should be rethought. So in chapter 5 and in the conclusion, I propose redrafting the basic blueprint of early Chinese thought as a network centered around the *Shi*.[56]

As discussed above and in the next chapter, the *Shi* pose enormous challenges to would-be translators, perhaps more so than any other early Chinese corpus. In lieu of translating the *Shijing* from scratch, in this book I have adapted Arthur Waley's 1937 translation of *The Book of Songs* reissued in 1996 (New York: Grove) and edited with additional translations by Joseph R. Allen. One idiosyncrasy of my use of the *Shijing* is that I have rendered all sound-symbolic binomes in *pinyin* with a suggested translation in brackets []. Given the difficulties inherent in translating these binomes,[57] I prefer to de-familiarize sound-symbolic binomes wherever they appear.

Citations of the Chinese text of the *Shijing* refer to the *Mao Shi zhuzi suoyin* 毛詩逐字索引 (*A Concordance to the Mao Shi*) and take the form {*Mao Shi* #}/{stanza #}.{line #}. Thus, "29/2.5–6" refers to the fifth and sixth lines of the second stanza of *Shi* number 29 in the received *Shijing*; "129/1–3.1" refers to the first lines of the first, second, and third stanzas of *Shi* number 129. Citations of all other primary sources follow a simplified format, for example, *Xunzi* 27.508 as opposed to *Xunzi jijie* 27.508 (i.e., chapter 27, 508). For the relevant editions, please consult the section in the bibliography called Primary Sources. All reconstructions of Old Chinese pronunciations follow Axel Schuessler (2009).

Readers will note that I have refrained from discussing looted manuscripts in this book. Thanks especially to the interventions of Anthony Barbieri-Low and Paul Goldin,[58] the question of whether early China scholars should conduct research using looted artifacts has become a topic of debate as more and more academic institutions in the People's Republic of China vie to secure their own manuscript corpora. The choice not to discuss looted materials is especially painful for a scholar of the *Shi* given the wealth of *Shi* material in the Shanghai Museum corpus (including the so-called *Kongzi on the Shi* [*Kongzi shilun* 孔子詩論] manuscript), the Qinghua University corpus (including a complete version of "Crickets" [Xi shuai 蟋蟀, #114]), and the Anhui University corpus, all of which offer insights into the use and circulation of *Shi* in the Warring States context.

In my first book, *Confucius Beyond the Analects*, I made the (less considered) decision to incorporate looted materials into my survey in the hopes of giving readers a maximally comprehensive view of early Kongzi material. However, this book calls for a different approach because I aim to reintroduce the *Shi* to students of early Chinese thought and, in the process, to prompt a conversation about how the subject should be framed. Regardless of one's view of the propriety of conducting research using looted artifacts, our introductory methods and models should demonstrate the best practices of our field. Given that looted artifacts fall short of that standard, I haven't incorporated such materials into my discussion, although I do occasionally reference studies of looted materials in the endnotes.

Chapter One

READING THE *SHI*

Before we talk about the *Shi*, we need to talk about how to begin talking about the *Shi*. Consider *Analects* (*Lunyu* 論語) 3/8:

> Zixia asked, " 'Sweet smile dimpling, / Lovely eyes twinkling, / Plain skin for painting"—what does [this *Shi*] mean?" Kongzi said, "The color comes after the plain." "So ritual [training also] comes after?" Kongzi said, "You inspire me, Shang! Now we can begin to talk about the *Shi* together!"
>
> 子夏問曰：巧笑倩兮，美目盼兮，素以為絢兮。何謂也？子曰：繪事後素。曰：禮後乎？子曰：起予者商也！始可與言詩已矣。[1]

This exchange speaks to the *Shi*'s importance in a few ways. First, it reveals *Shi* as objects of exegesis. *Shi* lines were opaque enough to necessitate comment and consequential enough to demand it. Second, it reveals *Shi* as sources of moral wisdom and "talk about the *Shi*" as a didactic discourse. Third, it highlights their social function. Kongzi's praise for Zixia isn't just a teacher's pride about a gifted student. It signals Zixia's initiation into an elite group distinguished by their ability to talk about the *Shi*.

For those of us who would like to go on talking about the *Shi* today, there's only one problem: the third of the three lines quoted by Zixia doesn't appear in the *Shijing*. The closest match is the second stanza of "A Splendid Woman" (Shuo ren 碩人, #57), which includes only the first two lines:

> Hands white as rush down, / Skin like lard,
> Neck long and white as a tree grub,
> Teeth like melon seeds, / Lovely head, beautiful brows.
> Sweet smile dimpling, / Lovely eyes twinkling.

> 手如柔荑，膚如凝脂，領如蝤蠐，齒如瓠犀，螓首蛾眉。巧笑倩兮，美目盼兮。(57/2)

The mismatch is especially galling given that the third line introduces the concept of the "plain" or "white" (*su* 素), which is the focus of Kongzi's comment. If we lack access to their version of the poem, how are we supposed to join Kongzi and Zixia in their club of *Shi* connoisseurs?

THE "SPECIAL CHARM" AND "SOCRATIC PLEASURES" OF THE *SHI*[2]

As noted in the introduction, the problem is that the largest collection of *Shi* available today—the *Shijing* 詩經—was one of four written recensions circulating in the Han period. At that time, our *Shijing* was known not as THE *Classic of Poetry* but as the *Mao Shi* 毛詩, that is, *The Shi [as transmitted and interpreted by a certain Mr.] Mao*, a tradition of exegesis said to have originated with Zixia himself. Moreover, the *Mao Shi* was the least authoritative *Shi* recension for much of the Han period owing to a lack of imperial recognition.[3] When the *Mao Shi* eventually did win out to become THE *Shijing*, thanks in part to Zheng Xuan's 鄭玄 (127–200 CE) adoption of the text for his own *Shi* commentary, its ascendancy precipitated the loss of the other recensions, thus rendering the study of the *Mao Shi*'s idiosyncracies that much more difficult.[4] Perhaps the author of *Analects* 3/8 quoted a version of "A Splendid Woman" from the Lu 魯, Qi 齊, or Han 韓 recension; if so, we have no way of verifying it.[5] Even worse, the likelihood that post-Mao editors retrospectively standardized *Shi* citations in transmitted texts composed prior to the *Mao Shi*'s ascendancy cautions against taking those citations as pure sources of a pre-Mao *Shi* tradition.[6]

Tracking the differences among a finite number of written versions, all but one of which are lost, is one challenge. Sorting through the variations that arose when bits and pieces of a tradition that "didn't depend solely on bamboo and silk" 不獨在竹帛 were transcribed from memory is another problem entirely.[7] Imagine for a moment that we could travel back in time and ask ten different literate individuals from across the Warring States to write out the same *Shi* poem. The tremendous variability of *Shi* material in excavated manuscripts teaches us to anticipate ten different transcriptions of the *Shi* in question, if not ten different poems.

Part of the problem has to do with the nature of the Chinese writing system.[8] The relatively restricted phonemic inventory of Old Chinese coupled with the lack of a standard orthography prior to the Qin and Han empires meant that a given word could be written in any number of ways depending on the writer's training, locale, and personal preferences. In the case of the *Shi*, their archaic language and hermeneutic indeterminacy compounded the problem further. If we were to ask our ten elites to recite the *Shi* in question, their recitations would most likely sound more similar than their transcriptions would look.[9] But on the page, we would expect to see different characters with the same pronunciation (e.g., "island" [*zhou* 州; *tu] for "boat" [*zhou* 舟; *tu]), variant characters with the same phonetic components but different semantic classifiers (e.g., *qiu* 求 or *qiu* 逑 for "mate" [*gu]), semantic variants, grammatical variants, graphic errors, and also wholly unrelated character variants.[10]

At higher levels of complexity, we would also anticipate lines of varying length and syntax and stanzas of varying length, number, arrangement, and rhyme scheme.[11] Consider "Drooping Boughs" (Jiu mu 樛木, #4):

> In the south is a tree with drooping boughs; / The cloth creeper binds it.
> Oh, happy is our prince; / Blessings and boons comfort him.
>
> In the south is a tree with drooping boughs; / The cloth creeper covers it.
> Oh, happy is our prince; / Blessings and boons protect him.
>
> In the south is a tree with drooping boughs; / The cloth creeper encircles it.
> Oh, happy is our prince; / Blessings and boons surround him!

> 南有樛木，葛藟纍之。樂只君子，福履綏之。
> 南有樛木，葛藟荒之。樂只君子，福履將之。
> 南有樛木，葛藟縈之。樂只君子，福履成之。

Like so many *Shi*, the poem's structure is extremely repetitive: only the (outlined) rhyme-bearing slots vary from one stanza to the next, all of which are synonyms. This redundancy raises a question: how many stanzas does "Drooping Boughs" need to have? Would a one-stanza version be too short? Would a version with four or more stanzas be too long?[12] What if we were to swap this version of "Drooping Boughs" with the second stanza of "In the South There Are Lucky Fish" (Nan you jia yu 南有嘉魚, #171)?

> In the south is a tree with drooping boughs; / The sweet gourds bind it.
> The prince has ale; / His lucky guests shall be feasted and comforted.

> 南有樛木，甘瓠纍之。君子有酒，嘉賓式燕綏之。

Repeat the same formula two or three more times while varying the rhymed slots and voila: another version of "Drooping Boughs."

The *Mao Shi* provides evidence of just this sort of variation in the eighteen poems with nonunique titles, including three versions of "Rising Waters" (Yang zhi shui 揚之水, #68, 92, 116):[13]

> Rising waters / Will float away bundled firewood.
> Those fine gentlemen / Are not with us defending Shen.
> Oh, the longing, the longing! / In what month shall I return home?

> 揚之水，不流束薪。彼其之子，不與我戍申。懷哉懷哉，曷月予還歸哉。(68/1)

> Rising waters / Will float away bundled brushwood.
> We have lost brothers— / It is only you and I.
> Do not believe what others say; / They surely will deceive you.

> 揚之水，不流束楚。終鮮兄弟，維予與女。無信人之言，人實迋女。(92/1)

Amid rising waters / White rocks *dzâuk-dzâuk [stand bright].
With white coat with red lappet, / I followed you to Wo;
And now that I have seen my prince, / Happy am I indeed.

揚之水，白石鑿鑿。素衣朱襮，從子于沃。既見君子，云何不樂。(116/1)

Still other *Shi* titles are obviously formulaic in nature, as if their poems were parallel instantiations of the same topoi. These include the eight poems with the title "Picking {flora}" (Cai 采, #13, 15, 72, 125, 167, 178, 222, 226), two of which are rather similar:

Where is the white aster gathered? / By the pools, on the little islands.
Where is it used? / In service to the lord.

于以采蘩，于沼于沚。于以用之，公侯之事。(13/1)

Where is the duckweed gathered? / By the banks of the southern dale.
Where is the water grass gathered? In those channeled pools.

于以采蘋，南澗之濱。于以采藻，于彼行潦。(15/1)

Other examples are the six titles with "{. . .} Winds" (Feng 風, #30, 32, 35, 41, 149, 201), five with "{. . .} Robes" (Yi 衣, #27, 75, 122, 133, 292), four with "{number} Month" (Yue 月, #154, 177, 192, 193), four with "The {. . .} of the Eastern Gate" (Dong men zhi 東門之, #89, 137, 139, 140), three with "Chopping {trees}" (Fa 伐, #112, 158, 165), and three with "{Cardinal direction} Mountains" (Shan 山, #101, 156, 205).[14]

The distribution of stanzas across *Shi* poems also varies. Whereas the *Mao Shi* treats "Martiality" (Wu 武, #285), "Bold" (Huan 桓, #294), and "Bestowal" (Lai 賚, #295) as three separate pieces, an episode from the *Zuo Tradition* (*Zuozhuan* 左傳) identifies them as "stanzas" (*zhang* 章) of a poem called "Martiality."[15] On the other hand, the *Zuo Tradition* also includes a number of episodes in which elites quote *Shi* by stanza as if the arrangement of stanzas within poems was relatively stable:

> In winter [in the year 613 BCE], our Lord [Wen of Lu] went to visit the Jin court and renewed the covenant [between our two states]. The Prince of Wei met with our lord at Ta and requested that he broker peace with Jin. As our Lord was returning home, the Liege of Zheng met with him at Fei, and requested that he broker a peace with Jin. Our Lord was successful on both counts.
>
> The Liege of Zheng and our Lord [Wen of Lu] held a banquet at Fei [at which this agreement was struck]. [The Zheng minister] Gongzi Guisheng recited [*Mao Shi* #181,] "The Wild Goose" [to seek recognition for Zheng's plight: "It is these wise men / Who say that we toil and labor" 維此哲人，謂我劬勞]. [The Lu minister] Ji Wenzi said, "Our unworthy ruler himself has yet to escaped this," and then recited [#204,] "The Fourth Month" ["in order to report his sorrows" 維以告哀 in sympathy]. Gongzi Guisheng then recited the fourth stanza of [#54,] "Gallop" [to request Lu's help: "Dominated by a great state, / Whom can we rely on? To whom can we go?" 控于大邦，誰因誰極]. Wenzi then recited the fourth stanza of [#167,] "Plucking Bracken" [to grant the request: "What great carriage is that? / It is our lord's chariot, / His war-chariot ready yoked, / Its four steeds *ŋap-ŋap* [so strapping]. / How could we dare stop or tarry?" 彼路斯何，君子之車。戎車既駕，四牡業業。豈敢定居]. The Liege of Zheng bowed, and our Lord bowed in response.
>
> 冬。公如晉朝且尋盟。衛侯會公于沓，請平于晉。公還，鄭伯會公于棐，亦請平于晉。公皆成之。鄭伯與公宴于棐。子家賦鴻鴈，季文子曰：寡君未免於此。文子賦四月，子家賦載馳之四章，文子賦采薇之四章。鄭伯拜，公荅拜。(Wen 13/598-599)[16]

Exchanges like these assume a high degree of textual stability, without which the encoding and decoding performed here would have been impossible.[17]

Now suppose we were to ask our ten elites to reflect on their ten transcriptions—what might they say? Would they recognize all of them as equally legitimate or would they argue over their quality or fidelity? If we can excuse the increasingly ridiculous nature of this thought experiment, my hunch is that our hypothetical test subjects would be fairly accommodating of textual difference. Early sources show elites reciting, quoting, discussing, and performing *Shi* but never critiquing the form or substance of others'

Shi quotations. Elsewhere we encounter critical statements like, "That's not a Kongzi saying" 非孔子之言也 or "I only accept two or three strips" 取二三策而已矣 of a text from the *Documents* (*Shu* 書) tradition.[18] But such things are never said about *Shi* quotations—why?

The cultural authority of the *Shi* as a literary lingua franca suggests one answer. Instead of debating the relative merits of their transcriptions, our ten educated representatives from around the Warring States might have used such an occasion to celebrate their shared cultural heritage. In the banquet scene from the *Zuo Tradition* translated above, the Zheng minister quotes "The Wild Goose" in the hopes of gaining the sympathies of Lu, which the Lu minister readily grants with a quotation of "The Fourth Month." In that context, claiming to know the *Shi* better than another would have undermined the spirit of mutual understanding on which the occasion depended. If the *Shi* were good for for bringing elites together, perhaps they were inappropriate vessels for highlighting difference.

The variability of the *Shi*, especially at the level of a poem as a whole, suggests another answer. I have used the word *transcription* to describe the process of writing down a *Shi* poem, but what if that is the wrong word? What if a *Shi* poem didn't exist in the minds of early elites as a fully elaborated poem? What if the core text of a *Shi* like "Rising Waters" was a loose template of a poem—a title, a theme, some core lines or couplets—that could be realized in any number of ways depending on the occasion? Consider the following *Zuo Tradition* episode:

> Lord Ping of Jin 晉平公 [557–532 BCE] and the princes feasted at Wen. He made the high officers dance, saying, "When singing a *Shi*, it must be the right sort." The *Shi* sung by Gao Hou of Qi wasn't the right sort. Enraged, Zhonghang Yan said, "The princes are not of one mind with us." He had the high officers swear a covenant with Gao Hou, but the latter escaped and returned to Qi. As a consequence, Shusun Bao, Zhongyang Yan of Jin, Xiang Xu of Song, Ning Zhi of Wei, Zijiao of Zheng, and the high officers of Lesser Zhu swore a covenant that said, "Together we shall chastise those who do not pay court."

> 晉侯與諸侯宴于溫，使諸大夫舞，曰：歌詩必類。齊高厚之詩不類。荀偃怒，且曰：諸侯有異志矣,使諸大夫盟高厚。高厚逃歸。於是叔孫豹，晉荀偃，宋向戌，衛甯殖，鄭公孫蠆，小邾之大夫，盟曰：同討不庭。(Xiang 16/1026)[19]

Unfortunately, the *Zuo Tradition* doesn't record the content of Gao Hou's recitation. But if fitting a *Shi* to the occasion" involved improvising or elaborating a known poetic template as opposed to quoting a preexisting poem from memory, then the question of textual difference becomes less pressing.[20]

Now imagine asking our ten hypothetical elites to interpret the written text of the *Shi* in question. Would they all understand it in the same way? Given the diversity of interpretations and interpretive strategies we find in early sources, probably not.[21] But the bigger problem for the modern reader isn't hermeneutic diversity so much as the relationship between interpretation and transcription. In our thought experiment, we have imagined asking ten elites to write down a *Shi* before asking them to explain its meaning, as if the text preceded the interpretation and existed independently of it. But there is reason to think that the opposite is true: a transcriber's sense of what a *Shi* was supposed to mean controlled its transcription.

Consider the Mao preface to "Ospreys Cry" (Guan ju 關雎, #1), translated below alongside the poem's first two stanzas and the accompanying Mao commentary. "Ospreys Cry" is the first of eleven poems in the "South of Zhou" subdivision of the "Airs of the States," so I have also included the relevant comments from the "Great Preface" (Da xu 大序) of the *Mao Shi*:[22]

Subdivision:	*The "Great Preface"*
"South from Zhou" 周南, the first eleven pieces of the "Airs of the States"	The transformation [of the eleven poems] from "Ospreys Cry" to "Unicorn's Hoofs" [#11] is the moral influence of a true king; thus, they are named after the Duke of Zhou [=the virtuous regent and uncle to King Cheng 成王, who was the son of the Zhou dynasty's founder]. "South" means that the transformation extends to the south from the north . . . [The poems] "South of Zhou" and "South of Shao" [illuminate] the Way of rectifying beginnings and the foundations of the royal transformation. This is why "Ospreys Cry" rejoices in finding a fine woman to marry the prince. Its concern is with advancing men of excellence, not being licentious with regard to sex, being loyal and retiring, longing for men of excellence and talent, and not having any thoughts of harming good men. This is the meaning of "Ospreys Cry."

READING THE SHI

關雎麟趾之化，王者之風，故繫之周公。南，言化自北而南也 . . . 周南召南，正始之道，王化之基，是以關雎樂得淑女以配君子。愛在進賢，不淫其色，哀窈窕，思賢才，而無傷善之心焉，是關雎之義也。[23]

Title:	**The preface to the poem:**
"Ospreys Cry" 關雎	It is [about] the virtue of the queen. It is the beginning of the "Airs [of the States]." It is the means by which [one] influences the world and rectifies [the relationships between] husbands and wives. Thus one applies it to the village heads and one applies it to the [lords of the vassal] domains. . . .[24]

后妃之德也，風之始也，所以風天下而正夫婦也，故用之鄉人焉，用之邦國焉。

The Mao text:	**The Mao commentary:**
Kron-kron [cry] the ospreys, On the river isle.	It is an evocative image. *Kron-kron* is the sound of harmony. "Ospreys" are fishhawks. They are devoted but maintain the [proper] separation. An "island" is a place where one can roost in a river. The queen rejoices in the virtue of the prince but without being unharmonious or licentious with regard to sex. She is cautious and steadfast and remains secluded just as the ospreys maintain separation in the poem. Only then does her moral influence transform the world. If a wife maintains the proper separation, then father and son are close; if a father and son are close, then ruler and subject are [mutually] respectful; if ruler and subject are [mutually] respectful, then the royal court is correctly disposed; if the royal court is correctly disposed, then the royal influence is complete.
關關雎鳩，在河之洲。	興也。關關，和聲也。雎鳩，王雎也，鳥摯而有別。水中可居者曰洲。后妃說樂君子之德，無不和諧，又不淫其色，慎固幽深，若關雎之有別焉，然後可以風化天下。夫婦有別則父子親，父子親則君臣敬，君臣敬則朝廷正，朝廷正則王化成。

*ʔiû?–liû? the fine woman, / A good mate for the prince.	*ʔiû?–liû? means retiring. "Noble" means fine. "Mate" means a companion. It says that the queen has the virtue of "Ospreys Cry," and that this retiring, loyal, fine woman is fit to be a good companion to a prince.
窈窕淑女，君子好逑。	窈窕，幽閒也。淑，善。逑，匹也。言后妃有關雎之德，是幽閒貞專之善女，宜為君子之好匹。
*Tshrəm-tshrai the xing plants; Attendants look for them.	Xing are water plants. Look for means seek. The queen has the virtue of "Ospreys Cry" and so she is able to supply the xing plants and furnish all the things required to serve the ancestral temple.
參差荇菜，左右流之。	荇，接余也。流，求也。后妃有關雎之德，乃能共荇菜，備庶物，以事宗廟也。
*ʔiû?–liû? the fine woman, / Waking, sleeping I seek her.	"Waking" means becoming conscious. "Sleeping" means going to bed.
窈窕淑女，寤寐求之。	寤，覺。寐，寢也。

As Martin Kern has shown, the Mao hermeneutic framework isn't confined to the "Great Preface" or the "little preface" (xiao xu 小序) to "Ospreys Cry." It also extends to the Mao character glosses and even the text itself.[25] This is most obvious in the text's handling of the rhymed binome yaotiao 窈窕 (*ʔiû?–liû?),[26] one of many instances in the Shi of the use of sound symbolism to describe nonauditory phenomena. These binomes aren't only notoriously difficult to translate, they are also among the most graphically unstable words in early Chinese texts.[27]

The Mao commentary glosses yaotiao as "retiring" (youxian 幽閒), that is, as an exemplar of chastity and modesty. However, other instances of yaotiao in the early literature reveal a very different meaning. In the opening lines of "Mountain Spirit" (Shan gui 山鬼) from the Verses of Chu (Chuci 楚辭) anthology, yaotiao refers to physical attractiveness:

> It is as if there is someone there in the mountain's recesses, /
> Clothed in climbing fig dodder about her waist.
> With a coy glance and an easy smile, / Finely alluring you yearn for me.

> 若有人兮山之阿，被薜荔兮帶女蘿。既含睇兮又宜笑，子慕予兮善窈窕。(3.79)

READING THE SHI

Likewise, the *Five Kinds of Conduct* (*Wu xing* 五行) manuscript from Mawangdui 馬王堆 tomb no. 3 (closed 168 BCE) glosses the lines "**krâu-{?} the fine woman, / Waking, sleeping I seek her*" 茭芍[淑女，寤]（眛）寐求之 as "about the longing for sex" 思色也.²⁸ Even the *Mao Shi* corroborates the sexualized reading of *yaotiao* in the first stanza of "Moon Rising" (Yue chu 月出, #143), which the Mao preface labels "a critique of the fondness for sex" 刺好色也:²⁹

> The moon rises white, / My lovely is so comely.
> Languidly **ʔiû?-kiu?* [attractive]! / My pained heart is consumed.

> 月出皎兮，佼人僚兮。舒窈糾兮，勞心悄兮。

The binome *yaojiu* 窈糾 (**ʔiû?-kiu?*) in the third line is a near homophone of *yaotiao*.

Why, then, did the *Mao Shi* embrace the sexual reading of *yaotiao* in "Moon Rising" but reject it in "Ospreys Cry"? The answer has to do with the different roles these poems perform within Mao hermeneutics. At the highest level, there is the *Mao Shi* reading of the "South from Zhou" poems as odes to the transformative powers of the Zhou dynasty's virtue. That framework controls the reading of "Ospreys Cry" as an ode to a chaste queen who maintains the proper degree of "separation" from her king. In turn, that reading dictates the glossing of *yaotiao* as "retiring" as opposed to "sexually attractive" or "seductive." Finally, that gloss seems to have determined the characters used to write *yaotiao* within the text of "Ospreys Cry." *Yao* 窈 means "distant," *tiao* 窕 "deep"; together, they reinforce the Mao commentary's praise for a queen who remains secluded and "separate" (*bie* 別) in the palace to avoid distracting her king. In contrast, "Moon Rising" appears within the "Airs of Chen" (Chen feng 陳風), a region at the southern edge of the Zhou state. Positioned at the periphery of Zhou society, these personas were free to express their sexual desires because they didn't have the burden of moral exemplarity.

The lesson for modern readers of the *Shijing* is that no written version of the *Shi* is sacrosanct. To transcribe some part of the *Shi* repertoire, one had to make a series of choices from a wide range of possible instantiations at every level of the text. The example of "Ospreys Cry" shows us that those choices were shaped by the transcriber's ideas about the meaning of the poem as a whole and its place within the *Shi* tradition. To quote Kern, "There are no original *Odes* available to us; all we have are the *Mao Odes*—that is, a text constructed through a particular interpretation."[30]

READING FROM THE MIDRANGE

Let's return to the question posed at the beginning of this chapter: how can modern readers of the *Shi* deal with these challenges? Is there a way to talk about the *Shi* tradition without falling into the Mao hermeneutic trap?

Pace Kern, I believe that there is, the key to which is reading the *Shi* against the grain of *Mao Shi* hermeneutics. The *Mao Shi* is organized to create 305 distinct objects of interpretation and thus 305 answers to the question of who first uttered a *Shi*, in what historical context, and with what intention (*zhi* 志). However, we aren't obliged to engage the *Shi* at that same level or with the same questions. We can let the boundaries of individual poems fade into the background to focus on themes, images, and topics across the anthology. We can replace the *Mao Shi* poem with the less hermeneutically bounded *Mao Shi* stanza as the primary unit of analysis, thus privileging clusters of parallel stanzas across poems over stanza sequences within poems. To minimize the influence of the Mao commentary in any given instance, we can read every line, phrase, character, and word against every other instance of that line, character, phrase, or word in the *Mao Shi* and beyond, as Kern demonstrates in the case of *yaotiao*. And we can prioritize elements with a higher intra- and intertextual profile in the hopes of basing our readings on the most stable or recognizable features of the *Shi* tradition.

In other words, we can try to short-circuit the operations of *Mao Shi* hermeneutics by declining its invitation to conceptualize the *Shijing* as 305 distinct poems. Instead, we try to read the anthology as one among many possible curations or crystallizations of the early *Shi* repertoire. As a consequence of this shift, the mode of *Shi* studies shifts from hermeneutics to poetics.[31] We read the *Shijing* not for its meanings but for its effects and for the poetic grammar that makes those effects possible.[32] My shorthand for this method is "reading from the midrange." Read too closely and we run the risk of attaching too much significance to the choices of the *Mao Shi*; read too distantly and we lose sight of the experience and ends of *Shi* poetics.

One consequence of flattening out the *Shi* tradition into a single repertoire or "one poetry," with "each extant text [within that tradition] as a single realization of many possible poems that might have been composed," is a loss of historical perspective.[33] Readers will note that my reading of the *Shi* mostly brackets a discussion of their origins and early history, including the many connections between the *Shijing* and epigraphic sources (including inscriptions on bronze ritual vessels) from the Western and Eastern Zhou periods.[34] Given the larger goal of this study, which is to trace the influence of the *Shi* worldview on the development of the intellectual tradition from the Warring States onward, I hope the trade-off is acceptable.[35] Early inscriptions illuminate the larger context out of which the verses and liturgies of the *Shi* emerged, but they can't explain why certain kinds of verses and liturgies were included in the *Shi* as opposed to others. For understanding the internal logic and dynamics of the *Shi* repertoire, we have to rely on the *Shijing* and other extant sources of *Shi* from the period.

One feature of the *Shi* tradition that allows us to create some distance from *Mao Shi* hermeneutics is its ubiquity. Fortunately, there is a lot of *Shi* material to work with. If we were to approach the elite literate culture of ancient China like archaeologists sorting cultures from pottery sherds, we might label it "the *Shi* culture."[36] By my rough estimate, excavated and transmitted sources through the end of the Han period preserve roughly 2,700 explicit *Shi* citations, of which only about 150, or 6 percent, have no obvious parallels in the received *Shijing*.[37] (Comparing "lost *Shi*" with the much greater amount of "lost *Documents*" material is illuminating.[38]) More than a third of all *Shijing* lines have at least one quotation in an early source. And although these quotations can vary significantly at the level of individual characters, especially in excavated manuscripts, there is a remarkable amount of overlap, thematically and syntactically, between these quotations and the received *Shijing*.

On the other hand, reading from the midrange comes with certain practical or material challenges. Figure 1.1 shows two pages from Ruan Yuan's 阮元 (1764–1849) 1816 woodblock print edition of the *Commentaries and Sub-Commentaries to the Thirteen Classics* (*Shisan jing zhushu* 十三經注疏), which is the basis of most modern editions. The large characters are the first four lines of "Ospreys Cry." Multiple layers of interlinear commentary follow each line: first are the semantic glosses of the Mao commentary,

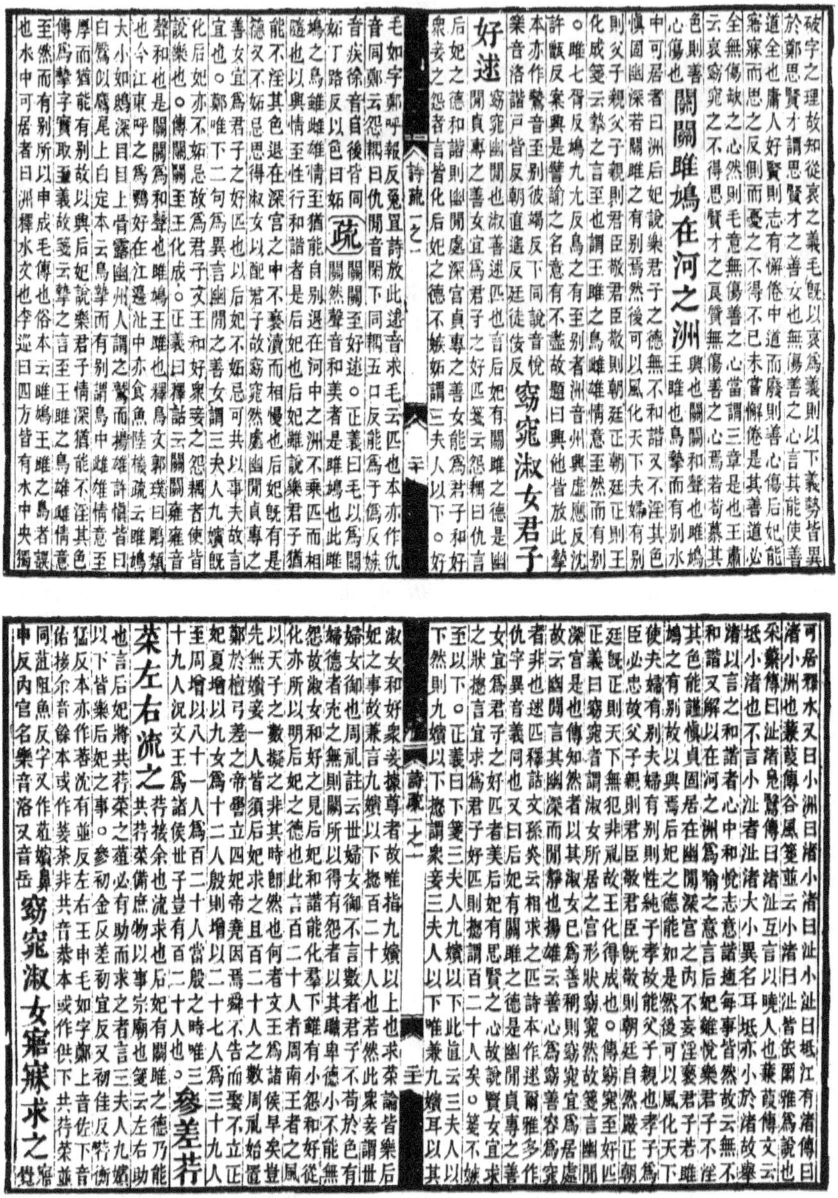

FIGURE 1.1. A woodblock print edition of the *Shijing*

next is Zheng Xuan's commentary, next are the phonological glosses of Lu Deming 陸德明 (ca. 550–630 CE). After line two comes the 1,115-character "sub-commentary" (*shu* 疏) of the *Corrected Meanings of the Five Classics* (*Wujing zhengyi* 五經正義), the monumental commentary project sponsored by the early Tang 唐 imperium and overseen by Kong Yingda 孔穎達 (574–648 CE).

In this format, "Ospreys Cry" looks like an archipelago drowning in a rising sea of verbiage. Clearly, this isn't a format designed to facilitate middle-distance reading—nor did it need to. For premodern audiences who had memorized the base text of the *Shijing* and could browse it at will, the point of the commentary was to make sense of the words already in their heads. Modern *Shijing* editions tend not to break up poems in the same way. In modern print editions, too, their commentarial apparatus makes for an extremely slow, patient, and close reading experience. By privileging the trees over the forest, the commentarial tradition ends up anchoring readers to the Mao hermeneutic framework.

My solution to this problem is to approach the *Shijing* primarily as a digital object—or, more precisely, as a single digital transcription in multiple formats. Positioning the *Shijing* in a digital space allows me to move more easily from one level of the text to another—be it the individual *Shi*, the stanza, the line, or its intertextual profile.[39] Using digital search tools, with just a few keystrokes I can create smaller subcollections from within the *Shijing* anthology, for example, all instances of "anxiety" (*you* 憂) or all couplets with a sound-symbolic reduplicating binome. Not unlike the Mao commentators more than two millennia ago, I shape the *Shijing* around the questions I'm most interested in—except that, where the *Mao Shi* insists on one interface, I change my interface on the fly. Whether because I started too late in life or because of the cultural and technological milieu in which I grew up, I long ago gave up on memorizing the *Shijing* in the traditional manner. I will never inhabit the *Shi* repertoire as fully as a classically trained scholar because I can't browse the corpus in my mind, recite poems on command, or compose new poems on *Shi* templates. Through digital texts, however, I can at least recapture something of their facility and ease of movement, what Lu Ji 陸機 (261–303 CE) once described as "roaming the groves and storehouses of literature" 遊文章之林府.[40]

"OSPREYS CRY" FROM THE MIDRANGE

What does a midrange reading look like in practice? Let us revisit the *Mao Shi* version of "Ospreys Cry," here translated in its entirety (minus the sound-symbolic binomes):

> *Kron-kron* [cry] the ospreys, / On the river isle.
> *ʔiûʔ-liûʔ* the fine woman, / A good mate for the prince.
> 1 關關雎鳩，在河之洲[*tu]。窈窕淑女，君子好逑[*gu]。

> *Tshrəm-tshrai* the *xing* plants; / Attendants look for them.
> *ʔiûʔ-liûʔ* the fine woman, / Waking, sleeping I seek her.
> 2 參差荇菜，左右流之[*ru]。窈窕淑女，寤寐求之[*gu]。

> I seek her but do not get her, / Waking, sleeping I long for her.
> How I pine! How I pine! / Now I toss, now I turn.
> 3 求之不得，寤寐思服 [*bək]。悠哉悠哉，輾轉反側[*tsrək]。

> *Tshrəm-tshrai* the *xing* plants, / Attendants gather them.
> *ʔiûʔ-liûʔ* the fine woman, / Stringed instruments cheer her.
> 4 參差荇菜，左右采之[*tshə̂ʔ]。窈窕淑女，琴瑟友之[*wəʔ]。

> *Tshrəm-tshrai* the *xing* plants, / Attendants pick them.
> *ʔiûʔ-liûʔ* the fine woman, / Bells and drum delight her.
> 5 參差荇菜，左右芼之[*mâuh]。窈窕淑女，鍾鼓樂之[*ŋrâukh]。

What makes "Ospreys Cry" a *Shi*? Like 90 percent of all *Shi* in the *Shijing*, it's composed of rhymed tetrametric couplets. Like 20 percent of all *Shijing* stanzas, every stanza but the third has a sound-symbolic binome in the first line. All five stanzas also feature some of the most common settings and categories of imagery, including birds, flowing water, foraging or harvesting, and music making.[41] All five stanzas appear to deal with courtship or marriage, among the most common topics in the *Shijing*.[42]

However, there's something anomalous about the structure of "Ospreys Cry."[43] As seen in "Drooping Boughs" earlier in this chapter, repetition is a hallmark of *Shi* poetics, especially in the "Airs of the States." But the repetition of "Ospreys Cry" is inconsistent because the opening stanza sets a pattern that is immediately dropped (the line "*?iû?–liû?* the fine woman" excepted). Instead, the dominant pattern begins in the second stanza and continues in the fourth and fifth. But even that pattern breaks down in the third stanza, whose first line repeats the last two characters of the second stanza (求之). Although common in the longer, more discursively complex pieces of the "Greater Court Songs," as a rule anadiplosis doesn't appear elsewhere in the anthology, nor do any other *Shi* interrupt an ABCD → ABCD → ABCD pattern with an ABCD → DEFG → ABCD pattern.[44]

The pattern of the first stanza of "Ospreys Cry" does appear elsewhere in the "Airs of the States":

> *Mên?-mên?* [Endlessly spreads] the cloth plant
> Along the banks of the river . . .
> *Mên?-mên?* the cloth plant / Along the margin of the river . . .
> *Mên?-mên?* the cloth plant / Along the lips of the river . . .
>
> 綿綿葛藟，在河之滸。. . . 綿綿葛藟，在河之涘。. . . 綿綿葛藟，在河之漘。(71/1–3.1–2)

> *Siuk-siuk* [Swish, swish] the tiger net,[45] / Hammered with a *têŋ-têŋ*.
> *Kiu?-kiu?* [dashing, daring] the martial men,
> Shield and rampart of the lord.
>
> *Siuk-siuk* [Swish, swish] the tiger net, / Spread where the paths meet.
> *Kiu?-kiu?* [dashing, daring] the martial men, / Good mates for the lord.
>
> *Siuk-siuk* [Swish, swish] the tiger net, / Spread deep in the woods.
> *Kiu?-kiu?* [dashing, daring] the martial men, / Belly and heart of the lord.
>
> 肅肅兔罝，椓之丁丁。赳赳武夫，公侯干城。
> 肅肅兔罝，施于中逵。赳赳武夫，公侯好仇。
> 肅肅兔罝，施于中林。赳赳武夫，公侯腹心。(7)

Syntactically, the opening couplet of each stanza of "Close the Cloth Plant Spreads" (Ge lei 葛藟, #71) closely parallels the opening couplet of "Ospreys

Cry": a sound-symbolic adjective for some natural phenomenon precedes a rhyme-bearing description of its location in relation to a "river" (*he* 河). The second stanza of "Tiger Net" (Tu ju 兔罝, #7) is an even better match. Not only does the line "Good mates for the lord" almost perfectly parallel "A good mate for the prince" from "Ospreys Cry," the binome *jiu-jiu* 赳赳 (*kiuʔ-kiuʔ) is a near homophone for the repeated binome *ʔiûʔ–liûʔ.

So what do we learn from this midrange reading of "Ospreys Cry"? In terms of its imagery, themes, and language, "Ospreys Cry" is a perfectly representative *Shi*. Syntactically, too, each couplet and stanza follow patterns of couplet and stanza construction seen throughout the *Shijing*. The wrinkle is that "Ospreys Cry" uses three such patterns where most other *Shi* use only one: (1) the first stanza; (2) stanzas two, three, and five; and (3) the anadiplosis from stanza two to three. In theory, each of these patterns might have been used to realize three different *Shi*; in the only extant version of "Ospreys Cry" available to us, they coexist awkwardly under a single title. Unfortunately, reconstructing the history of the *Mao Shi* arrangement is impossible given the poem's limited intertextual profile. Although certain lines from the *Mao Shi* version of "Ospreys Cry" are quoted in Warring States and early Western Han manuscripts, they're never explicitly attributed to "Ospreys Cry."[46]

The most interesting finding is the overlap with "Tiger Net," as shown in the following table:

*ʔiûʔ–liûʔ the fine woman,	**Kiuʔ-kiuʔ* the martial men,
Good mate for the prince.	Good mates for the lord.
窈窕淑女，君子好逑。	赳赳武夫，公侯好仇。
*ʔiûʔ–liûʔ{ʔ} diuk nraʔ / kwən–tsə ʔ hûʔ gu	**kiuʔ–kiuʔ maʔ pa / klôŋ gô hûʔ gu*

On the surface, these are two different couplets. At the level of the repertoire, they're two versions of the same template. Note that the second half of the template is more stable than the first. Here and throughout the *Shi* repertoire, the dominant perspective is that of the "prince" (*junzi* 君子; 184 instances in 159 stanzas across 62 *Shi*) or "lord" (*gong* 公 or *hou* 侯; 141 instances in 112 stanzas across 58 *Shi*). For the ruling elite, marriageable women and companionable men both belong to the category of "good mates." In the *Shi*, there are few things worse than being a lonely lord with "no one at your back, no one at your side, . . . no one to be your assistant, no one to be your minister" 無背無側, . . . 無陪無卿 (255/4.6,8). As we will see in the next chapter, the *Shi* worldview depended on blurred distinctions like this one.

Chapter Two

A POETRY OF RETURN

The Kongzi of *Analects* (2/2) famously summarizes the *Shi* tradition with a three-character line from "Stout" (Jiong 駉, 297/4.7):

[Kong]zi said, "A single saying encapsulates the three hundred *Shi*: 'O without slip.'"

子曰：詩三百，一言以蔽之，曰：思無邪。[1]

This chapter offers a theory of the *Shi* tradition's ideology and poetics. Unlike Kongzi, I can't claim to summarize the *Shi* so pithily or comprehensively, nor do I think that a corpus as large and diverse as the *Shi* could ever be confined within a single theory. My more modest goal is to outline a flexible framework that clarifies more than it obscures, that accommodates more poems than not, and that suggests new ways of understanding the *Shi* tradition's intellectual historical significance.

SHI KINETICS

To read the *Shijing* from beginning to end is to experience various different movements—across the anthology as a whole, over the course of individual poems, in *Shi* imagery, and in the arrangement of stanzas and couplets. The *Shi* at every level are a profoundly kinetic poetry.

The most immediately obvious movement is the journey through the "Airs of the States," the first division of the anthology. This movement begins in the Zhou heartland with the eleven poems of the "South of Zhou" (Zhou nan 周南) subdivision and the fourteen poems "South of Shao" (Shao nan 召南), and then jumps to thirteen other areas in and around the Yellow River Valley and North China Plain. Progressing through these fifteen regions, we experience the full territorial extent of the Western Zhou state.

The performance of territorial sovereignty in ancient China often took the form of a ritualized "inspection tour" (*xun* 巡/*xun shou* 巡守), wherein a ruler paraded to the far reaches of his domain or to a strategic or ritual site therein. These tours often included the ascent of a sacred mountain to perform the sovereign's panoptic gaze, sacrifices to mountain and river spirits, and gatherings of local elites in the inspected regions. In the *Shijing*, two liturgical artifacts of that practice are "He Proceeds" (Shi mai 時邁, #273) and "Celebration" (Ban 般, #296); other early accounts include the "Canon of Shun" (Shun dian 舜典) chapter of the *Exalted Documents* and the stele inscriptions of the Qin First Emperor:

> [The king] proceeds through his domain;
> May mighty Heaven treat him as its son!
> Truly the succession is with Zhou. / See how they tremble before him!
> Not one fails to tremble and quake.
> Submissive, yielding are all the Spirits,
> Likewise the rivers and high hills. / Truly he alone is monarch.
> Bright and glorious is Zhou; / He has succeeded to the seat of power.

> 時邁其邦，昊天其子之。實右序有周，薄言震之。莫不震疊，懷柔百神。及河喬嶽，允王維后。明昭有周，式序在位。(273/1.1–10)

> How mighty is this Zhou [king]! / He ascends the high mountains,
> The narrow ridges and towering peaks;
> Truly he follows the [Yellow] River that gathers [all waters].

All under Heaven / Assemble in response
To the mandate of this Zhou [king].

於皇時周！陟其高山，隋山喬嶽。允猶翕河。敷天之下，裒時之對，時周之命。(296)

In the second month of the year, [Shun] went on an inspection tour of the royal domains to the east as far as the Grand Mountain [Mount Tai], where he conducted sacrifices to Heaven and to the spirits of the mountains and rivers in the proper order. Thereupon he had an audience with the eastern vassal lords.

歲二月，東巡守，至于岱宗，柴望秩于山川，肆覲東后。(*Shangshu* 3.71)

In His twenty-sixth year,
[The Qin First Emperor] first unified All under Heaven.
There was none who was not respectful and submissive.
He personally tours the distant multitudes,
Ascends this Grand Mountain [i.e., Mt. Tai]
And all around surveys the [world at the] eastern extremity.
The attending officials meditate on His feats,
Trace the roots and origins of His deeds and achievements
And respectfully recite His merits and virtuous power.

廿有六年，初并天下，罔不賓服。親輮遠黎，登茲泰山，周覽東極。從臣思跡，本原事業，祗誦功德。[2]

Many of these elements can be found throughout the *Shi*, and in the "Airs" in particular: verbs of "climbing" verbs (*zhi* 陟, *sheng* 升, etc.; 19 stanzas across 13 poems), mountains (95 stanzas across 63 poems), verbs of "gazing" or "observing" (*wang* 望, *guan* 觀, etc.; 56 stanzas across 36 poems), rivers (110 stanzas across 55 poems), and references to "processions" (*mai* 邁)

or "campaigns" (*zheng* 征; 35 stanzas across 22 poems). The "Airs" don't simply take us on a tour of the Zhou domain; in the aggregate, they simulate the experience of a parading sovereign.

Moving through the four divisions of the *Shijing*, one finds a progression through different sectors of Zhou society, from outer to inner and lower to upper. This movement unites the various roles and categories of Zhou society to create a sense of universality and "wholeness,"[3] thus complementing the Zhou state's territorial extension with its social penetration. The tour begins in the "Airs" with the lowest rungs of society. There are scenes of farming, foraging, hunting, dancing, and other communal activities. Many pieces have a curiously off-stage quality; at the heart of the "Airs" is a fascination with life at the margins. "The Cloth Plant Spreads" (Ge tan 葛覃, #2) shows a woman making and washing clothes in preparation to visit her parents but concludes prior to the visit itself. Pieces about soldiers on the march show more interest in the drudgery of campaigns than in battles. Still other pieces are set in the "wilds" (*ye* 野; #23, 94), outside of "gates" (*men* 門; #40, 89, 93, 137–141), or in the dead of night (#13, 21, 82, 100).[4] Not coincidentally, the "Airs" is the only division to feature female personas.

If the generic subject of the "Airs" is the commoner at the margins, in the "Lesser Court Songs," it's the "prince" (*junzi* 君子) in the upper echelons of Zhou society. There are banquet scenes, military campaigns, odes to virtuous leaders, and poems of admonishment by (would-be) advisers. Then, with the "Greater Court Songs," we ascend to the royal house, the center stage of Zhou society. We are introduced to the Zhou dynasty's founders—King Wen 文王 and King Wu 武王—and its most illustrious ancestors beginning with Hou Ji 后稷, the demigod inventor of agriculture. The Zhou kings are also the "Sons of Heaven" (*tianzi* 天子); thus, as we enter the Zhou royal house, our gaze is lifted upward toward Heaven and the ancestor spirits. Finally, with the "Ritual Hymns" we enter the most sacred space of all—the ancestral temple—wherein the Zhou kings secured the protection of their ancestors.

At the level of individual *Shi*, too, numerous pieces are organized as multistage journeys or circuits. "Bring out the Carts" (Chu ju 出車, #168) is voiced by soldiers who "bring out the carts" 出我車 and "set up the standards" 設此旐矣 in the first two stanzas, "build a fort on the frontier" 城彼朔方 in the third, lament the length of the campaign in the fourth and fifth, and "return home" 還歸 in the sixth. The ritual liturgy of "Thorny Caltrop"

(Chu ci 楚茨, #209) opens in the fields and storehouses with the harvesting and storing of grain for use in the ancestral sacrifice before "proceed[ing] to the autumn and winter sacrifices" 以往烝嘗 in the second stanza.[5] In the second and third stanzas, the ancestor spirits are enticed to "return" (*huang* 皇) and "arrive" (*ge* 格) at the ancestral temple, where they receive offerings from the living.[6] With the announcement of the ceremony's conclusion in the beginning of the fifth stanza, the ancestors "return" (*gui* 歸) to Heaven. The "entrance" (*ru* 入) of the musicians in the final stanza marks the start of the feast in which the clan celebrates the successful completion of the rites and the promise of another year of good harvests.

"Birth to the People" (Sheng min 生民, #245), which tells the origin myth of Hou Ji 后稷 or "Lord Millet" as Zhou progenitor and demigod inventor of agriculture, traces another kind of circuit. Hou Ji is conceived in the first stanza of the poem when his mother "treads on the big toe of the footprint of [the high-god] Di" 履帝武敏歆 (245/1.6). After his birth in the second stanza, his abandonment by his mother in the third, and his maturation in the fourth, he plants the crops that mature in the sixth, at which point Hou Ji "carries [the harvest] in his arms, carries it on his back / And brings it home to begin the sacrifices" 是任是負．以歸肇祀 (245/6.7–8). The poem culminates in the eighth stanza with the smell of the offerings rising up to Di in Heaven:

> High we load the stands, / The stands of wood and of earthenware.
> When the fragrance begins to rise / Di on high is very pleased:
> "What smell is this, so strong and good?"
> Hou Ji founded the sacrifices,
> And without blemish or flaw / They have gone on till now.

> 卬盛于豆，于豆于登。其香始升，上帝居歆。胡臭亶時，后稷肇祀。庶無罪悔，以迄于今。

Hou Ji's journey ends as the ongoing sacrifices to Di begin. Hou Ji is a gift from Di on high, which the Zhou people repay by sending offerings back up to Di.

Other *Shi* are organized around the looping or retrograde motion of repetition.[7] Even in *Shi* with rigidly repetitive structures, as in "Plantain" (Fu yi 芣苢, #8) and "Off in a Boat" (Er zi cheng zhou 二子乘舟, #44)

below, the interplay between repeated and varied elements foregrounds movement and action:

Tshə́ʔ-tshə́ʔ [thick, thick] the plantain; / Here we go plucking it
Tshə́ʔ-tshə́ʔ the plantain; / Here we go holding it.

Tshə́ʔ-tshə́ʔ the plantain; / Here we go collecting it.
Tshə́ʔ-tshə́ʔ the plantain; / Here we go picking it.

Tshə́ʔ-tshə́ʔ the plantain; / Here we go filling aprons with it.
Tshə́ʔ-tshə́ʔ the plantain; / Here we go tucking it.

采采芣苢，薄言采之。采采芣苢，薄言有之。
采采芣苢，薄言掇之。采采芣苢，薄言捋之。
采采芣苢，薄言袺之。采采芣苢，薄言襭之。

The two of you went off in a boat,
Bəm-bəm [flowing, floating] into the distance.
Longingly I think of you; / My heart within *jaŋh-jaŋh* [dismal, doleful].

The two of you went off in a boat, / *Bəm-bəm* off and away.
Longingly I think of you. / Oh may you come to no harm!

二子乘舟．汎汎其景．願言思子．中心養養．
二子乘舟．汎汎其逝．願言思子．不瑕有害．

Repetition creates the background against which the varied elements—mostly rhymed verbs—pop. In "Plantain," the effect enhances the buzz and bustle of the scene; in "Off in a Boat," it highlights the separation that occasions the persona's grief.

So many of the images we find in the opening couplets of *Shi* stanzas likewise convey a sense of movement and flow. By my count, eighty-seven initial couplets across forty-three *Shi* feature flowing water. Forty-eight stanzas across twenty-nine *Shi* open with blowing winds or falling precipitation. Another twenty-three couplets across fourteen *Shi* describe the movements of the sun, moon, or stars. Three dozen more across twenty-one *Shi* feature various kinds of birds in flight. Five dozen stanzas across twenty-eight *Shi* open with horses and/or carriages. The foraging depicted in "Ospreys Cry" and other poems is often prefaced by descriptions of the movements required to get there:

I climbed that southern hill, / To pluck the fern shoots.

陟彼南山，言采其蕨。(14/2.1–2)

I am going to gather the dodder / In the village of Mei.

爰采唐矣，沬之鄉矣。(48/1.1–2)

There in the oozy ground by the Fen [River] / I was plucking the sorrel.

彼汾沮洳，言采其莫。(108/1.1–2)

I went through the wilds / To pluck the dockleaf.

我行其野，言采其蓫。(188/2.1–2)

On the flipside, images of thwarted or aberrant movement tend not to bode well. In the lament of "Wings Flapping" (Xiao bian 小弁, #197), a road "overgrown with weeds" 鞫為茂草 (197/2.2), a "trapped hare" 投兔 (197/6.1–2), and a "dead man on the path" 行有死人 (197/6.3–4) all accentuate the persona's despair. In "Alignment in the Tenth Month" (Shi yue zhi jiao 十月之交, #193), we learn that "The sun and moon foretell disaster / When they do not follow their [normal] path" 日月告凶，不用其行 (193/2.1–2). The carpe diem poem "On the Mountain Is the Thorn-Elm" (Shan you shu 山有樞, #115) makes a similar point:

On the mountain is the thorn-elm; / On the low ground the white elm-tree.
You have long robes, / But you do not sweep or trail them.

You have carriages and horses, / But do not gallop or race them.
When you are dead / Another man will enjoy them.

On the mountain is the cedrela; / On the low ground the privet.
You have courtyard and house, / But you do not sprinkle or sweep them.
You have bells and drums, / But you do not play or beat them.
When you are dead / Another man will treasure them.

On the mountain is the varnish tree; / On the low ground the chestnut.
You have ale and food; / Why do you not daily play your zither,
And perhaps once in a way be merry, / Once in a way sit up late?
When you are dead / Another man will enter your house.

山有樞，隰有榆。子有衣裳，弗曳弗婁。子有車馬，弗馳弗驅。宛其死矣，他人是愉。

山有栲，隰有杻。子有廷內，弗洒弗埽。子有鐘鼓，弗鼓弗考。宛其死矣，他人是保。

山有漆，隰有栗。子有酒食，何不日鼓瑟。且以喜樂，且以永日。宛其死矣，他人入室。

"Robes" (*yi* 衣), "carriages" (*ju* 車) and "horses" (*ma* 馬), "bells" (*zhong* 鐘), "drums" (*gu* 鼓), "zithers" (*qin* 琴), and "ale" (*jiu* 酒) are the standard trappings of elite society in the *Shi*. To participate fully in that society, however, owning them isn't enough. These possessions are also conveyances that transport us with and through the world. One wears robes out to "trail" them along the ground; one "gallops" and "races" horses; and one cleans one's home, prepares food, and plays music to welcome guests. And if a person chooses not to go with the flow, eventually another man will "enter his house" and enjoy his things, and the world will move on without him.

A very different kind of movement is the abrupt and often puzzling transition from a stanza's opening image to its human.

In the wilds there is a dead deer; / With white rushes we wrap it.
There was a lady longing for the spring; / A fair man of service seduced her.

野有死麕，白茅包之。有女懷春，吉士誘之。(23/1)

Tshâŋ-tshâŋ [thick] grow the rush leaves; / White dew turns to frost.
He whom I love / Must be somewhere along this stream.

蒹葭蒼蒼，白露為霜。所謂伊人，在水一方。(129/1.1–4)

Seŋ-seŋ [supple] the horn bow; / Swiftly its ends fly back.
Brothers and kinsmen by marriage / Ought not to keep their distance.

騂騂角弓，翩其反矣。兄弟昏姻，無胥遠矣。(223/1)

The significance of these "stimuli" or "evocative images" (*xing* 興) is a central problem in *Shijing* scholarship and the study of Chinese literature more broadly. At the microlevel, there's the question of an image's relationship to the poem as a whole. Is the carcass of "In the Wilds is a Dead Doe" (Ye you si jun 野有死麇, #23) being carved up into meat as a gift for the lady of the second couplet, as Zheng Xuan suggests?[8] Is it meant to emphasize's a lady's lost virtue, as read by Waley?[9] It's hard to say. At the macrolevel, such images have prompted a wider discussion about the foundational assumptions of the Chinese literary tradition versus that of the West, especially as they relate to the possibility of metaphor and allegory.[10] If "there are no disjunctures between true reality and concrete reality, nor between concrete reality and literary work" in Chinese literary thinking, and if a poem is "a *literal reaction* of the poet to the world around him and of which he is an integral part," then the images can't refer to anything beyond the poet; somehow they must be integral to the experience that prompted the *Shi*.[11]

For our purposes, the meaning of *Shi* imagery matters less than its effect. A *Shi* stanza is like a battery: take one of these images, transition abruptly to a standard *Shi* topic (love, marriage, praise of a lord, a campaign, etc.), wrap it up with repetition and rhyme—that "semantic glue" which "bind[s] together and identif[ies] things that under other circumstances tend to fly apart"—and a poetic voltage is generated.[12] That voltage is the tension between obvious categorical difference (the natural versus the human, peasant life versus elite concerns) and the artificial sense of synchronicity or complementarity produced by syntax and rhyme. (This is what those who see the Chinese worldview as essentially holistic miss about *Shi* imagery: without an implicit sense of categorical difference, the poetry doesn't work.[13]) And like the electric tension in a battery, the poetic tension of a *Shi* stanza induces a current: it prompts us to make sense of it, to make connections for ourselves.

THE MANY HOMECOMINGS OF THE *SHI*

Shi kineticism has an obvious aesthetic payoff, but its ultimate value is ideological. The *Shi* set the world in motion in order to assimilate a particular kind of movement to the movements of celestial bodies, rivers, fauna, and so on, and thus to naturalize it. That movement is *gui* 歸, "to go/come home." Not only do *gui* and its synonyms (*huan* 還, *fu* 復, *fan* 反, etc.) pervade the *Shi* tradition, as a heuristic *gui* illuminates the core commitments of the *Shi* worldview and helps us parse seemingly disparate themes and scenarios.

The movements of *gui* are manifold in the *Shi*. At one end of the spectrum are the more mundane returns and reunions of families and lovers, which feel the most relatable from a cross-cultural perspective.[14] We feel the excitement of a wife preparing to visit the home of her birth, the love-sickness of a woman begging to marry the man she loves, and the filial anxiety of a royal messenger far from home:

> I will go to my matron, / I will tell her I am going home.
> Here I lather my shift, / Here I wash my dress.
> Which things are clean and which not? / I am going to comfort my parents.

> 言告師氏，言告言歸。薄汙我私，薄澣我衣。害澣害否，歸寧父母。(2/3)

> I am wearing my unlined coat all of brocade,
> I am wearing my unlined skirt all of brocade.
> Oh uncles, young and old, / Let me go with him back to his home!

> 裳錦褧裳，衣錦褧衣。叔兮伯兮，駕予與歸。(88/4)

> I yoke these white horses with the black manes,
> I gallop away *tshəm-tshəm [fast and fleet].
> How could I not long to return home?!
> This is why I made this song, / To tell how I long to care for my mother.
>
> 駕彼四駱，載驟駸駸，豈不懷歸。是用作歌，將母來諗。(162/5)

The Hou Ji myth from "Birth to the People" is another example. For all its mythological and sociocultural import, at its core the poem is the story of an orphan who wants nothing more than to reconnect with a distant father (Di), and who goes so far as to invent agriculture and rites of sacrifice just to please daddy. In these poems, there's little effort to rationalize the instinct to *gui*. To paraphrase the rhetorical question of "Four Steeds" (Si mu 四牡, #162) above and several other *Shi*, how could these personas *not* long for home?[15] Or to borrow an example from another literary tradition, Homer didn't need to justify Odysseus's desire to return to his family in Ithaka. The trick was explaining why it took ten long years to get there.

The accumulation of mundane homecomings in the *Shi* is the cover for a certain sleight of hand, an expansion of the range of homes to which people *gui*. Especially in the eulogies of the "Greater Court Songs," *gui* is also the act of going home or submitting to a good king. The implicit argument is that our instinct to submit to royal virtue is as powerful as the instinct to return home and thus that the love we feel for a king is akin to familial love. Even when not described explicitly as a *gui*, the Zhou kings' pull is unmistakable:

> Far away we draw from that wayside pool, / Scooping there, pouring here,
> So that we can steam the grain.
> *Qi-di* [happy] prince, / Father and mother to the people.
>
> Far away we draw from that wayside pool, / Scooping there, pouring here,
> So that we can wash the vessels.
> *Qi-di* [happy] prince, / Where the people return.
>
> Far away we draw from that wayside pool, / Scooping there, pouring here,
> So that we can clean the receptacles.
> *Qi-di* [happy] prince, / Where the people rest.

泂酌彼行潦，挹彼注兹，可以餴饎。豈弟君子，民之父母。[16]
泂酌彼行潦，挹彼注兹，可以濯罍。豈弟君子，民之攸歸。
泂酌彼行潦，挹彼注兹，可以濯溉。豈弟君子，民之攸墍。(251)

When [King Wen] built the Magic Tower,
When he planned it and founded it,
All the people worked at it; / In less than a day they finished it.
When he built it, there was no goading;
Yet the people came in throngs like children.

經始靈臺，經之營之。庶民攻之，不日成之。經始勿亟，庶民子來。(242/1)

[The Zhou king] receives Heaven's blessing,
From the four directions they come to wish him well:
"For 10,000 years, / May your luck never fail!"

受天之祜，四方來賀。於萬斯年，不遐有佐。(243/6)

Splendid were the works of [King Wen] / Within the walls of Feng,
Meeting place for all peoples / A sure buckler was our sovereign and king.
Oh, glorious our sovereign and king!

The Feng River flowed to the East / In the course made for it by Yu,
Meeting place for all peoples.
A pattern was our great king. / Oh, glorious our great king!

To [King Wen's] capital at Hao, to the Moated Mound From west, from east, / From south, from north /
No one did not submit. / Oh, glorious the great king!

A POETRY OF RETURN

王公伊濯，維豐之垣，四方攸同。王后維翰，王后烝哉。
豐水東注，維禹之績，四方攸同。皇王維辟，皇王烝哉。
鎬京辟廱，自西自東，自南自北，無思不服。皇王烝哉！(244/4–6)

From his position at the center of Zhou society, a good king has a magnetism or gravity as powerful as any natural cycle. In "At the Wayside Pool" (Jiong zhuo 泂酌, #251), he is the parent, home, and refuge of his people; likewise, "The Magic Tower" (Ling tai 靈臺, #242) says of King Wen's subjects that they "came in throngs like children." In "Renowned Was King Wen" (Wen wang you sheng 文王有聲, #244), the flow of the Feng River mirrors the flow of subjects to the king.

Some *Shi* even credit the Zhou kings with creating the possibility of home itself. The first stanza of "Spreading" (Mian 綿, #237) opens in "the ancient past" (*gu* 古) with a Zhou ancestor "scraping shelters, scrapings holes [for his people], / before there were any houses" 陶復陶穴，未有家室 (237/1.5–6). But when he and Lady Jiang "came to look for a home" 聿來胥宇 (237/2.5–6) in the environs of Mount Qi 岐山 (in modern-day Shaanxi), he received a divination "saying, 'Stop,' saying, 'Here,' / Build your house at this place" 曰止曰時．築室于茲 (237/3.5–6), whereupon he founded the Zhou capital. Recall, too, that the orphaned Hou Ji doesn't "go home" (*gui*) until the sixth stanza of "Birth to the People" after he grows and harvests the crops that are offered to Di in sacrifice. The implication is that the ruler-managed cycle of planting, growing, harvesting, and sacrificing establishes the basic structure of Zhou society, without which the people would be homeless. The same idea animates the proto-almanac "Seventh Month" (Qi yue 七月, #154):

> In the seventh month the Fire[star] ebbs;
> In the ninth month we hand out the coats.
> In the days of the first month, sharp frosts;
> In the days of the second month, keen winds.
> Without coats, without serge, / How should we finish the year?
> In the days of the third month, we plow;
> In the days of the fourth month, out we step
> With our wives and children, / Bringing hampers to the southern acres
> Where the field hands come to take good cheer.

> ...
> In the days of the second month, we hack the ice *druŋ-druŋ* [thwack thwack],
>   In the days of the third month, we bring it into the cold shed.
>   In the days of the fourth month very early, / We offer lambs and garlic.
>   In the ninth month are shrewd frosts;
>   In the tenth month, we clear the stack grounds.
>   With twin pitchers we hold the village feast, / Killing for it a young lamb.
>   Up we go into their lord's hall, / To raise the drinking cup of buffalo horn:
>   "May [our lord] live for ever and ever!"
>
> 七月流火，九月授衣。一之日觱發，二之日栗烈。無衣無褐，何以卒歲。三之日于耜。四之日舉趾，同我婦子。饁彼南畝，田畯至喜。 ...
> 二之日鑿冰沖沖，三之日納于凌陰。四之日其蚤，獻羔祭韭。九月肅霜，十月滌場。朋酒斯饗，曰殺羔羊。躋彼公堂，稱彼兕觥，萬壽無疆。(154/1,8)

By having the peasants "go up" to the lord and offer him ale, the ultimate product of the agricultural activities described in the first seven stanzas, "Seventh Month" positions the lord at the center of Zhou society. Juxtaposed with so many other celestial movements, seasonal transitions, and human activities, the peasants' *gui* is natural and inevitable.

Tracing the flow of people from periphery to center is one way that the *Shi* legitimize the Zhou kings. Another is offering a rudimentary theory of royal magnetism to fill in the gap in our intuitions about political submission. That theory is one of the foundational conceits of early Chinese thought: that "virtue" is "power" (*de* 德). A true king need only cultivate his virtue because virtue, like charisma, has a tangible, quasi-magical effect on others:

> Now this King Wen, / So circumspect and reverent,
> Illustriously served Di on high / And enjoyed many blessings.
> His virtue unfailing, / He received [the submission of] the myriad domains.
>
> 維此文王，小心翼翼，昭事上帝，聿懷多福。厥德不回，以受方國。(236/3)

Oh, mighty is the man,
On all sides men will take their lesson from him.
Conspicuous are the movements of virtue,
In all lands men will conform to them.
He who takes counsel widely is final in his commands,
Farsighted in his plans, timely in their announcing,
Scrupulously attentive to decorum
Will become a pattern to his people.

無競維人，四方其訓之。有覺德行，四國順之。訏謨定命，遠猶辰告，敬慎威儀，維民之則。(256/2)

Virtue compels movement and it compels the senses. Virtue has a "sound" (*yin* 音; 29/3.4, 241/4.3, etc.) and a conspicuously "bright" (*ming* 明; 241/7.2, 255/4.7, etc.) or "shining" (*zhao* 昭; 161/2.4) appearance:

Then came King Wen; / Di took the measure of his heart,
Spread abroad the sound of his virtue.
His virtue shone bright, / So bright, so good,
Well he led, well he lorded / As king over this great land.

維此王季；帝度其心，貊其德音。其德克明，克明克類，克長克君，王此大邦。(241/4.1-7)

Good kings actively "manifest" (*xian* 顯; 249/1.2, 288/1.12, etc.) or "illuminate" (*ming* 明; 299/4–5.2) their virtue, which is then "followed" (*shun* 順; 243/4.2, 256/2.3-4, etc.) and "cherished" or "longed for" (*huai* 懷; 241/7.2, 254/7.5) as dearly as other *Shi* personas cherish their loved ones.[17]

However, the virtue possessed by a king or dynasty isn't immutable. Virtue must be "sought" (*qiu* 求; 273/1.13) and "cultivated" (*xiu* 脩; 235/6.2) lest it be "forgotten" (*wang* 忘; 83/2.6, 201/3.5), "warped" (*hui* 回; 208/2.5, 236/3.5, etc.), or "overturned" (*dianfu* 顛覆; 256/3.3). We are told that "virtue is as light as a hair [yet] few people can lift it" 德輶如毛，民鮮克舉之 (260/6.2-3) and that the preceding Shang 商 dynasty fell to the Zhou because it failed to preserve its virtue:

> King Wen said, "Come! / Come, you Yin and Shang!
> You rage and seethe in the center of the realm
> And count the hoarding of resentment as virtue.
> You do not make bright your virtue
> So that you have no one at your back, no one at your side;
> Your virtue is not bright,
> And so you have no one to be your assistant, no one to be your minister.

> 文王曰咨，咨女殷商。女炰烋于中國，斂怨以為德。不明爾德，時無背無側；爾德不明，以無陪無卿。(255/4)

In losing their moral authority, the Shang kings reversed virtue's polarity and caused others to find a new home with the Zhou.

Human beings aren't the only ones to feel the pull of the Zhou kings' virtue:

> [The god] Di on high in sovereign might / Looked down majestically,
> Gazed down upon the four quarters, / And sought peace for the people.
> Already in two kingdoms [i.e., Xia and Shang]
> The governance had been all awry;
> Then every land / He tested and surveyed.
> Di on high examined them / And hated the laxity of their rule.
> So he turned his gaze to the west
> And here [in Zhou] made his dwelling place.

> 皇矣上帝，臨下有赫，監觀四方，求民之莫。維此二國，其政不獲。維彼四國，爰究爰度。上帝耆之，憎其式廓，乃眷西顧，此維與宅。(241/1)

Herein lies another explanation for the Zhou kings' magnetism: they establish a home for the gods on earth. Of course, the *Shi* repeatedly observe that the Zhou kings serve at the behest or "command" (*ming* 命) of Heaven (*Tian* 天):

> Di shifted his bright power;
> To fixed customs and rules he gave a path.
> Heaven set up for himself a match on earth;
> Its charge was firmly awarded.

帝遷明德，串夷載路。天立厥配，受命既固。(241/2.9–12)

May you never shame your ancestors, / But rather tend their virtue,
That forever you may be a match for [Heaven's] command
And bring to yourselves many blessings.
Before Yin lost its armies / It was the match of Di on high.
Take Yin as your mirror: / The great command is not an easy thing.

無念爾祖，聿脩厥德，永言配命，自求多福。殷之未喪師，克配上帝。宜鑒于殷，駿命不易。(235/6.1–8)

But there is also an implied *gui* in the description of the Zhou king as the "match" or "mate" (*pei* 配; *phâih) of Heaven. A homophone in Old Chinese for "wife" or "consort" (*fei* 妃; phâi), *pei* also refers to one's spouse, that is, the person one makes a home with. Elsewhere the Zhou king is referred to as the "Son of Heaven" (*Tianzi* 天子), as in the opening stanza of "The Many People" (Zheng minn 烝民, #260):

Heaven birthed the many people; / They have distinctions, they have rules.
The people cling to customs, / They are fond of fine virtue.
Heaven, looking upon the land of Zhou, / Sent a radiance to earth below.
To protect this Son of Heaven / It created Zhong Shan Fu.

天生烝民，有物有則。民之秉彝，好是懿德。天監有周，昭假于下。保茲天子，生仲山甫。(260/1)

Here Heaven actively "protects" (*bao* 保) the king just as fathers elsewhere in the *Shi* "protect their house and home" 保其家室 (213/2-3.6) or "protect and maintain [their] posterity" 保艾爾後 (172/5.6). Regardless of whether the Zhou kings are the mates or sons of Heaven, the message is the same: the royal family is also a divine family. Gods and kings come together to form a home at the center of the world.

The logic of home and homecoming also runs through descriptions of the ancestral sacrifice, wherein a clan's living members entice their deceased ancestors to "return" (*huang* 皇; 209/2.8) to earth and "come to" (*li* 戾; 280/1.12) or "arrive at" (*ge* 格; 209/3.10) the ancestral temple. Properly propitiated, the ancestor spirits then return to Heaven to "requite [their descendants] with great blessings" 報以介福 (209/2–3.11):

> The rites have all been accomplished,
> The bells and drums have given warning.
> The offering descendant goes to his seat,
> The officiant conveys the message:
> "The Spirits are all drunk. / The august impersonator may now rise!"
> Drums and bells send him off.
> The divine protectors [the ancestor spirits] go home.
> Attendants and noble wives / Clear and remove [the dishes] without delay.
> Fathers and brothers / All together banquet among themselves.

> 禮儀既備，鍾鼓既戒。孝孫徂位，工祝致告。神具醉止，皇尸載起。鼓鍾送尸，神保聿歸。諸宰君婦，廢徹不遲。諸父兄弟，備言燕私。(209/5)[18]

Because the dead can't reside with the living, the reunion must be temporary. To quote the *Zuo Tradition* "When a ghost [*kwəi?*] has somewhere to return [*kwəi*], it doesn't become vengeful" 鬼有所歸，乃不為厲.[19] The spirits *gui* to Heaven but remain bound to the living by blood and the logic of "reward" or "reciprocity" (*bao* 報). The concluding banquet then reinforces the kinship of the living "fathers and brothers."

The upshot of this poetics of homecoming is a vision of society united at every level by the innate and universal impulse to *gui*. Lovers *gui* to each other, brides and grooms *gui* to their new homes together, children *gui* to their parents, subjects *gui* to virtuous rulers, the dead *gui* to their living descendants, and Di and Heaven *gui* to virtuous kings to create a home at the center of the world. The happy scenes of conviviality and cooperation we find throughout the *Shi* are the proof of that vision's appeal:

> **Siuk-siuk* [Swish, swish] the tiger net, / Spread deep in the woods.
> **Kiu?-kiu?* [dashing, daring] the martial men, / Belly and heart of the lord.

> 肅肅兔罝，施于中林。赳赳武夫，公侯腹心。(7/3)

The king's hosts *thân-thân [thronging, surging],
As if flying, as if winged,
Like the River, like the Han / Steady as a mountain,
Flowing onward like a stream,
*Mên?-mên? [endless, ceaseless], *lək-lək [ruly, orderly],
Immeasurable, unassailable, / Mightily they marched through Xu.

王旅嘽嘽，如飛如翰。如江如漢，如山之苞。如川之流，綿綿翼翼。不測不克，濯征徐國。(263/5)

They clear away the grass, the trees;
Their ploughs *drak-drak [digging, tilling].
In a thousand pairs they tug at weeds and roots,
Along the low grounds, along the ridges.
There is the master and his eldest son,
There the headman and overseer.
They mark out, they plough. / Deep the food baskets that are brought;
[The men] think fondly of the women, / And they cleave to their men.

載芟載柞，其耕澤澤。千耦其耘，徂隰徂畛。侯主侯伯，侯亞侯旅，侯彊侯以，有嗿其饁。思媚其婦，有依其士。(290/1.1–10)

At their most idyllic, the *Shi* present a vision of society in which everyone experiences the contentment of belonging to a collective anchored to a virtuous lord.

Of course, the *Shi* don't just show us images of virtuous kings and happy subjects. Many *Shi* are voiced by personas who are denied a homecoming for one reason or another. *Gui* in the *Shi* has aspect, grammatically speaking: either the movement of *gui* is complete, in which case the personas are fully integrated within their families or communities, or the movement is ongoing, in which case they suffer the torment of not belonging. This bipolarity creates yet another kind of movement across the *Shijing* anthology: a seesawing oscillation between *Shi* of being home and *Shi* of being away from home, and thus between *Shi* of contentment and *Shi* of anxious separation.

This bipolarity is an old problem in the commentarial tradition. According to the "Great Preface" to the *Mao Shi*, there are two types of *Shi*: the "correct" (*zheng* 正) *Shi* from the Zhou dynasty's heyday and the "mutated" (*bian* 變) *Shi* that arose "when the kingly way declined, ritual and propriety were abandoned, good governance and education were lost, each domain had its own government, and every family had its own customs" 至于王道衰，禮義廢，政教失，國異政，家殊俗 (1.16). The *Mao Shi* thus presents the *Shi* as a grand morality play about the history of the Zhou dynasty, with each poem praising or blaming particular figures and moments in that history.

In contrast, I read moral judgment as an incidental feature of the *Shi* genre. *Shi* of separation or estrangement lend themselves to moral critique, of course, but that isn't their raison d'être. Being home/wanting to go home and belonging/estrangement are complementary aspects of the imperative to *gui*. Showing the pull of exemplary kings on the people is one way to illustrate that imperative; the other is to illustrate the consequences of not *gui*-ing by cutting personas off from their loved ones:

> **Tshə̂ʔ-tshə̂ʔ* [thick, thick] the cocklebur,
> But even a shallow basket I did not fill.
> Sighing for the man I long for / I laid it there on the king's road.

> 采采卷耳，不盈頃筐。嗟我懷人，寘彼周行。(3/1)

> Even the rising waters / Cannot float away bundled firewood.
> Those fine gentlemen / Are not with us defending Shen.
> Oh, the longing, the longing! / In what month shall I return home?

> 揚之水，不流束薪。彼其之子，不與我戍申。懷哉懷哉，曷月予還歸哉。(68/1)

A POETRY OF RETURN

The cloth plant grows, covering the thorn bush,
The bindweed spreads over the wilds.
My lovely one is here no more. / Who am I with? I dwell alone.
. . .
Summer days, / Winter nights—/ A hundred years hence
I will go home to his house.
Winter nights, / summer days—/ A hundred years hence
I will go home to his chamber.

葛生蒙楚，蘞蔓于野。予美亡此，誰與獨處。...
夏之日，冬之夜。百歲之後，歸于其居。
冬之夜，夏之日。百歲之後，歸于其室。(124/1,4-5)

The dominant emotion in these excerpts is the "longing" (*huai* 懷) for reunion, a word which appears forty-two times across thirty-eight stanzas in twenty-eight *Shi*. In dozens of other *Shi*, it's *you* 憂, the "anxiety" or distress that only homecoming can dispel:

ʔiau-ʔiau [Chirp, chirp] goes the cicada,
Lhiâuk-lhiâuk [hop, skip] goes the grasshopper.
Before I saw my prince
My anxious heart *thruŋ-thruŋ* [thronged with worry].
But now that I have seen him, / Now that I have met him,
My heart is at rest.

喓喓草蟲，趯趯阜螽。未見君子，憂心忡忡。亦既見止，亦既覯止。我心則降。(14/1)

The Qi *ju-ju* [ripples, popples]; / Oars of juniper, boat of pine wood.
Come, yoke the horses, let us drive away,
That I may be rid at last of my anxiety.

淇水滺滺，檜楫松舟。駕言出遊，以寫我憂。(59/4)

The mayfly's wings / Are dressed *tshraʔ-tshraʔ* [brilliantly bright].
My heart is anxious; / Come back to me and stay.

蜉蝣之羽，衣裳楚楚。心之憂矣，於我歸處。(150/1)

These excerpts from "Cicada" (Cao chong 草蟲, #14) and "Mayfly" (Fu you 蜉蝣, #150) also happen to feature the two most common formulas in the *Shi*: the lines "[my] anxious heart is __" 憂心__, with twenty-seven instances across fourteen poems, and "[my] heart is anxious" 心之憂矣, with twenty-six instances across eleven poems.

In the more aristocratic milieu of the "Lesser Court Songs," anxiety takes a different form. Elites don't suffer the common loneliness of soldiers on the march or women awaiting their husbands' return. Separation for elites is more figurative than literal, more existential than occasional. These *Shi* of estrangement or alienation give voice to their personas' grievances against their lords, neighbors, and/or Heaven, as in "Wings Flapping":

Wings flapping, those small crows,
Flying homeward *di-di* [flock on flock].
All people are nourished; / I alone am in distress.
Why this curse from Heaven? / What is my offense?
My heart is anxious, / What can I do or say?

Diûk-diûk [Even runs] the highway,
But now it is overgrown with weeds.
My heart is anxious and pained, / My ponderings make me sick of heart.
With deep sighs, I need to sleep; / It's not just anxiety, but also age.
My heart is anxious; / My head pounds, fevers rage.

Certainly the mulberry and catalpa / Are to be remembered and adored.
Whom do we revere if not our fathers?
Whom do we need if not our mothers?
But I do not know a father's roughness / Or a mother's softness.[20]
If Heaven gave me this life, / How was I born under such a star?
...
Look there, a trapped hare, / Perhaps someone will save it.
Along the path, a dead man lies, / Perhaps someone will bury him.

My lord has a heart / Cruel and callous to our lot.
My heart is anxious; / My tears fall because of it.

弁彼鸒斯，歸飛提提。民莫不穀，我獨于罹。何辜于天，我罪伊何。心之憂矣，云如之何。
踧踧周道，鞫為茂草。我心憂傷，惄焉如擣。假寐永歎，維憂用老。心之憂矣，疢如疾首。
維桑與梓，必恭敬止。靡瞻匪父，靡依匪母。不屬于毛，不罹于裏。天之生我，我辰安在。...
相彼投兔，尚或先之；行有死人，尚或墐之。君子秉心，維其忍之。心之憂矣，涕既隕之。(197/1–3,6)

"Wings Flapping" generates a sense of alienation in several ways. As in *Shi* of separation, the dominant emotion is an "anxiety" amplified by sighing, sleeplessness, pain, and tears. The crows coming home to roost (*gui*) in the first stanza only intensifies the "isolation" or "loneliness" (*du* 獨) of a persona denied that chance. He is more akin to the trapped rabbit or unburied corpse of the sixth stanza, a sorry thing that is perilously, shamefully out of place. Like Hou Ji, the persona is also an orphan: Heaven "birthed" him only to "curse" him; he has a father and mother but "does not know" them. And the once level "highway" or "way of Zhou" (*Zhou dao* 周道) is too choked with weeds to permit a return home.[21]

As in "Wings Flapping," another hallmark of estranged or sundered *Shi* personas is the shift from the happy "we" to the suffering "I." In a worldview predicated on homecoming and belonging, true happiness can only be experienced in the first-person plural. To be denied homecoming is to be denied membership in that "we"; thus, these "solitary" (*du* 獨) personas must voice their pain in the first-person singular:

Tall stands that pear-tree; / Its leaves *sraʔ-sraʔ* [glossy, sheeny].
Alone I walk *kwaʔ-kwaʔ* [forlorn]. / True indeed, there are other men;
But they are not like the children of one's own father.
Hey, you that walk upon the road, / Why do you not join me?
A man without brothers, / Why do you not help him?

有杕之杜，其葉湑湑。獨行踽踽，豈無他人，不如我同父。嗟行之人，胡不比焉。人無兄弟，胡不佽焉。(119/1)

There are those with tasty ale / And also fine dishes.
Who gather together with neighbors / And with relatives so numerous.
To think of me all alone, / My anxious heart *ʔən-ʔən [pained, strained].

彼有旨酒，又有嘉殽。洽比其鄰，昏姻孔云。念我獨兮，憂心慇慇。(192/12)

*Ju-ju [on and on] is my malady, / So very painful.
In the four directions there is abundance; / I alone dwell in anxiety.
The people are all at ease; / I alone dare not rest.

悠悠我里，亦孔之痗。四方有羨，我獨居憂。民莫不逸，我獨不敢休。(193/8)

The "I" of these stanzas isn't a natural or stable entity. In the *Shi*, (nearly) every "I" would much rather rejoin the "we."[22] Not even the high god Di of "Sovereign Might" is immune to this imperative. When Di tells King Wen, "I long for [your] shining virtue" 予懷明德 (241/7.2), he (it?) uses the same language as other sundered personas. First-personhood in the *Shi* is a defective state, a side effect of separation or alienation. These voices aren't individuals (in the sense of ontologically indivisible beings) so much as splintered collectives or the dismembered.[23]

Individuation is painful in the *Shi*, but it isn't necessarily abnormal, as the example of romantic longing shows. As long as a person can't be with a mate, feeling whole is impossible:

That mad boy / Will not eat with me.
Yes, it is all because of you / That I cannot take my rest.

彼狡童兮，不與我言兮。維子之故，使我不能餐兮。(86/1)

Outside the Eastern Gate / There are girls like clouds;
But though there are girls like clouds
There is none on whom my heart dwells.
The one in the white jacket and gray scarf / Alone could cure my woe.

出其東門，有女如雲。雖則如雲，匪我思存。縞衣綦巾，聊樂我員。(93/1)

The cloth plant grew till it covered the thorn bush;
The bindweed spread over the wilds.
My lovely one is here no more. / With whom? No, I sit alone.

葛生蒙楚，蘞蔓于野。予美亡此，誰與獨處。(124/1)

By that swamp's shore / Grow reeds and lotus flowers.
There is a man so fair—/ Well made, big, and stern.
Waking, sleeping I can do nothing; / Face to pillow I toss and turn.

彼澤之陂，有蒲菡萏。有美一人，碩大且儼。寤寐無為，輾轉伏枕。(145/3)

However, as the proto-almanac of "Seventh Month" makes clear, the heartache occasioned by courtship isn't a threat to the social fabric. On the contrary, lovesickness is a normal, even necessary, feature of communal life:

> In the seventh month the Fire ebbs;
> In the ninth month I hand out the coats.
> But when the spring days grow warm / And the oriole sings
> The girls take their deep baskets
> And follow the path under the wall / To gather the soft mulberry leaves.
> The spring sun *dri-dri* [warms, thaws],
> They gather the white aster in crowds.

A girl's heart is sick and sad / Till with her lord she can go home.

七月流火，九月授衣。春日載陽，有鳴倉庚。女執懿筐，遵彼微行，爰求柔桑。春日遲遲，采蘩祁祁。女心傷悲，殆及公子同歸。(154/2)

From the perspective of "Seventh Month," lovers' heartache is all for the good because it anticipates and ultimately reinforces the marriage bonds through which communities reproduce themselves. The greater the heartache, the stronger the bond.

Another prosocial individuation can be seen in *Mao Shi* 286–289, which feature the only instances of the first-person singular pronouns *yu* 余 and *zhen* 朕 in the "Zhou Ritual Hymns":

Pity me, the little child, / Inheritor of a House unfinished,
Gweŋ-gweŋ [forlorn, alone] and troubled.
O august father, / All my days I will be pious,
Bearing in mind those august forefathers
Who ascend and descend in the courtyard. / It is I, the little child,
Who will be reverent early and late.
O august kings, / The succession shall not be forgotten!

閔予小子，遭家不造，嬛嬛在疚。於乎皇考，永世克孝，念茲皇祖。陟降庭止，維予小子，夙夜敬止。於乎皇王，繼序思不忘。(286)

Here, then, I come, / Betake myself to the bright ancestors:
"Oh! So anxious, / I have not yet achieved good order.
Help me to complete it.
In continuing your plans, I have been idle. / It is I, the little child,
Who am not yet equal to the troubles assailing our House.
You who roam in the courtyard, up and down,
You who ascend and descend in their houses,
Grant me a boon, o august father!
Protect and enlighten this my person.

訪予落止，率時昭考。於乎悠哉，朕未有艾，將予就之。繼猶判渙。維予小子，未堪家多難。紹庭上下，陟降厥家，休矣皇考，以保明其身。(287)

In the context of the ancestral cult, the "little child" is the male clan head whose authority over the living derives from his special relationship to the dead.[24] As the oldest son of the most recently deceased clan head, he is in the best position to oversee the ancestral sacrifices and ask for blessings from the ancestors. He is the "little child" because he still grieves for his father, the only moments of respite coming during the ancestral sacrifice when his father comes down from Heaven to enjoy the offerings. Only in death will he rise up to join his father in Heaven, at which point his own son will become the new "little child." In the meantime, he remains in a state of constant "disquiet" (*you* 悠, *ju; see 287/1.3), a rhymed synonym for "anxiety" (*you* 憂; *ʔu). In this way, the bereaved "little child" of the "Ritual Hymns" is just a special instance of the sundered son topos. As with the analogy between rulers and parents, blurring the distinction between bereavement and separation has the effect of naturalizing "filial piety" (*xiao* 孝) toward the dead as a core value of the ancestral cult.

OF WRINKLES AND GLITCHES

The *Shi* don't merely use sundered or estranged personas as proof of the universal impulse to go home. At the heart of *Shi* poetics is a fascination with personas who are trapped between conflicting modes of *gui*. These voices are wrinkles in the social fabric or glitches in the system, figures who obey the imperative to *gui* but are denied a true homecoming through no fault of their own. This fascination gives the *Shi* their ethical and psychological depth.

One such wrinkle is the toiling soldier or "man on the march" (*zhengfu* 征夫),[25] a scenario accounting for more than thirty poems and roughly 10 percent of all stanzas.[26] At one end of the subrepertoire are pieces that describe military campaigns as glorious triumphs. The king or general marshals the troops who march in lockstep to victory, as in "Always Mighty in War" (Chang wu 常武, #263):

The king roused his war might, / He thundered and raged.
He advanced his tiger officers / Fierce as ravening tigers.

> ...
> The king's hosts *thân-thân [thronged, surgeed],
> As if flying, as if winged,
> Like the River, like the Han, / Steady as a mountain,
> Flowing onward like a stream,
> *Mên?-mên? [endless, ceaseless], *lək-lək [ruly, orderly],
> Immeasurable, unassailable, / Mightily they marched through Xu.

> 王奮厥武，如震如怒。進厥虎臣，闞如虓虎。...
> 王旅嘽嘽，如飛如翰。如江如漢，如山之苞。如川之流，綿綿翼翼。不測不克，濯征徐國。(263/4.1-4, /5)

But there are even more pieces that describe the plight of common soldiers torn between their allegiance to the king and their desire to return home to their loved ones. They perform "the king's service" (*wang shi* 王事) but at great cost:

> We bring out the carts / On to those pasture grounds.
> From where the Son of Heaven is
> Orders have come that we are to be here.
> The drivers are told / To get the carts loaded up.
> The king's service brings many hardships / It makes swift calls upon us.
>
> We bring out our carts / On to those outskirts.
> Here we set up the standards, / There we raise the oxtail banners.
> The falcon banner and the standards / All *bâts-bâts [flying, fluttering]
> Our anxious hearts *tshiau?-tshiau? [mourning, sorrowing],
> The drivers are worn out.
> ...
> Long ago, when we started,
> The ale millet and cooking millet were in flower.
> Now that we are on the march again / Snow falls upon the mire.
> The king's service brings many hardships
> We have no time to rest or bide.

> 我出我車，于彼牧矣。自天子所，謂我來矣。召彼僕夫，謂之載矣。王事多難，維其棘矣。

我出我車，于彼郊矣。設此旐矣，建彼旄矣。彼旟旐斯，胡不旆旆。憂心悄悄，僕夫況瘁。...

昔我往矣，黍稷方華。今我來思，雨雪載塗。王事多難，不遑啟居。(168/1–2,4)

The burden of a campaign isn't just borne by the soldiers. It also brings anxiety and hardship to those left behind:

> I climb that wooded hill, / And look toward where my father is.
> My father is saying, "Alas, my son is on service;
> Day and night he knows no rest.
> Grant that he is taking care of himself,
> So that he may come back and not be left behind!"

陟彼岵兮，瞻望父兮。父曰嗟予子行役，夙夜無已。上慎旃哉，猶來無止。(110/1)

> The soldiers are on the march
> Painfully they struggle through the wilds.
> In dire extremity are the strong men,
> But pity these wives, left all alone.

之子于征，劬勞于野。爰及矜人，哀此鰥寡。(181/1)

A handful of pieces (e.g., 181/2) do give soldiers a happy homecoming. On the whole, however, the *Shi* are much more interested in the pain of separation than in the joys of reunion. In "Northern Gate" (Bei men 北門, #40), the trauma even extends beyond the return:

> The king's business came my way;
> Government business of every sort was put upon me.
> When I came in from the outside
> The people of my house all turned on me and scolded me.
> Well, it's over now. / No doubt it was Heaven's doing,
> So what's the good of talking about it?

> 王事適我，政事一埤益我。我入自外，室人交遍讁我。已焉哉！天實為之，謂之何哉。(40/2)

The poem doesn't answer the rhetorical question. But its interest in the soldier's plight is clear: his *gui* is a homecoming only in the most superficial sense because he has come home to a family who doesn't welcome him. "Eastern Hills" (Dong shan 東山, #156) subjects its persona to an even crueler fate:

> When I went to the eastern hills, / *Lhû-lhû* [so long] I did not return.
> Now I am come from the east; / How the drizzling rain mists!
> The fruit of the bryony, / Spreads over the eaves of my house.
> There are sowbugs in the rooms, / Spiders in the doorways.
> The paddock shows signs of wild deer, / Glinting are the glow worms.
> These are not things to be feared, / But to be cherished.
> ...
> When I went to the eastern hills, / *Lhû-lhû* [so long] I did not return.
> Now I come from the east; / How the drizzling rain mists!
> The oriole is flying, / Glinting are its wings.
> This one is going [to her new] home.
> Bay and white, sorrel and white her steeds.
> Her mother has tied the strings of her girdle;
> All things proper have been done for her.
> Her new marriage is very festive; / Her old marriage, what of that?

> 我徂東山，慆慆不歸。我來自東，零雨其濛。果臝之實，亦施于宇。伊威在室，蠨蛸在戶。町畽鹿場，熠燿宵行。不可畏也，伊可懷也。...
> 我徂東山，慆慆不歸。我來自東，零雨其濛。倉庚于飛，熠燿其羽。之子于歸，皇駁其馬。親結其縭，九十其儀。其新孔嘉，其舊如之何。(156/2,4)

This soldier has returned home to find his house in shambles and his wife remarried. The pleading, aporetic question of the final line is more than just a pathos-inducing punctuation mark. It's also a challenging question for an ideology premised on the imperative to *gui*: what are people to do when their loved ones don't uphold their end of the bargain? What if a person becomes homeless through no fault of his or her own?

Perhaps the most powerful statement on the toll of military service is "What Plant Is Not Faded" (He huang bu cao 何草不黃, #234), which sharply critiques the triumphalist rhetoric of "Always Mighty in War" and the "Greater Court Songs" generally:

> What plant is not faded? / What day do we not march?
> What man is not taken / To defend the four borders?
>
> What plant is not wilting? / What man is not taken from his wife?
> Pity us soldiers, / Alone treated as if we are not people!
>
> We are not buffalos, we are not tigers / To be led to these desolate wilds.
> Pity us soldiers, / Day and night without rest!
>
> The fox bumps and drags / Through the tall, thick grass.
> The corvéed carts / Are moving along the highway.
>
> 何草不黃？何日不行？何人不將，經營四方？
> 何草不玄？何人不矜？哀我征夫，獨為匪民。
> 匪兕匪虎，率彼曠野。哀我征夫，朝夕不暇。
> 有芃者狐，率彼幽草。有棧之車，行彼周道。

Recall that "Always Mighty in War" likens the king's officers to tigers and his armies to rivers and mountains. In that poem, the king's hosts are so fierce and unrelenting as to appear inhuman. For the persona of "What Plant Is Not Faded," that is precisely the problem. The soldiers are "people" (*min* 民), not tigers, and wish to be treated accordingly. As a rule, the ruler centrism of the *Shi* tradition makes it a relatively inhospitable space for exploring the limits of sovereign power. But in "What Plant Is Not Faded" at least, the critique is clear: submitting to a ruler (*gui*) isn't at all the same as going home to one's family (*gui*).

The most horrifying poem in the *Shijing*, "Yellow Bird" (Huang niao 黃鳥, #131) pushes the logic of *gui* to the breaking point:

> "Kio" sings the oriole / As it lights on the thorn bush.
> Who followed Lord Mu? / Yanxi of the clan Ziju.
> Now this Yanxi / Was the pick of all our men;

But as he drew near the tomb shaft
*Toih-toih [quivering, shivering] he trembled.
That blue one, Heaven, / Destroys all our good men.
If he could be ransomed / A hundred would take his place.

交交黃鳥，止于棘。誰從穆公，子車奄息。維此奄息，百夫之特。臨其穴，惴惴其慄。彼蒼者天，殲我良人。如可贖兮，人百其身。(13/1)

The Mao commentary to "Yellow Bird" understands it as a "criticism" (*ci* 刺) of Lord Mu of Qin 秦穆公 (r. 659–621 BCE) for requiring Yanxi (and the victims of the second and third stanzas) to serve as his assistant in the afterlife. But the poem itself seems less interested in Lord Mu's culpability than in his posthumous power of attraction. In literally the ultimate act of *gui*, Yanxi "follows" (*cong* 從) his lord and "draws near" (*lin* 臨) his grave in preparation to be sacrificed. No one experiences this movement as a happy homecoming; if anything, "Yellow Bird" plays like a scene from a horror movie. A trembling Yanxi is pulled inexorably into the grave pit and away from the community that loves him. However, his sacrifice has a payoff. Despite their revulsion, the onlookers stand united in their admiration for Yanxi and their willingness to trade a hundred of themselves for one of him. Heaven's cruelty ultimately confirms the strength of the Zhou social fabric.

Marriage in the *Shi* is often an engine of social cohesion but not always, especially when viewed from the bride's perspective. The first nuptial glitch occurs after a wedding when the wife "goes home" (*gui*) for the first time to her husband's clan. But as this entails leaving the home of her birth and "distancing herself from her brothers and parents" 遠兄弟父母 (59/2.4), neither the bride nor her birth family necessarily experiences this *gui* as a happy homecoming. As in "Swallow, Swallow" (Yan yan" 燕燕, #28), it's also an occasion for tears:

The swallows are flying, / *Tshrai-drai [flapping, fluttering] their wings.
This one is going [to her new] home, / Far we escort beyond the field.
We gaze after her in vain, / Our tears flowing like rain.

The swallows are flying, / Now up, now down.

A POETRY OF RETURN

This one is going [to her new] home, / Far we go with her.
Gaze after her, cannot see her, / And stand here weeping.

燕燕于飛，差池其羽。之子于歸，遠送于野。瞻望弗及，泣涕如雨。燕燕于飛，頡之頏之。之子于歸，遠于將之。瞻望弗及，佇立以泣。(28/1–2)²⁷

Saying farewell to the family of her birth is something that every bride must endure. In the otherwise joyful wedding scene of "Magpie's Nest" (Que chao 鵲巢, #12), the image of a parasitic cuckoo laying its eggs in another bird's nest warns of the challenge of assimilating into a new family:

Now the magpie had a nest, / But the cuckoo lived in it.
This one is coming [to her new] home; A hundred coaches meet her

維鵲有巢，維鳩居之。之子于歸，百兩御之。(12/1)

Perhaps the most tragic voices in the *Shi* belong to women trapped in unhappy marriages. These personas are the counterparts of the veterans who return to an unwelcoming home:

Why do you not cherish me, / But rather treat me as an enemy?
You have spoilt my virtue; / What is used, no merchant will buy.
Once in times of peril, of extremity / With you I shared all troubles.
But now that you are well nurtured, well fed,
You treat me as though I were a poison.

不我能慉，反以我為讎。既阻我德，賈用不售。昔育恐育鞫，及爾顛覆。既生既育，比予于毒。(35/5)

Three years I was your wife, / Never neglecting my work.
I rose early and went to bed late, / Never idling.
First you took to finding fault with me, / Then you became violent with me.

My brothers disowned me, / "Ho, ho," they laughed.

三歲為婦，靡室勞矣。夙興夜寐，靡有朝矣。
言既遂矣，至于暴矣。兄弟不知，咥其笑矣。(58/5)

Mên?-mên? [Endlessly spreads] the cloth plant
Along the banks of the river.
Far from big brothers, from little brothers / I must call a stranger "Father."
Must call a stranger "Father"; / But he does not heed me.

Mên?-mên? the cloth plant / Along the margin of the river.
Far from big brothers, from little brothers / I must call a stranger "Mother."
Must call a stranger "Mother"; / But she has nothing to do with me.

綿綿葛藟，在河之滸。終遠兄弟，謂他人父。謂他人父，亦莫我顧。
綿綿葛藟，在河之涘。終遠兄弟，謂他人母。謂他人母，亦莫我有。(71/1-2)

All of these mistreated women are blameless in the eyes of the *Shi*, as when the persona of "Valley Wind" (Gu feng 谷風, #35) states in the first stanza that she has "never disobeyed the sound of virtue" 德音莫違. The problem is that the wives' faithfulness isn't reciprocated (*bao* 報) by their husbands and also that they lack the power to do anything about it. In the words of "The Beck" (Si gan 斯干, #189), "[a girl's] only care is the ale and food / And not troubling her father and mother" 唯酒食是議，無父母詒罹 (189/9.6–7).

A darker variation on this theme is "Cypress Boat" (Bo zhou 柏舟, #26):

Tossed is that cypress boat, / Wave tossed it floats.
Krêŋ?-krêŋ? [Tossing, turning] I cannot sleep. / But secret is my anxiety.
Ale I have, all things needful, / For play, for sport.

My heart is not a mirror, / To reflect what others will.
Brothers too I have; / I cannot be snatched away.

But lo, when I told them of my plight
I found that they were angry with me.

My heart is not a stone; / It cannot be rolled.
My heart is not a mat; / It cannot be folded away.
I have borne myself *lis-lis [prim and proper]
In rites more than can be numbered.

Anxious heart *tshiau?-tshiau? [mourning, sorrowing],
I am harassed by a host of small men.
I have borne vexations very many, / Received insults not few.
In the still of night I brood upon it;
In the waking hours I rend my breast.

O sun, ah, moon, / Why are you changed and dim?
My heart's anxiety / Is like an unwashed dress.
Silently I ponder my lot; / I cannot up and fly away.

汎彼柏舟，亦汎其流。耿耿不寐，如有隱憂。微我無酒，以敖以遊。
我心匪鑒，不可以茹。亦有兄弟，不可以據。薄言往愬，逢彼之怒。
我心匪石，不可轉也。我心匪席，不可卷也。威儀棣棣，不可選也。
憂心悄悄，慍于群小。覯閔既多，受侮不少。靜言思之，寤辟有摽。
日居月諸，胡迭而微。心之憂矣，如匪澣衣。靜言思之，不能奮飛。

Even at their lowest, the sufferers of the *Shi* never abandon the hope of a literal or figurative homecoming—except for this persona, who in the final couplet longs instead for an escape up and away.[28] The image of the "unwashed dress" (*fei huan yi* 匪澣衣) accentuates her hopelessness: unlike the happier wife of "The Cloth Plant Spreads" (*Ge tan* 葛覃, #2), she has no opportunity to "wash [her] dress" (*huan wo yi* 澣我衣; 2/3.4) in preparation to return to the home of her birth. And as in "What Plant Is Not Faded," the breakdown in the logic of *gui* opens up a space for critique. Just as the soldiers insist that they aren't mindless animals, the persona of "Cypress Boat" insists that she has a "heart" or "mind" (*xin* 心) of her own. Given their larger ideological commitments, the *Shi* have little solace to offer her. But through marginalized voices like this one, *Shi* authors could at least acknowledge the human costs of the imperative to *gui*. This is the tradition at its darkest but also its most humanistic.

The elite counterparts of the suffering soldiers or unhappy wives of the *Shi* are the male personas of the "Lesser Court Songs" and "Greater Court Songs" who serve unjust or inept lords, as in "Rain Without Limit" (Yu wu zheng 雨無正, #194):

> *Gû?-gû?* [broad and vast] is mighty Heaven,
> Yet it keeps its virtue from us.
> It rains down death and famine,
> Brings war and destruction to all domains.
> Foreboding Heaven is a cruel affliction,
> It does not ponder, does not plan.
> It pays no attention to the guilty, / Who have admitted their crimes.
> But the ones who are innocent, / These, without exception, suffer.
>
> The house of Zhou was destroyed,
> There was no place to rest or reside.[29]
> The great left their homes, / No one knows our toils.
> The three high ministers / All refuse to serve at dawn or at dusk.
> Princes and vassal lords
> All refuse to meet in the morning or at night.
> One wished they could be good,
> But no, they continue their wayward ways.
> . . .
> "Go serve in office," is what they say;
> But it is so difficult, so dangerous.
> Some orders cannot be carried out,
> And thus you incur the Son of Heaven's blame.
> Other orders can be carried out,
> But rancor can reach even to your friends.
>
> They say you should return to the royal city,
> But you say, "I have no house or home."
> So lonely I weep until my eyes bleed;
> Of these words not one does not pain.
> In the past when you moved away,
> Who was there to build a house for you?

A POETRY OF RETURN

> 浩浩昊天，不駿其德。降喪饑饉，斬伐四國。旻天疾威，弗慮弗圖。舍彼有罪，既伏其辜。若此無罪，淪胥以鋪。
>
> 周宗既滅，靡所止戾。正大夫離居，莫知我勚。三事大夫，莫肯夙夜。邦君諸侯，莫肯朝夕。庶曰式臧，覆出為惡。...
>
> 維曰予仕，孔棘且殆。云不可使，得罪于天子。亦云可使，怨及朋友。
>
> 謂爾遷于王都，曰予未有室家。鼠思泣血，無言不疾。昔爾出居，誰從作爾室。(194/1-2,6-7)

Whether figurative or literal, the persona's claim to "have no house or home" epitomizes the plight of those who obey the imperative to *gui* without reaping its benefits. He is compelled to "serve" (*shi* 仕) but feels alienated from king and friends. The opening line of the second stanza also ties his plight to the fall of the Western Zhou capital in 771 BCE and the move to the eastern capital in Luoyi 洛邑 (modern-day Luoyang, Henan province). His homelessness is an aftereffect of the destruction of the Zhou ancestral temple, the home of the Zhou on earth.

The key difference between elite male lamenters and their female or nonelite counterparts is that these men have the agency to vent their frustrations openly and unapologetically:

> Jiafu made this complaint / To delve the king's disorder.
> If you would change your heart,
> The myriad domains would be well nourished.
>
> 家父作誦，以究王訩。式訛爾心，以畜萬邦。(191/10)

> I am not an eagle or a falcon / That soars up into Heaven.
> I am not a sturgeon or a snout fish / That hides away in the deep.
> On the hill grows the bracken, / In the lowlands, the red thorn.
> A prince makes his song / To report his sorrows.
>
> 匪鶉匪鳶。翰飛戾天。匪鱣匪鮪，潛逃于淵。
> 山有蕨薇，隰有杞桋。君子作歌，維以告哀。(204/7-8)

[The king's] plans are not far-reaching,
Thus [I] offer this great remonstration.

猶之未遠，是用大諫。(254/1.7–8)

Complaint (*song* 誦/訟), *report* (*gao* 告), and *remonstration* (*jian* 諫) are bureaucratic terms of art. As defined in the *Offices of Zhou* (*Zhou guan* 周官 or *Zhou li* 周禮), complaints are legitimate grievances submitted by one's subjects, reports are the passing of information from inferiors to superiors, and remonstrations are admonishments of rulers by their officials.[30] Given the Han account of the *Shi* as artifacts of the Zhou state's domestic intelligence-gathering apparatus, such complaints might have been solicited and consumed by Zhou kings as a way to accommodate criticism.

The empowerment of elite male critics undercuts the pathos of their *Shi*, as does their overt didacticism:

> Mighty Heaven now inconstant, / Brings down on us this hardship;
> Mighty Heaven now uncaring / Brings down on us this great pain.
> My lord if strict in rule / Would bring relief to the people's hearts.
> My lord if peaceful / Would dispel hatred and anger.
> ...
> When your cruelty is in full form, / We will indeed meet your spears;
> But if you are constant and kind to us,
> Then we would pledge ourselves to you.

昊天不傭，降此鞠訩。昊天不惠，降此大戾。君子如屆，俾民心闋。君子如夷，惡怒是違。...
方茂爾惡．相爾矛矣．既夷既懌．如相酬矣．(191/6,8)

> When disorder first came, / Calumny did soon reign.
> Now that disorder has come again, / My lord puts his faith in slander.
> But if my lord were angry with them, / Disorders would quickly end.
> If my lord brought us good fortune, / Disorders would quickly cease.

亂之初生，僭始既涵。亂之又生，君子信讒。君子如怒，亂庶遄沮。君子如祉，亂庶遄已。(198/2)

Heaven has brought on this hardship;
Don't be so *hŋans-hŋans* [gratified, satisfied]!
Heaven has brought on this turmoil;
Don't be so *slat-slat* [slack, lax]!
Harmonious words, / Make for a united people.
Easy words, / Make for a tranquil people.

天之方難，無然憲憲。天之方蹶，無然泄泄。辭之輯矣，民之洽矣。辭之懌矣，民之莫矣。(254/2)

Note the explicit and implicit if-then conditionals in these stanzas. The conceit of a didactic literature is that lessons can be learned and mistakes corrected. So, too, in these admonishments, misrule is cast as a temporary wrinkle in the social fabric, something that can be smoothed out with the requisite care and attention—provided, of course, that a ruler "has mounts and wings, / Men of piety and men of virtue, / To guide and fly him" 有馮有翼，有孝有德，以引以翼 (252/5.1–3) along the right path.

WISDOM IN THE *SHI*

The word *wisdom* hasn't been mentioned in this chapter thus far, and for good reason: the *Shi* worldview doesn't require human beings to comprehend the forces to which they are subject. It's much more important for those forces to be inexorable than to be knowable. According to "Sovereign Might," not even the Zhou kings needed to understand the dynamics of virtue:

Di said to King Wen: / "I long for your bright virtue.
You have high renown but do not put on airs,
You are great but without changing your former ways.
Neither understanding nor knowing,
You [merely] follow the precepts of Di."

帝謂文王，予懷明德。不大聲以色，不長夏以革。不識不知，順帝之則。(241/7)

As guarantors of the Zhou sociopolitical order, the gods demand compliance, not understanding. The final stanza of "King Wen" (Wen wang 文王, #235) goes one step further to suggest that Heaven is essentially unknowable:

> The workings of High Heaven / Are without sound, without smell.
> Make King Wen your model
> And the 10,000 domains will put their faith in you.

> 上天之載，無聲無臭。儀刑文王，萬邦作孚。(235/7.5–8)

Because later peoples can't know Heaven directly, their only recourse is to emulate the former mates of Heaven, beginning with King Wen. Here the silence and odorlessness of Heaven stand in sharp contrast to the "brilliance" (*zhao* 昭; 235/1.2) and "illustriousness" (*xian* 顯; 235/1.5) of King Wen. As noted above, part of virtue's conceit is that it compels recognition as much as submission. Recognizing the virtuous requires no intellectual work because virtue is so powerfully self-evident.

Nevertheless, the *Shijing* anthology includes a number of poems whose personas evince an interest in wisdom. Not surprisingly, the vast majority of these passages are found within *Shi* of estrangement. If the Zhou sociopolitical order precludes the need for wisdom, then only those excluded from that order feel its lack. Wisdom is a virtue in the breach; consequently, every performance of wisdom in the *Shi* is also a lament.[31]

One of the oldest and most widely attested forms of wisdom literature across the ancient world is the instruction text, wherein an older authority figure passes on his wisdom to a representative of the next generation, usually a prince.[32] Common features of instruction texts include generational markers, exhortations to listen with humility, and articulations of a conservative ethos ("What I tell you are the old ways"), all of which can be found in the final stanzas of "Grave" (Yi 抑, #256):

> Alas, my son, / That you do not yet know right and wrong!
> When I have not led you by the hand, / I have pointed at the thing itself.
> When I have not face-to-face declared it to you,
> I have whispered it in your ear.
> You may say to me, "You don't know yet,"
> But I have held you in my arms.

A POETRY OF RETURN

The people are short of supplies;
Who knew it early but deals with it late?

Oh, mighty Heaven so bright, / My life is joyless!
Seeing you so *môŋ-môŋ [blind, benighted]
My heart is *tshâmʔ-tshâmʔ [hurt, irked].
I instruct you *tun-tun [again and again];
But you listen to me *mrâuk-mrâuk [aloof and stiff].
You do not treat my talks as lessons,
But on the contrary regard them as a joke.
You may say, "You don't know yet," / But I am in truth a very old man.[33]

Alas, my son, / What I tell you are the old ways.
If you listen to my advice / You will have small cause to repent.
Heaven is sending us calamities; / It is destroying the realm.
You do not have far to go for an example;
Mighty Heaven does not change.
By perverting your virtue, / You reduce the people to great extremity.

於乎小子，未知藏否。匪手攜之，言示之事。匪面命之，言提其耳。借曰未知，亦既抱子。民之靡盈，誰夙知而莫成。

昊天孔昭，我生靡樂。視爾夢夢，我心慘慘。誨爾諄諄，聽我藐藐。匪用為教，覆用為虐。借曰未知，亦聿既耄。

於乎小子，告爾舊止。聽用我謀，庶無大悔。天方艱難，曰喪厥國。取譬不遠，昊天不忒。回遹其德，俾民大棘。(256/10–12)

Whereas instruction texts typically accompany normal transfers of power from one generation to the next, in "Grave," as in the other elite laments of *Mao Shi* #191–200 and 253–257 (excepting 255), the problem is that Zhou society has become disintegrated from top to bottom and center to periphery. Heaven "does not extend its virtue" 不駿其德 (194/1.2) to the people and "the hundred princes" 凡百君子 (194/3–4.5), the political elites immediately below the king, behave irresponsibly.

As in "Grave," whose persona complains that his instructions are mistaken for jokes, a common theme of these poems is misrecognition. In other *Shi* we encounter sundered or estranged personas who crave the sympathetic "understanding" or "recognition" (*zhi* 知) of others.[34] But the elite lamenters of the *Shi* must also contend with the indiscriminate punishments of Heaven and the falsehoods, slander, and misperceptions of their peers:

> Foreboding Heaven is a cruel affliction,
> Neither pondering, neither planning.
> It pays no attention to the guilty, / Who have admitted their crimes.
> But the ones who are innocent, / These, without exception, suffer.
>
> 旻天疾威，弗慮弗圖。舍彼有罪，既伏其辜。若此無罪，淪胥以鋪。(194/1)

> Yes, you say the mountains are low, / But they have hills and ridges.
> The lies and rumors of others, / Why does no one stop them?
> We call in the elders for counsel, / Ask them to divine our dreams;
> They all say, "We are sagely," / But who can tell cock raven from hen?
>
> Yes, you say that Heaven is high, / Yet you dare not but stoop under it.
> Yes, you say the earth is solid, / But you dare not but tiptoe on it.
> The one who cries out these words / Has good sense and good grounds.
> Take pity on the people now; / Why be such snakes and serpents?
>
> 謂山蓋卑，為岡為陵。民之訛言，寧莫之懲。召彼故老，訊之占夢。具曰予聖，誰知烏之雌雄。
> 謂天蓋高，不敢不局。謂地蓋厚，不敢不蹐。維號斯言，有倫有脊。哀今之人，胡為虺蜴。(192/5-6)

> Our tortoise shells are exhausted, / They do not offer good counsel.
> Counselors we have so very many, / Yet with them nothing is achieved.
> Debates fill the court with words,
> But with failure who dares take the blame?
> We are like nontravelers planning an excursion—/ Useless on the road.

我龜既厭，不我告猶。謀夫孔多，是用不集。發言盈庭，誰敢執其咎。如匪行邁謀，是用不得于道。(195/3)

Misrecognition is a symptom of a fractured polity. Virtue's power (*de*) is that it aligns people in a single direction. When that power fails, the people no longer move or act as one, resulting in a multiplicity of purposes and perspectives. Whereas other *Shi* extol the virtues of "the prince" (*junzi* 君子) in the singular, the "hundred princes" (*fan bai junzi* 凡百君子; 194/3-4.5, 200/7.5) of elite lamentations are agents of confusion and disorder. The diversity of voices gives rise to a multitude of "words" (*yan* 言), "counsels" (*mou* 謀), and "plans" (*you* 猶) at court.[35] Against this backdrop, the value of the "wise" (*zhe* 哲) or "sagely" (*sheng* 聖) man lies in his ability to sort through the cacophony to distinguish good men from bad, true talk from false, and right plans from wrong.

In a magisterial survey of notions of wisdom through the ages, Aleida Assman illuminates a key dynamic of wisdom literature in various cultural contexts. Critiquing recent efforts in the social sciences to define wisdom as an object of empirical research, Assmann instead approaches the topic from the outside in to argue that wisdom thrives within a particular kind of ecosystem:

> In a space that is rationally ordered and institutionally controlled, there is little room for wisdom . . . Nor can wisdom flourish where the world is conceived as totally contingent. If there is no order at all, if every move is unexpected and erratic, if every next moment is the manifestation of the utterly new, wisdom has no chance. The special ingenuity of wisdom lies in the gift for recognitions. But recognition presupposes a pattern, however difficult it may be to detect. We may assume that wisdom flourishes in an intermediary space that is neither tightly structured by fixed rules nor totally given over to arbitrariness and confusion. It is expelled from a world in which order is firmly established; it belongs to a world in which order is to be discovered. Order is invisible but assumed to be there; it takes the sensitivity of wisdom to detect or restore it.[36]

Had Assmann incorporated the *Shijing* into her survey, she would have found ample support for her theory. The Zhou sociopolitical order at its height is a prime example of "a space that is rationally ordered and institutionally controlled," hence Di's praise for King Wen as "neither understanding nor knowing" in "Sovereign Might" and the overall lack of interest in wisdom. The elite lamentations of the *Shi* exist in Assmann's "intermediary space" in which order has collapsed but not irretrievably so. The system of the Zhou founders is still there to be activated by those who understand it.

Assmann's notion of wisdom as a middle-ground virtue helps us make sense of the seesawing movement between *Shi* of belonging and *Shi* of separation or alienation, or between *gui* in the perfective and *gui* in the imperfective aspect. As a rule, the *Shijing* avoids mixing these two poles at the level of the poem or stanza. But a few stanzas lump them together as if their authors were mindful of the bipolarity:

> Here there is a wise man: / When I tell him the dicta and sayings,
> He follows the movements of virtue. / Over there is a fool:
> He instead says I am wrong / And to each his own mind.

> 其維哲人，告之話言，順德之行。其維愚人，覆謂我僭，民各有心。(256/9.5–10)

> Here there is a kindly lord, / To whom all the people look.
> His heart full of far-ranging plans, / He selects his ministers with care.
> Over there is a wayward [lord], / Who thinks only he can do good.
> Having his very own thoughts, / He drives the people to lunacy.
> . . .
> Here there is a sage / Who looks out over a hundred leagues.
> Over there is a fool / Who instead delights in lunacy.
> It is not that words are inadequate;
> Why then do you shirk [from doing the right thing]?

> Here there is a good man, / Neither sought after nor advanced.
> Over there is a cruel man, / Both looked after and promoted.
> The people are needy and distressed;
> What is the cause of such bitterness?

> A gale wind finds its course / Through the steep, deep valley.

Here there is a good man, / His every action praiseworthy.
Over there is a wayward man, / Marching on in depravity.

維此惠君，民人所瞻。秉心宣猶，考慎其相。維彼不順，自獨俾臧。自有肺腸，俾民卒狂。

...

維此聖人，瞻言百里。維彼愚人，覆狂以喜。匪言不能，胡斯畏忌。

維此良人，弗求弗迪。維彼忍心，是顧是復。民之貪亂，寧為荼毒。

大風有隧，有空大谷。維此良人，作為式穀。維彼不順，征以中垢。 (257/8,10–12)[37]

The fact that these seesawing here/there stanzas include some of the very few mentions of "wise men" (*zhe ren* 哲人), "sages" (*sheng ren* 聖人), and "fools" (*yu ren* 愚人) in the *Shi* is telling.[38] Wisdom needs the seesaw because it thrives at the fulcrum. To demonstrate his ability to differentiate good from bad, a wise man needs both.

Shi poetry in general isn't wisdom literature. However, these stanzas and elite lamentations more generally suggest a way of reading *Shi* as wisdom literature. From the bipolarity of being home/being away from home, it is but a small leap to a bipolarity of moral praise/censure. This is precisely the leap made by the "Great Preface" to the *Mao Shi*, with its distinction between "correct" and "mutated" *Shi*, with the Mao commentator in the role of the wise man. The elite lamentations of the *Shi* not only taught early exegetes how to read the *Shi* as a repertoire of positive and negative exemplars, they also showed them how to represent themselves as discerning men of wisdom.

CONCLUSION

In the long and storied history of sweeping East–West comparisons, some of the most influential entries over the last few decades belong to David L. Hall and Roger T. Ames, who, in their 1987 book *Thinking Through Confucius*, listed certain "uncommon assumptions" or "distinctive presuppositions" of the Confucian—and, thus, the Chinese—philosophical tradition versus the Anglo-European tradition, including:

- "An ontology of events" versus an ontology of substances, one consequence of which is to "[preclude] the consideration of either agency or act in isolation from the other. The agent is as much a consequence of his act as its cause" (15).
- The immanence of classical Chinese metaphysics and the mutual interdependence of Heaven, earth, and man. Where Western metaphysics prefers dualistic and essentializing explanations, Chinese metaphysics deals in "conceptual polarities" and "contextualist interpretations of the world in which events are strictly interdependent" (19).
- The socially embedded self. "The distinction between Western forms of individualism and the Confucian concept of the person lies in the fact that difference is prized in Western societies as a mark of creativity and originality, while in China the goal of personality development involves the achievement of interdependence through the actualization of integrative emotions held in common among individuals" (23).

Setting aside the validity of their generalizations about the Chinese or Western case, there are some nontrivial parallels between Hall and Ames's list and my own theory of *Shi* poetics, both of which are attempts to trace the basic parameters of early Chinese thought. Their focus on events or "processes"[39] isn't far removed from my argument that the *Shi* parse the world in terms of movement and flow. The many juxtapositions of the movements of nature with the movements of human society could be read as evidence of the immanence of Chinese metaphysics. And the idea that Confucian self-cultivation is about interdependence as opposed to independence could just as easily be applied to notions of personhood in the *Shi*.

Obvious methodological differences aside, what separates my account from that of Hall and Ames is how we interpret these findings. For Hall and Ames, they are the pre-philosophical givens of Chinese culture, "those usually unannounced premises held by the members of an intellectual culture or tradition that make communication possible by constituting a ground from which philosophic discourse proceeds" (11). In the context of this study, they are artifacts of an ideology whose overriding goal was the concentration of political authority in the hands of the Zhou kings.[40] Naturalizing the tenets of the Zhou state's legitimating ideology as essential features of Chinese civilization, as Hall and Ames do, is precisely the goal of *Shi* poetics.

A POETRY OF RETURN

What does this conclusion imply about the origins and early history of the *Shi* tradition? At a bare minimum, my reading would seem to assume a degree of centralized planning on the part of early *Shi* recorders or compilers. Given the pro-Zhou orientation of the *Shijing* and its references to the fall of the Western Zhou capital, the most obvious locale for that planning is the court of the Eastern Zhou dynasty (770–256 BCE), which might have invested in *Shi* as a way of maximizing its ritual and cultural authority in response to the loss of its political and military dominance.[41] In such a scenario, the emphasis on *gui* might have been intended to persuade Spring and Autumn–era elites to return to the Zhou fold. Given that so many of the aristocratic lineages of the Spring and Autumn period (771–476 BCE) were descended from the Zhou royal house, representations of filial affection might have reminded aristocrats of their obligations to the Zhou ancestral cult. At some point, the success of a proto-*Shijing* tradition and the continued decline of the Zhou kings might have resulted in the tradition's unmooring from the Eastern Zhou court. At this second stage, the anthology might have transformed into the more fluid and loosely bounded repertoire observed in Warring States sources. Older material might have been adapted to new purposes, and newer poems organized on older templates might have entered the repertoire. With the centralization of the Qin and Han empires, that repertoire become an anthology once more. But this is mere speculation.

Zooming out from the early Chinese context, this chapter's framework suggests a way to contextualize the *Shi* within a global history of human thought, especially as it relates to the rise of early states and agrarian societies. The *Shi* in the aggregate don't just make an argument for going home to the Zhou kings. By naturalizing the idea of home itself, they advance a very old and familiar narrative:

> Historical humankind has been mesmerized by the narrative of progress and civilization as codified by the first great agrarian kingdoms. As new and powerful societies, they were determined to distinguish themselves as sharply as possible from the populations from which they sprang and that still beckoned and threatened at their fringes. In its essentials, it was an "ascent of man" story. Agriculture, it held, replaced the savage, wild, primitive, lawless, and violent world of hunter-gatherers and nomads. Fixed-field

crops, on the other hand, were the origin and guarantor of the settled life, of formal religion, of society, and of government by laws. Those who refused to take up agriculture did so out of ignorance or a refusal to adapt. In virtually all early agricultural settings the superiority of farming was underwritten by an elaborate mythology recounting how a powerful god or goddess entrusted the sacred grain to a chosen people.[42]

As outlined by James Scott, the early agrarian state was anything but natural or inevitable. Mobile peoples fiercely resisted permanent settlement. Early city dwellers were far more malnourished and diseased than hunters and foragers. Over the long sweep of human evolution, the experience of living a sedentary life under a state has been the exception, not the rule.

I have argued that the *Shi* juxtapose human activities with natural movements in order to naturalize the former. But the present discussion suggests that that formulation isn't specific enough: the *Shi* naturalize sedentism and statism against the mobile and stateless. Crucially, the *Shi* don't seem to deny the possibility of a life lived on the move. From foragers to campaigners, messengers to kings, *Shi* personas traverse the landscape in all sorts of ways. Recall, too, the curiously offstage or liminal quality of the "Airs of the States," which are so often set before or after important ceremonies, outside city gates, or in the uncultivated "wilds" (*ye* 野). Images of wild flora and fauna might even reflect an awareness of the tempo of the hunter-gatherer lifestyle versus that of the farmer or city dweller.[43] Against this backdrop, the *Shi* (disingenuously) represent the sedentary Zhou lifestyle not as form of bondage but as the culmination of the most natural movement of all, the movement of *gui*. Personas who travel away from home are miserable and want nothing more than to bring their travels to an end. To those tempted by the promise of a life lived beyond the confines of the fragile Zhou state, the *Shi* guarantee them an anxious, tormented homesickness. In short, the *Shi* obsession with movement might spring from early agriculturalists' anxieties about the appeal of the nonsedentary, stateless lifestyle.

Chapter Three

SHI POETICS BEYOND THE *SHI*

In the last chapter, I read the *Shi* as artifacts of a more or less coherent ideology. In this chapter, I test that reading by looking for traces of *Shi* poetics in other sources. As I hope to show, early elites didn't simply use the *Shi* as a repertoire of memorable lines or as a venue for showcasing their cultural bona fides. The *Shi* inculcated certain habits of thought and expression that reverberated throughout the early literature.

Demonstrating influence in an ancient context isn't easy due to the sketchiness of our sources. In many of the texts quoted below, *Shi* are referenced explicitly; for others, the determination of influence hinges on the interpretation of intertextual parallels. In still other cases, I show how later texts use the key terms and themes of *Shi* poetics (*return, anxiety*, etc.) in ways that parallel, complement, and problematize the *Shi*. With respect to the *Laozi*, I argue that its poetics stand in such sharp contrast to the *Shi* as to suggest a deliberate oppositionalism. Can I prove that all of these authors were directly responding to the *Shi* when they composed their texts? Definitely not. But recall that what ultimately motivates this effort is the remarkable pervasiveness of the *Shi* in early sources, which establishes a prima facie case for the *Shi* tradition's influence on early thinkers. Given the overall picture, the question is how and where to look for that influence.

Looking ahead to chapter 5 and the conclusion, we can also read this chapter as an experimental introduction to early Chinese thought. Standard introductions to Warring States philosophy tend to carve it up into different thinkers, schools, or -isms, thereby privileging diversity over similarity and neater categorizations over messier heuristics. In keeping with a network theoretical approach, the movement of this chapter is more meandering than programmatic, more "rhizomatic" than "arborescent."[1] Each of this chapter's eight sections tugs on strings tied to the *Shi* tradition and follows them through the early literature without regard for the usual sorts of intellectual historical or literary categories. Imperial edicts are read alongside treatises, the classics alongside noncanonical texts, poetry alongside prose, Kongzi alongside Laozi, and so on. The goal isn't to exhaust all possible connections but to suggest ways of linking the *Shi* to texts, themes, and figures with a high degree of networkability in their own right, thus maximizing the connectivity of a *Shi*-centric model.[2]

EARLY POETRY

The most obvious place to look for the influence of *Shi* poetics is the realm of poetry. Below are three early anecdotes that culminate in the recitation of verse. After summarizing each episode, I ask a simple question: are these verses *Shi* poems?[3]

We begin with the first extended narrative of the *Zuo Tradition*, the story of Lord Zhuang of Zheng 鄭莊公 (r. 743–701 BCE), who nearly falls victim to a coup d'état at the hands of his mother and younger brother.[4] After the coup fails, Lord Zhuang dismisses his mother from the capital and swears an oath: "Until we reach the Yellow Springs [i.e., the land of the dead], we won't see each other!" 不及黃泉，無相見也. Regretting this decision, he follows a subject's advice to "dig into the earth as far as the springs and to meet [his mother] in a tunnel" 闕地及泉，隧而相見, thereby satisfying the letter of his oath. The episode culminates with the happy reunion of mother and son:

> On entering the tunnel, the lord recited, "Within the great tunnel, / Our joy *luŋ-luŋ* [flows, pours]." On exiting the tunnel, Lady Jiang recited, "Beyond the great tunnel, / Our joy *slat-slat* [spreads, extends]." Thereupon they were mother and son as in the beginning.[5]

公入而賦：大隧之中，其樂也融融。姜出而賦：大隧之外，其樂也洩洩。遂為母子如初。(Yin 1/10–16)

The episode ends quoting "Drunk with Wine" (Ji zui 既醉, #247): "With filial sons aplenty, / A good thing is given you forever" 孝子不匱，永錫爾類 (247/5.3–4).

Our second example is the tragedy of Jie Zhitui 介之推 (or Jie Zitui 介子推), one of a handful of supporters who followed Prince Chong'er 重耳 into exile and helped him win back the throne as Lord Wen of Jin 晉文公 (r. 636–628 BCE). When the time comes for Chong'er to reward his followers in the *Zuo Tradition* account, Jie Zhitui alone "doesn't speak of remuneration and remuneration doesn't come to him" 不言祿，祿亦弗及.[6] Angered, he dies in self-imposed exile rather than "eat [the lord's] food" 不食其食. In the *Annals of Lü Buwei* (*Lüshi chunqiu* 呂氏春秋) version, he is said to have "recited verses" (*fu shi* 賦詩) and "hung a written copy from [Chong'er's] gates" 懸書公門 before fleeing into the mountains:

> A dragon is flying / He circles the world.
> Five serpents escort him / They give him assistance.
> The dragon comes home / And claims his position.
> Four serpents escort him / And claim condensation.
> One serpent ashamed / Dies parched in the wilds.[7]

> 有龍于飛，周遍天下。五蛇從之，為之丞輔。龍反其鄉，得其處所。四蛇從之，得其露雨。一蛇羞之，橋死於中野。(12.3/634–635)

The episode ends with Lord Wen offering a reward for information about Jie Zhitui's whereabouts but failing to locate him.

Our final example is an episode from chapter 8 of the *Grand Scribe's Records* (*Shiji* 史記), the "Basic Annals of Emperor Gaozu" (Gaozu benji 高祖本紀):

> Emperor Gaozu was returning home [to his capital in Chang'an in 195 BCE] when he stopped in [his hometown of] Pei [in modern-day Anhui province]. Preparing a banquet in the Pei palace, he summoned all his former acquaintances, young and old alike, to drink their fill. He also gathered 120 children

of Pei to teach them songs. At the height of the banquet, Gaozu played his zither and sang his own verses:

> A great wind rises, clouds fly up and away.
> Having conquered the world, I return to my hometown.
> Where shall I find fearsome warriors to guard my realm?

He then said to the elders of Pei, "A wandering son is sad for his hometown. Although I have made my capital in Guanzhong [at Chang'an], 10,000 years hence my soul will still think fondly of Pei."

> 高祖還歸，過沛，留。置酒沛宮，悉召故人父老子弟縱酒，發沛中兒得百二十人，教之歌。酒酣，高祖擊筑，自為歌詩曰：大風起兮雲飛揚，威加海內兮歸故鄉，安得猛士兮守四方！謂沛父兄曰：游子悲故鄉。吾雖都關中，萬歲後吾魂魄猶樂思沛。(8.389–390)

The episode continues with Gaozu exempting the people of Pei from all tax obligations.

Do any of these verses count as *Shi*? Although labeled *shi*/*Shi* 詩, Jie Zhitui's and Emperor Gaozu's recitations clearly don't belong in the capital-S *Shi* repertoire. The *Shi* tradition's quotidian sensibilities don't allow for flying dragons and serpents à la Jie Zhitui's poem, and the meter of Emperor Gaozu's song (two tri- or tetrametric hemistichs separated by a caesura) marks it as an artifact of Han song culture. Formally speaking, the most *Shi*-like verses are those of Lord Zhuang and his mother because they resemble "Within the Ten-Acre Field" (Shi mu zhi jian 十畝之間, #11):

> Within the ten-acre field, / A mulberry-picker *grên-grên* [lolls, loafs]:
> "If you're going, I'll return with you."
>
> Beyond the ten-acre field, / A mulberry-picker *slat-slat* [slacks, lax]:
> "If you're going, I'll go away with you."

> 十畝之間兮，桑者閑閑兮，行與子還兮。
> 十畝之外兮，桑者泄泄兮，行與子逝兮。

Note the overlapping contrast "within" (*zhong* 中/*jian* 間) and "beyond" (*wai* 外), and the parallel use of the sound-symbolic binome *xie-xie*, written as 浟浟 (*slat-slat) in the *Zuo Tradition* and 泄泄 (*slat-slat) in the *Shijing*. This *Shi* or one like it could have been the template.

On the other hand, the verses of Jie Zhitui and Gaozu seem to participate more fully in *Shi* poetics, beginning with their opening imagery. No fewer than a dozen stanzas across nine poems in the *Mao Shi* open with an image of something "in flight" (*yu fei* 于飛) like the dragon in Jie Zhitui's song, and another seventeen stanzas across eight poems feature winds as in Gaozu's.[8] Both songs also describe a "return" (*fan* 反, *gui* 歸) to a "hometown" (*xiang* 鄉, *guxiang* 故鄉) after a period spent wandering the world. There's also a familiar wrinkle in both cases: Gaozu and Jie Zhitui come home but don't experience a true homecoming. For Jie Zhitui, a lack of recognition keeps him from assuming his rightful place and forces him into exile. For Gaozu, the situation is more complicated.

As one of only two dynastic founders in Chinese history born a commoner, Gaozu's biography throws a very large wrench into the *Shi* tradition's vision of dynastic centrality. Unlike the Zhou founders and the Qin First Emperor, Gaozu was not an aristocrat and so didn't have the benefit of a predynastic capital. When the time came to establish a capital, he chose to build Chang'an 長安 near the ruins of the Qin capital in the Guanzhong 關中 region nearly five hundred miles from his home district of Pei. Consequently, Gaozu in this episode is a man torn between two places—or, more accurately, between one and all places. As a man of Pei, he doesn't experience the imperial capital as a true home; as ruler of the world, his return to Pei is necessarily temporary and thus bittersweet.

The verses of Lord Zhuang and his mother make no mention of homecoming, as one would expect from a *Shi* like "Within the Ten-Acre Field." Instead, the return takes place outside the verses when Lord Zhuang and his mother enter the tunnel and reunite underground. The narrative satisfies the dictates of *Shi* poetics, with the verses reinforcing the action and upping the emotional stakes.

So the short answer is that no, these verses aren't *Shi*. But they're not not *Shi* either. Whoever composed these episodes clearly had a good grasp of *Shi* poetics both in terms of how to compose verses (start with an opening image, organize the action around *gui*, etc.) and when it was appropriate to invoke them (to punctuate problematic homecomings). At the same time, their authors clearly didn't think of *Shi* poetics as strict rules to be applied in rote fashion. In their hands, the *Shi* were a flexible framework for dealing with thorny questions of identity, place, and personal obligations.

Not only do these episodes reveal the flexibility of *Shi* poetics, they also demonstrate the use of *Shi*-style verse to push the limits of the *Shi* ideology. Nowhere do the *Shi* contemplate the possibility of a commoner like Gaozu rising up from among the people to become Son of Heaven. Jiu Zhitui manages to do something that the estranged personas of the *Shi* cannot: he disobeys the imperative to *gui* and chooses to die alone in the wilderness rather than stick by his lord, even one as successful and virtuous as Lord Wen of Jin.[9] Like the Qu Yuan 屈原 legend (see chapter 4), the Jie Zhutui episode shows authors thinking through the possibilities of individual autonomy within and against the centralizing ideology of the *Shi*.

The other lesson of these episodes is that the operations of *Shi* poetics weren't restricted to verse. In the *Zuo Tradition*, the verses and narrative work in tandem to realize the reunion of mother and son. For Gaozu and Jie Zhitui, too, the narrative elements reinforce the action of the verses, and vice versa. So, too, for the case studies of this chapter, we will see that the influence of *Shi* poetics extends across multiple genres of writing.

"THE WAY HOME" (*DAO* 道)

If there is a single word that signals an early author's participation in the world of didactic discourse, it's *dao* 道 (road, path; The Way). Early thinkers routinely framed their arguments as roadmaps to the figurative "Way" or "Path" for rulers to achieve peace and prosperity, for men of service (*shi* 士) to assist their rulers, and for individuals to realize their potential.

How did *dao* become such a central concept in early Chinese thought? Talk of a figurative or abstract *dao* can be found in every canonical tradition and in a wealth of noncanonical texts. Many of these texts also use *dao* used in reference to literal roads, paths, or channels. But only in the *Shi* is it possible to trace the emergence of a figurative *dao* from a literal *dao* that was also an object of interest in its own right.

As integral parts of the Zhou state's political, military, and economic infrastructure, roads in the *Shi* are potent symbols of Zhou sovereignty.[10] "Spreading" (Mian 綿, #237) treats the creation of roads as a key moment in the Zhou dynasty's rise after incursions from barbarian tribes forced an exodus to the environs of Mount Qi 岐 in the Wei 渭 River valley:

> Now [the Zhou] did not suppress their grudge,
> Nor let fall their high renown;
> The oak forests were laid low / Roads were opened up.
> The Kun tribes scampered away; / Oh, how they panted!
>
> 肆不殄厥慍，亦不隕厥問。柞棫拔矣，行道兌矣。混夷駾矣，維其喙矣。(237/8)[11]

Here roads facilitate the projection of Zhou military power. In "Han is Mighty" (Han yi 韓奕, #261), the juxtaposition of roads with an investiture ceremony highlights their role in bringing king and subjects together:

> Mighty is Mount Liang, / It was Yu who fashioned it.
> Conspicuous are its paths.
> The Lord of Han received a charge, / The king in person delivered it.
>
> 奕奕梁山，維禹甸之，有倬其道。韓侯受命，王親命之。(261/1.1–5)

This idea is even more explicit in the "Hounds of Lü" (Lü ao 旅獒) chapter of the *Exalted Documents*, in which the opening of roads allows far-flung peoples to obey the call of the Zhou kings' virtue: "It was when [Zhou] conquered Shang that they opened up roads to the nine Yi tribes and eight Man tribes, and the Western Lü brought hounds in tribute" 惟克商，遂通道于九夷八蠻，西旅底貢厥獒 (13.386). *Dao* are the infrastructure created by kings to bring people to the center (*gui*) or—in the case of campaigns and inspection tours (*xun* 巡)—the center to the periphery.[12]

Roads play an even bigger role in *Shi* poetics. Recall that within *Shi* of separation, the *dao* (or *lu* 路 or *hang* 行) isn't just any path. It's the road back to the sundered persona's loved ones:

> Look up at the sun, the moon. / *Ju-ju* [on and on] I long for you.
> But the road is long; / How could I possibly come?
>
> 瞻彼日月，悠悠我思。道之云遠，曷云能來。(33/3)

My four steeds *phəi-phəi [trekking, treading],
The highway is long and winding.
How could I not long for home? / But the king's business never ends. /
My heart is sick and sad.

四牡騑騑，周道倭遲。豈不懷歸，王事靡盬，我心傷悲。(162/1)

Of course, the roads of the *Shi* also facilitate the separation of people from their loved ones. Within *Shi* poetics, however, the focus is overwhelmingly on roads as pathways of return. The phrase *zhou dao* 周道 in "Four Steeds" (Si mu 四牡, #162) can be read either as a literal "highway" or "great road" connecting the territories of the Zhou domain or (following the Mao commentary and Zheng Xuan) as a metaphor for the Western Zhou sociopolitical order ("the Way of Zhou"). The former derives from the meaning of *zhou* 周 as a "circle" or "circuit"; thus, a *zhou dao* is a road that "encompasses" the realm. In the traveler's lament of "Four Steeds," the literal meaning seems more active. But when the elite persona of "Wings Flapping" complains that the *Zhou dao* 周道 "is overgrown with weeds" 鞫為茂草 (197/2.1–2), the meaning is more ambiguous. Regardless, the ambiguity of *Zhao dao* (or *Zhou lu* 周路 [Zhou road] or *Zhou hang* 周行 [Zhou path])[13] in the *Shi* likely enhanced the sense of *dao*'s significance.[14]

As separation for alienated personas is more figurative than literal, so, too, is their way home, as the third stanza of "Foreboding" (Xiao min 小旻, #195) makes explicit:

Our [divinatory] tortoise shells are exhausted,
They do not offer good counsel.
Master planners we have so very many, / Yet with them nothing is achieved.
Debates fill the court with words, / But who dares take the blame for failure?
We are like nontravelers planning an excursion—/ Useless on the road.

我龜既厭，不我告猶。謀夫孔多，是用不集。發言盈庭，誰敢執其咎。如匪行邁謀，是用不得于道。[15]

Note the use of *ru* 如 ("to be like") to mark the simile of the final couplet. Given the ubiquity of the metaphorical *dao* in later sources, "Foreboding" would seem to reflect an earlier stage in the concept's development. It's hard to imagine the authors of, say, the *Laozi* pausing to observe that *dao* is metaphorical as opposed to literal.

In short, a *Shi*-centric reading of *dao* reveals an overlooked nuance. Like a moving walkway, the *dao* of the *Shi* has a direction or flow. *Dao* isn't just "The Way" but "The Way Home," the path back to a state of integration and belonging. This isn't to suggest that all mentions of *dao* in the early literature carry this nuance. Especially when subordinated to other nouns, as in "the Way of Heaven" (*Tian dao* 天道) or "the Way of Yao and Shun" (堯舜之道), *dao* is simply shorthand for the workings of, and the conduct appropriate to, a particular domain. But there are also moments when the *dao*'s homeward orientation is palpable. One such moment is *Laozi* section 25:

> There is something turbidly formed, / Born before Heaven and Earth,
> So silent, so still.
> Standing alone it does not change,
> It can be considered the mother of the world.
> I don't yet know its name. / We give it the sobriquet "Way." /
> Forced to give it a first name, I call it "The Great."
> "The Great" is "What Moves On."
> "What Moves On" is "Distant." / The "Distant" is "What Turns Back."

> 有物昆（混）成，先天地生。繡（寂）呵繆（寥）呵，獨立〔而不改〕，可以為天地母。吾未知其名也，字之曰道。吾強為之名曰大。大曰筮（逝），筮（逝）曰遠，遠曰反（返）。(section 25/348–350)[16]

First, the *Dao* "moves on" or "away" (*shi* 逝), a verb that appears twenty-two times in the *Shijing* (and in numerous *Shi* citations) but very rarely in early Chinese prose. As it moves away, the *Dao* becomes "distant" (*yuan* 遠), a common theme in *Shi* of separation. Finally, it "turns back" (*fan* 返) toward its point of origin—in other words, it performs a return (*gui*). *Laozi* section 25 thus represents the *Dao* as a journey away and back again in an oscillating cycle of separation and reunion.

Other examples of the use of *dao* to describe a return include the following:

> The "Heavenly man" does not separate from his ancestor. The "spiritual man" does not separate from his essence. The "accomplished man" does not

separate from his true self. The "sage" takes Heaven as his ancestor, virtue as his root, and the Way back [to ancestor and root] as his gate, and he manifests [these aspects] amid changes and transformations.

不離於宗，謂之天人；不離於精，謂之神人；不離於真，謂之至人。以天為宗，以德為本，以道為門，兆於變化，謂之聖人。(*Zhuangzi* 33.1066)

When orders issue from the ruler's mouth, officers receive and enact them. Day and night, they do not rest, communicating them to the lowest reaches of the bureaucracy, imbuing the people's hearts with them, and extending them to the four quarters of the world, until they come full circle and return [*gui*] to the ruler—such is the circular Way. If orders come full circle, then they make the impermissible permissible and the bad good; nothing impedes them. Thus, the ruler devotes his life to his orders, for they determine his worth as well as his security.

令出於主口，官職受而行之，日夜不休，宣通下究，濊於民心，遂於四方，還周復歸，至於主所，圜道也。令圜則可不可善不善無所壅矣。無所壅者，主道通也。故令者，人主之所以為命也，賢不肖安危之所定也。(*Lüshi chunqiu* 3.5/174–175)[17]

Yuezheng Zichun said, "... I heard from Zengzi, who heard it from Kongzi, that 'parents give a whole life and the child returns it whole.' Not damaging oneself or harming one's body can be called 'filial.' The princely man does not take a single step in which he forgets this. But I have forgotten the Way back to filiality, and that is why I am anxious."

樂正子春曰：．．．．吾聞之曾子，曾子聞之仲尼：父母全而生之，子全而歸之，不虧其身，不損其形，可謂孝矣。君子無行咫步而忘之。余忘孝道，是以憂。(*Lüshi chunqiu* 14.1/737–738)

The Way back is like a great road—how could it be hard to recognize? The problem with people is simply that they don't look for it. Go home and look for it. There will be teachers aplenty.

夫道若大路然，豈難知哉？人病不求耳。子歸而求之，有餘師。(*Mengzi* 6B/2)

Note the association of *dao* and *gui* in the *Annals of Lü Buwei* and *Mengzi* excerpts. In the first *Annals of Lü Buwei* passage in particular, the movement of the *dao* is explicitly described as a circuit or a return journey. In the second *Annals of Lü Buwei* passage and the *Zhuangzi*, *gui* isn't a literal movement so much as it is a return to one's roots, be it an ancestor or one's parents. Also note the simile that opens the excerpt from the *Mengzi*. Whereas "Foreboding" explicitly marks the use of *dao* as a metaphor; for the author of *Mengzi* 6B/2, the metaphorical usage of *dao* is so well established that he has to mark its literalization as a "great road."

Of the many sources that correlate *dao* with *gui*, perhaps the most famous is a poem from the "Great Plan" (Hong fan 洪範) chapter of the *Exalted Documents*, which is also among the most cited *Documents* passages in the early literature:

> Neither partial nor slanted, / Keep the royal principles,
> Be without favorites, / Keep to the royal way.
> Be without enemies, / Keep to the royal path,
> Nothing partial, nothing partisan.
> The royal way is *lâŋʔ-lâŋʔ* [broad and wide],
> Nothing partisan, nothing partial.
> The royal way is *breŋ-breŋ* [true and smooth],
> No turning, no tilting, / The royal way is straight and true.
> Gathering [all] at the [sovereign] ridgepole,
> Returning [all] to the [sovereign] ridgepole.

無偏無陂，遵王之義。無有作好，遵王之道。無有作惡，遵王之路。無偏無黨。
王道蕩蕩，無黨無偏。王道平平，無反無側。王道正直。會其有極，歸其有極。(12.368–369)

(As it happens, the *Mozi* attributes lines 7–10 to the "Zhou *Shi*."[18]) Here the smoothness and straightness of the royal *dao* is what facilitates the "return" and the "gathering" of people to the king in the center, symbolized in the "Great Plan" by the "ridgepole" (*ji* 極) or topmost beam of a roof. The section concludes with the statement that "the Son of Heaven acts as father and mother to the people, thereby serving as king of the world" 天子作民父母，以為天下王.

"FATHER AND MOTHER TO THE PEOPLE"

It probably isn't a coincidence that this last line from "Great Plan" parallels one of the most widely quoted couplets from the *Shi* tradition, the lines "**Khâiʔ-dîh* [happy] prince, / Father and mother to the people" 豈弟君子，民之父母 from the first stanza of "At the Wayside Pool" (Jiong zhuo 泂酌, #251):

> Far away we draw from that wayside pool,
> Scooping there, pouring here,
> So that we can steam the grain.
> **Khâiʔ-dîh* [happy] prince, / Father and mother to the people.
>
> Far away we draw from that wayside pool,
> Scooping there, pouring here,
> So that we can wash the vessels.
> **Khâiʔ-dîh* [happy] prince, / Where the people return.
>
> Far away we draw from that wayside pool,
> Scooping there, pouring here,
> So that we can clean the receptacles.
> **Khâiʔ-dîh* [happy] prince, / Where the people rest.
>
> 泂酌彼行潦，挹彼注茲，可以饋饎。豈弟君子，民之父母。
> 泂酌彼行潦，挹彼注茲，可以濯罍。豈弟君子，民之攸歸。
> 泂酌彼行潦，挹彼注茲，可以濯溉。豈弟君子，民之攸墍。[19]

I count at least two dozen explicit citations in early sources, more than for any other *Shi* couplet but one.[20] However, it isn't simply the number of citations that is significant. Many authors also use the couplet as a prompt for further discussion as if the notion of the ruler as parent required unpacking.

One such example is the opening of the "Kongzi at Leisure" (Kongzi xianju 孔子閒居) chapter of the *Ritual Records* (*Liji* 禮記):

> Kongzi was at leisure with Zixia in attendance. Zixia asked, "I venture to ask about the *Shi* that says, '*Khâiʔ-dîh* [happy] prince, / Father and mother to the people.' What sort of person can be called 'father and mother to the people?'"

> 孔子閒居，子夏侍。子夏曰：敢問詩云：凱弟君子，民之父母。何如斯可謂民之父母矣？(51.1626)[21]

Another is this edict issued by Emperor Wen 文帝 (r. 180–157) in 167 BCE:

> The *Shi* say, "*Khâiʔ-dîh* [happy] prince, / Father and mother to the people." But now when someone commits a crime, [mutilating] punishments are meted out before the person has received instruction. He might wish to reform his conduct but has no path [home] to follow. We are extremely grieved by this. Punishment that extends to the severing of limbs and the carving of skin, for which there is no respite until death, is unjustifiably cruel and inimical to virtue. How is this consistent with the idea of being a 'father and mother to the people'? Let mutilating punishments be abolished.

> 詩曰：愷悌君子，民之父母。今人有過，教未施而刑加焉。或欲改行為善而道毋由也。朕甚憐之。夫刑至斷支體，刻肌膚，終身不息，何其楚痛而不德也。豈稱為民父母之意哉！其除肉刑。(*Shiji* 10.427–428)[22]

Emperor Wen's argument against mutilating punishments is that they permanently damage people who might otherwise reintegrate into Han society. A true parent doesn't deny his children a homecoming.

An anecdote from the *Guanzi* 管子 features a very different use of the couplet by an early Chinese ruler. The anecdote opens with Lord Huan of Qi 齊桓公 (r. 685–643) declaring his wish to "restore" (*fu* 復) the property of subjects who borrowed money to bankroll his wars. The "subterfuge" (*miu shu* 繆數) he and Guanzi settle on is to shower the moneylenders with gifts, honors, and invitations to court. When the moneylenders question this generosity, Lord Huan's representatives deliver the following message:

> I have heard that the *Shi* say, '*Khôiʔ-dîh* [happy] prince, father and mother to his people.' I have [recently] had the battle of Zhengqiu, and I have learned that you lent money to my poorest people so that they could supply my most urgent needs and meet my demands, and so that they had the means to plow and plant in spring and tend their fields in summer, thereby funding their lord's endeavors. It is all because of your strength. This is why I have given you jade discs and invited you to court, so that I might repay you in some small way. You are truly 'fathers and mothers to the people.' "

> 寡人聞之詩曰：愷悌君子，民之父母也。寡人有崢丘之戰，吾聞子假貸吾貧萌，使有以給寡人之急，度寡人之求，使吾萌春有以傳耜，夏有以決芸，而給上事，子之力也。是以式璧而聘子，以給鹽菜之用。故子中民之父母也。(83.1492–1493)

The final line is Lord Huan's trump card, an invitation to become "princes" à la "At the Wayside Pool" and join him as parents to the people. Powerless to resist, the moneylenders "tear up their [loan] contracts and erase their books" 折其券而削其書 and proceed to share their wealth with the poor, thus signaling their acceptance of the moral obligations of the parent-to-the-people ideal. In the end, Lord Huan and Guanzi successfully weaponize "At the Wayside Pool" against war profiteers.

As in the excerpt from "Great Plan" above, there are even more passages that compare virtuous rulers to parents without explicitly citing the *Shi*, including the postface to the *Annals of Lü Buwei*:

> The Marquis of Wenxin [=Lü Buwei] said, "Once I succeeded in learning the substance of the Yellow Emperor's instruction to Zhuanxu, which is that there is a great circle above and a great square below. If you can model yourself on these, then you will be a father and mother to the people."

> 文信侯曰：嘗得學黃帝之所以誨顓頊矣，爰有大圜在上，大矩在下。汝能法之，為民父母。(12.654)

As chancellor and regent to the underaged First Emperor of Qin and thus the most powerful person in the (Chinese) world at this time, Lü Buwei 呂不韋 (d. 235 BCE) was in a unique position to certify which ideas mattered in the late third century BCE. And according to his postface (which is arguably the earliest authorial statement known from early China), all 100,000 characters of Lü Buwei's compendium are nothing more than a guide to becoming a parent to the people. Another unmarked usage is this *Guanzi* passage:

> The man of mercy grants many pardons, which is easy initially but creates difficulties later on, eventually bringing countless disasters. The man of law embraces the initial difficulty in order to make things easier later on, eventually bringing countless blessings. Thus, the man of mercy is the enemy of the people and the man of law is the father and mother to the people.
>
> 惠者，多赦者也，先易而後難，久而不勝其禍：法者，先難而後易，久而不勝其福。故惠者，民之仇讎也；法者，民之父母也。(16.298)

Here we find an author using the parent-to-the-people ideal against the spirit of "At the Wayside Pool." "Mercy" (*hui* 惠) is a common term in the *Shi*, particularly in the "Greater Court Songs" and "Ritual Hymns."[23] However, this author rejects the affective dimension of parenthood and instead redefines the ideal around a commitment to *fa* 法 (law). His parent is a strict disciplinarian, not a caring nurturer.

What made the couplet from "At the Wayside Pool" so special? Why did the notion of the ruler as parent interest so many authors? One answer is that it mixed categories in a way that many found challenging, especially those who viewed the strict delineation of social and political roles as the essence of good order. The *Han Feizi* 韓非子 criticizes Ru 儒 and Mohists on the grounds that they "all praise the former kings for indiscriminately caring for all under Heaven, and for looking upon the people as a father and mother would" 今儒、墨皆稱先王兼愛天下，則視民如父母 (49.1096). It goes on to argue that a ruler who allows himself to be guided by familial "affection" or "concern" (*ai* 愛) only invites chaos. The Kongzi of *Analects* 12/11 likewise insists on the distinction between rulers and parents in response to a question about "good governance" (*zheng* 政): "A lord acts as lord, subjects as subjects, fathers as fathers, and sons as sons"

君君，臣臣，父父，子子.²⁴ By that logic, treating a ruler as a parent or a subject as a child is inimical to good order.

We need look no further than the *Shi* for evidence of the same tension. As noted in chapter 2, "At the Wayside Pool" is one of the most explicit statements in the *Shi* on the power of a virtuous ruler to compel the "return" or "submission" (*gui*) of his people. The poem's imagery amplifies that power in a few respects, beginning with the movement "far away" (*jiong* 泂) and back again that anticipates the "return" of the second stanza and the "rest" of the third. The identification of the prince as "father and mother" underscores the same movement insofar as "parents" (*fumu* 父母) in the *Shi* represent the home that sundered personas long for:²⁵

> The king's business never ends;
> I cannot plant my cooking millet and wine millet.
> Where can my father and mother look to for support?
> *Ju-ju* [on and on] blue Heaven stretches; / When will this all be settled?

> 王事靡盬，不能蓺稷黍，父母何怙。悠悠蒼天，曷其有所。(121/1.3–7)

> I climb those northern hills / And pluck the boxthorn.
> *Kri?-kri?* [toiling, moiling] the men of service,
> Early and late upon their tasks.
> The king's business never ends; / I am anxious for my father and mother.

> 陟彼北山，言采其杞。偕偕士子，朝夕從事。王事靡盬，憂我父母。(205/1)

"Bustard's Plumes" (Bao yu 鴇羽, #121) and "Northern Hills" (Bei shan 北山, #205) highlight the problem with the prince/parent equivalence: these men don't serve the king as wholeheartedly as they care for their parents. Their bodies belong to the king but their hearts belong to their families. If these men truly thought of their king as a parent à la "At the Wayside Pool," what would they have to complain about?

In the last chapter, I suggested that the lines "Are we buffaloes, are we tigers / That our home should be these desolate wilds?" from "What Plant

Is Not Faded" can be read as a critique of the dehumanizing rhetoric of the "Greater Court Songs." There's a human cost to forcing people to march in lockstep at the beck and call of a king: men aren't mindless automatons. Read against "At the Wayside Pool" and the analogy between political and familial *gui* in the *Shi*, these stanzas suggest a parallel critique. Likewise, the frequent problematization of the "father and mother to the people" ideal in early sources indicates that the inclusion of rulers among the objects of *gui* wasn't uncontroversial. Implicit in the controversy was an acknowledgment that a king who claims the role of parent to the people usurps their flesh-and-blood parents, thus robbing the people of a fundamental part of their humanity.

WATER (*SHUI* 水)

The other important piece of the parent-to-the-people puzzle is water, which is the common thread of "At the Wayside Pool." Water falls from Heaven, collects in the roadside cistern, is "scooped" and "poured" by the people, grows and cooks the grain, and cleans the vessels, presumably as part of a ritual offering to the spirits in Heaven.[26] Water mediates the reciprocal relationship between Heaven as giver of life and man as giver of offerings. In this way, the flow of water through "At the Wayside Pool" concretizes the flow of virtue (*de* 德) as it springs from the prince, envelops his people, and sweeps them along in a current of prosocial conduct, all of which redounds to the glory of the prince. As a synecdoche for the entire complex of images and relationships in "At the Wayside" pool, "Happy prince, / Father and mother to the people" is an apt tagline.

Numerous early sources likewise compare virtue's attraction to flowing water and filial love:

> The people [of Qi] suffer grievously but there is someone who will give them comfort and respite. They will love [the Chen 陳 clan] like their father and mother and they will return to them like flowing water. Even if they wished not to win the people, how could they avoid it?

> 民人痛疾，而或燠休之。其愛之如父母而歸之如流水。欲無獲民，將焉辟之？(*Zuozhuan* Zhao 3/1233–1234)

As for the world's relationship to Lord Huan, the people of distant states looked on him as a father and mother and the people of nearby states followed him like flowing water.

天下之於桓公，遠國之民望如父母，近國之民從如流水。(*Guanzi* 20.439–440)

[In ancient times] the hundred surnames all loved their superiors. The people returned to them like flowing water and loved them like fathers and mothers.

百姓皆愛其上，人歸之如流水，親之歡如父母。(*Xunzi* 10.190)

When soldiers of principle arrive [to punish a state], the people of neighboring states return to them like flowing water and the people of the punished state look on them as their father and mother. Their territory grows and their subjects become ever more numerous. Without blades meeting in battle, the people submit as if transformed.

義兵至，則鄰國之民歸之若流水，誅國之民望之若父母。行地滋遠，得民滋眾，兵不接刃而民服若化。(*Lüshi chunqiu* 7.5/418)

The people returned to [Zichan 子產] like water flowing downhill and cared for him like a filial son honoring his father and mother.

民歸之，如水就下；愛之、如孝子敬父母。(*Hanshi waizhuan* 3.24/109)

When the government is good, the people are pleased, and when the people are pleased, they return to it like flowing water and feel as close as they do toward their parents.

夫政善則民說，民說則歸之如流水，親之如父母。(*Da Dai Liji* 74.207)

Here as elsewhere, the pairing of water and family metaphors seems axiomatic to early conceptions of virtuous rulership. Given the wealth of "father and mother to the people" citations in early sources, "At the Wayside Pool" might be the locus classicus of that association.

With water, we arrive at a concept of special significance in the early Chinese context, what Sarah Allan has called "the most powerful metaphor in early Chinese philosophical thinking."[27] As Allan shows, many of the most important concepts and arguments in the early tradition are dripping with water imagery, including the *Laozi*:

> The highest good is like water. Water is good at benefiting the myriad things and possesses tranquility. It occupies places that most find loathsome; thus it comes close to the Way.
>
> 上善治（似）水。水善利萬物而有靜。居眾之所亞惡，故幾於道矣。(section 8/253–255)

> The reason why the rivers and seas can be kings of all lesser streams is because they are adept at being below them; thus they can be kings of all lesser streams. Thus, when the sage desires to be above the people, he is always below them with his words; when he wishes to go before the people, he is always after them in his person.
>
> 〔江〕海之所以能為百浴（谷）王者，以其善下之，是以能為百浴（谷）王。是以聖人之欲上民也，必以其言下之；欲先〔民也〕，必以其身後之。(section 66/145–147)[28]

Attached to the *Laozi* materials excavated in 1993 from a tomb discovered in the village of Guodian 郭店 (near Jingmen 荊門 city, Hubei 湖北 province) and dated to about 300 was an untitled text subsequently labeled "The Great Unity Gives Birth to Water" (Tai yi sheng shui 太一生水). Where the *Laozi* offers water as a metaphor for the "highest" (*shang* 上) or most efficacious form of (non)action, "The Great Unity Gives Birth to

Water" presents it as a literal flow and the most foundational movement of the cosmos:

> The Great Unity gives birth to water, and water returns to join with (/assist) the Great Unity, thereby forming Heaven. Heaven returns to join with the Great Unity, thereby forming Earth. Heaven and Earth 【...】, thereby forming the spiritual and luminous. The spiritual and luminous further join with each other, thereby forming *yin* and *yang*. *Yin* and *yang* further join with each other, thereby forming the four seasons . . .
>
> Thus, the Great Unity is stored in water and mobilized in the four seasons:
>
> Cycling and 【...】 anew, 【...】 the mother of the myriad things.
> Alternately empty and full, it thereby weaves together as the warp of the myriad things.
>
> This is something which Heaven cannot destroy, Earth cannot bury, and to which *yin* and *yang* cannot give final form. When a noble man knows this, this is what we call 【...】.[29]

太一生水，水反（薄/輔）太一，是以成天。天反薄太一，是以成地。天地【…】也，是以成神明。神明復相薄也，是以成陰陽。陰陽復相薄，是以成四時。…

是故太一藏於水，行於時：
周而又【…】萬物母。
一缺一盈，以紀為萬物經。
此天之所不能殺，地之所不能埋，陰陽之所不能成。君子知此之謂
【…】

Here, too, the basic movement is a "turning back" or "return" (*fan* 反). And although the final character of this excerpt is missing in the manuscript,[30] the text's overall message is clear: if the cosmos has a literal flow, then a grasp of fluid dynamics is a precondition for wisdom.[31]

Perhaps the best demonstration of water's protean symbolism is an anecdote tradition featuring Kongzi "observing" or "contemplating" (*guan* 觀) water, with versions in the *Analects*, *Garden of Persuasions* (*Shuiyuan* 說苑), *Elder Dai's Ritual Records* (*Da Dai Liji* 大戴禮記), *Family Sayings of*

Kongzi (*Kongzi jiayu* 孔子家語), *Mengzi* (x2), and this episode from the *Xunzi*:³²

> Kongzi stood contemplating the eastward flow of water. Zigong asked him, "Why does a princely man always stand and contemplate water whenever he sees it?" Kongzi said, "Like virtue, water flows everywhere to all living beings and does so effortlessly. Like propriety, it flows downhill, and whether straight or meandering always follows the lay of the land. Like the Way it *kwâŋ-kwâŋ* [flows on and on] and never runs out. Like courage it responds like an echo when sluiced or channeled, and it rushes into a gorge a hundred meters down without hesitation. Like the law, it is always even when poured into a container. Like rectitude, it does not require a level when full. Like discernment, it proceeds bit by bit when slowed down. Like moral transformation, it freshens and purifies as it flows in and out. Like the will, it always flows east even when split into 10,000 streams. This is why when I see a large body of water I always stand and contemplate it."

> 孔子觀於東流之水。子貢問於孔子曰：君子之所以見大水必觀焉者，是何？孔子曰：夫水遍與諸生而無為也，似德。其流也埤下，裾拘必循其理，似義。其洸洸乎不淈盡，似道。若有決行之，其應佚若聲響，其赴百仞之谷不懼，似勇。主量必平，似法。盈不求概，似正。淖約微達，似察。以出以入以就鮮絜，似善化。其萬折也必東，似志。是故見大水必觀焉。(*Xunzi* 28.524–526)

In this context, Kongzi's laconic statement at *Analects* 6/23 that "a wise man delights in water" 知者樂水 makes a little more sense. In text after text, Kongzi matches his observations of fluid dynamics to his knowledge of human virtues, thus showing that the "princely man" exists in a permanent state of "flow" (*liu* 流). A wise man like Kongzi aspires to understand and emulate water's ever-changing, endlessly adaptable movements.

The most spectacular example of water viewing in the early literature is Mei Cheng's 枚乘 (d. ca. 140 BCE) *Seven Stimuli* (*Qi fa* 七發), wherein an anonymous visitor cures a sheltered and ailing prince with vivid descriptions of seven superlative experiences. In the sixth stimulus, the visitor re-creates the experience of "observing" (*guan* 觀) the tidal bore of the Qiantang River 錢塘 in modern-day Hangzhou 杭州, the world's largest. Below is an excerpt of that performance:

When it first rises, a torrent pours forth like a flock of swooping white egrets. As it advances slightly, it becomes vast and gleaming white, like a white carriage and team with curtains and canopy displayed. The wave swells and scatters like clouds, as jumbled as the piled-up baggage of the three armies. It runs to the side and rises rapidly; it is light and graceful, like a command chariot directing the troops. A team of six water dragons follows in the River God's wake. All alone it gallops, like a huge rainbow, front and rear strung together . . . Such magical things are eerie and baffling and cannot be described completely. It only makes one stumble, confused, and apprehensive. This is the strangest sight in the world.

其始起也，洪淋淋焉，若白鷺之下翔。其少進也，浩浩溰溰，如素車白馬帷蓋之張。其波涌而雲亂，擾擾焉如三軍之騰裝。其旁作而奔起也，飄飄焉如輕車之勒兵。六駕蛟龍，附從太白。純馳浩蜺，前後駱驛。. . . 神物怪疑，不可勝言。直使人踣焉，洞闐悽愴焉。此天下怪異詭觀也。(*Quan Han wen* 20.7a/239)[33]

In the *Seven Stimuli*, observing the waters of the tidal bore has a payoff beyond the aesthetic. The experience "confuses and befuddles, frightens and terrifies, rushes and surges, befuddles and baffles, is strange and eerie, deep and vast, broad and boundless" 怳兮忽兮，聊兮慄兮，混汩汩兮，忽兮慌兮，俶兮儻兮，浩瀇瀁兮，慌曠曠兮 but ultimately leads to a cleansing of mind and body:

[The observer] can cast out indolence, purge filth, resolve doubts, and open up the ears and eyes. At this time, although one might have a chronic, long-term illness, it still will straighten a hunchback, raise up the lame, give sight to the blind and hearing to the deaf so that they can go and observe it.

揄棄恬怠，輸寫淟濁，分決狐疑，發皇耳目。當是之時，雖有淹病滯疾，猶將伸傴起躄，發瞽披聾而觀望之也。(*Quan Han wen* 20.7a/239)[34]

On one level, this section is just a conceit on the part of an author-performer who implicitly claims the power to re-create the experience of the tidal bore itself. But the sixth stimulus can also be read as Mei Cheng's contribution to water-viewing literature, all the more so when read against the seventh and final stimulus:

I will present you with men of methods and techniques who are resourceful and ingenious, men like Zhuang Zhou [Zhuangzi], Wei Mou, Mo Di [Mozi], Yang Zhu, Bian Juan, and Zhan He. I will have them discuss the rarefied things of the world and make sense of right and wrong for the myriad creatures. Kong[zi] and Lao[zi] will survey them and Mengzi will tally everything up [so that] you will not make a single mistake in ten thousand [decisions]. These are the most essential sayings and wondrous Ways of the world—does the Crown Prince wish to hear them?

將為太子奏方術之士，有資略者，若莊周、魏牟、楊朱、墨翟、便蜎、詹何之倫，使之論天下之精微，理萬物之是非。孔老覽觀，孟子持籌而算之，萬不失一。此亦天下要言妙道，太子豈欲聞之乎？ (*Quan Han wen* 20.7b–8a/239)

The climax of the performance is a demonstration of his mastery of the wisdom of Laozi, Kongzi, and others, with the preceding sixth stimulus serving as the proof of his intellectual credentials. If a wise man in early China is someone who speaks compellingly about water, then Mei Cheng's protagonist has all other wise men beat.

This reading dovetails with Sarah Allan's analysis of the famous exchange at *Mengzi* 6A/2 between Mengzi and Gaozi 告子 concerning human nature (*xing* 性):

Gaozi said, "Human nature is like fast-moving water. Channel it eastward and it will flow to the east; channel it westward and it will flow to the west. Human nature is indifferent to good versus bad just as water is indifferent to east versus west."

Mengzi said, "Water is indifferent to east versus west, but is it indifferent to up versus down? The goodness of human nature is like the downward flow of water. All people are good; all water flows downward. Now, you could strike water and make it leap up high so that it goes over your head, or you could drive and channel it up into the mountains. But would this have anything to do with the nature of water? It's the circumstances that make it so. When people can be turned bad, their nature is [forcibly distorted in] the same way."

告子曰：「性猶湍水也，決諸東方則東流，決諸西方則西流。人性之無分於善不善也，猶水之無分於東西也。」孟子曰：「水信無分於東西，無分於上下乎？人性之善也，猶水之就下也。人無有不善，水無有不下。今夫水、搏而躍之，可使過顙；激而行之，可使在山。是豈水之性哉？其勢則然也。人之可使為不善，其性亦猶是也。」

Mengzi 6A/2 has been a lightning rod for scholars intent on assessing the nature and quality of debate in early China. Much of the conversation has focused on the question of whether arguments by analogy are legitimate, or whether Arthur Waley was right when he stated that "[a]s a controversialist [Mengzi] is nugatory."[35] However, what the modern debate misses about *Mengzi* 6A/6 is that it's a contest, not a debate. To quote Allan, Mengzi triumphed "not for the trivial reason that his rhetoric was more ingenious than that of his opponent, but *because he had a better understanding of water than Gaozi*."[36] By using the water analogy with superior skill and insight, Mengzi establishes his authority to speak about human nature and other topics. Like the protagonist of the *Seven Stimuli*, Mengzi proves himself a superior water talker and thus a more perspicacious observer of the world's currents.

Returning to the argument of this chapter, there is reason to think that this tradition of performative water talking grew out of the *Shi*. As noted in chapter 2, water is one of the most common images in the *Shijing*, appearing in over a hundred stanzas across dozens of poems. A number of these stanzas open with a persona viewing a body of water:

> Look[37] there at the spring waters, / Flowing into the Qi River.
> My love is in Wei, / No day but I think of him.
>
> 毖彼泉水，亦流于淇。有懷于衛，靡日不思。(39/1.1–4)
>
> . . .
>
> I think of the branching spring, / Long now I sigh for it.
> I think of Mei and Cao, / My heart *ju-ju* [longs on and on].
>
> 我思肥泉，茲之永歎。思須與漕，我心悠悠。(39/4.1–4)

> Look there at the little bay of the Qi, / The river grass *yi-yi* [so delicately waving].

Delicately fashioned is my lord, / As if cut, as if filed,
As if chiseled, as if polished.

瞻彼淇奧，綠竹猗猗。有匪君子，如切如磋，如琢如磨。(55/1.1–4)

Examine those spring waters; / Sometimes clear, sometimes foul.
Every day we meet fresh disasters. / How can we possibly have enough?

相彼泉水，載清載濁。我日構禍，曷云能穀。(204/5)

Look there at the Luo River, / Its waters *ʔaŋ-ʔaŋ [running deep].
Our lord has come, / Blessings heaped upon him thick as thatch.
In his madder knee-caps so red / He is raising the king's six hosts.

瞻彼洛矣，維水泱泱。君子至止，福祿如茨。韎韐有奭，以作六師。(213/1.1–4)

Oh, delight in the waters of the Pan [palace], / Come, pluck the watercress.
The Lord of Lu has come / With his steeds *kauʔ-kauʔ [strong, sturdy].
His steeds *kauʔ-kauʔ [strong, sturdy],
His fame *tiauʔ-tiauʔ [illustrious].
He glances, he smiles, / So patiently he teaches us.

思樂泮水，薄采其藻。魯侯戾止，其馬蹻蹻。其馬蹻蹻，其音昭昭。載色載笑，匪怒伊教。(299/2)

The link between thinking (*si* 思/*nian* 念) and water viewing is most explicit in "Spring Waters" (Quan shui 泉水, #39), in which the sight of the waters flowing off into the distance prompts thoughts of the persona's beloved. In the complaint of "Fourth Month" (Si yue 四月, #204), the endlessly suffering persona seems jealous of the spring waters' occasional purity. The title "Waters of the Pan" (Pan shui 泮水, #299) refers to the semicircular moat surrounding the "Pan palace" (Pan gong 泮宮), a ritual structure whose construction was a privilege granted to the vassal lords of the Zhou.[38] Not coincidentally, the *Outer Traditions of the Han Shi* caps its own version of the "wise man contemplates water" tradition with a quotation of this very *Shi*, the implication being that the *Shi* taught wise men to "delight in water" (*le shui* 樂水).[39]

Elsewhere in the *Shijing*, "Liu the Duke" (Liu gong 劉公, #250) highlights the political dimension of water viewing as a performance of the sovereign gaze:

> Stalwart was Liu the Duke. / He reached the Hundred Springs
> And gazed at the wide plain, / Climbed the southern ridge,
> Looked upon the citadel, / And the lands for the citadel's army.
> Here he made his home, / Here he lodged his hosts,
> Here they were *ŋən-ŋən [at ease, at peace],
> Here they were *ŋaʔ-*ŋaʔ [happy, glad].
>
> Stalwart was Liu the Duke. / In his lands broad and long,
> He noted the shadows and the height of the hills,
> Examined which parts were in the shade, which in the sun,
> And observed the flowing spring waters. (250/3,/5.1–5)

> 篤公劉，逝彼百泉。瞻彼溥原，迺陟南岡。乃覯于京，京師之野。
> 于時處處，于時廬旅。于時言言，于時語語。…
> 篤公劉，既溥既長，既景迺岡，相其陰陽，觀其流泉。(250/3,5.1–5)

Here, we might also recall chapter 2's discussion of royal inspection tours (*xun* 巡) and their ritualized "ascents" (*zhi* 陟) of mountains and surveys of lands and rivers. If the *Shi* taught wise men to delight in water, early kings taught *Shi* poets to associate water viewing with authority.

THE *SHI* AND KONGZI

As the most quoted figure in early China, Kongzi connects dozens of early sources (including numerous excavated manuscripts) in a wide swath of genres from the Warring States through the early imperial period and beyond. As I have argued elsewhere, " 'Kongzi' was the symbolic hub of a metatradition of thinking about the raw ingredients of early Chinese discourse," a voice early authors would borrow in order to "situate" (*chu* 處) or "fix" (*ding* 定) the meaning of various canonical and noncanonical traditions.[40] With the rise of the *Analects* as an instrument of imperial legitimacy and the composition of the first Kongzi biography around 100 BCE, that voice eventually became tied to a particular collection of sayings and a particular narrative of Kongzi's life and times.

Something that the pre- and post-*Analects* versions of Kongzi have in common is their unwavering commitment to the *Shi*. Kongzi was classical China's foremost *Shi* champion.[41] In source after source, he comments on the meaning and significance of the *Shi*, quotes the *Shi* as proof texts, and explicitly promotes their study, as when he says to his son at *Analects* 16/13, "If you don't learn the *Shi*, you'll have no way to speak" 不學詩，無以言. As General Wenzi of Wei 衛將軍文子 tells Zigong 子貢 in a dialogue from the *Elder Dai's Ritual Records*, "I have heard that when [Kong]zi imparted his teachings, he prioritized the *Shi*" 吾聞夫子之施教也，先以詩 (60.107).

Kongzi's statements on the *Shi* are well documented.[42] Less appreciated is the fact that the relationship between Kongzi and the *Shi* wasn't unidirectional: early authors invoked Kongzi to talk about the *Shi*, but they also used *Shi* to talk about Kongzi. Below are the opening lines of the eulogy appended by Sima Qian 司馬遷 (d. ca. 87 BCE) to his biography of Kongzi in the *Grand Scribe's Records*:

> The *Shi* have it, "The lofty mountain looms, / The great road marches on." My heart goes back to him but cannot reach him. When I read the writings of Kongzi, I imagine seeing what he was like as a man. (47.1947)

> 詩有之：高山仰止，景行行止。雖不能至，然心鄉往之。余讀孔氏書，想見其為人。

On one level, Sima Qian quotes this *Shi* couplet as a simple tribute to Kongzi's greatness. Kongzi is the towering mountain for Sima Qian to look up to and the great road for him to follow. However, read against the fifth stanza of "Axle-Pin" (*Ju xia* 車舝, #218), the mention of "heart" (*xin* 心) and the desire to "see" (*jian* 見) Kongzi suggests a deeper meaning:

The lofty mountain looms, / The great road marches on.
The four horses *phəi-phəi* [trekking, treading],
The six reins like zither strings.
The sight of your new bride / Comforts our hearts.

高山仰止，景行行止。四牡騑騑，六轡如琴。覯爾新昏，以慰我心。(218/5)

As in the last couplet, the juxtaposition of acts of "seeing" (見/覯/瞻/望) with descriptions of the onlookers' "hearts" is a common formula in the *Shi*, appearing in at least two dozen stanzas across more than a dozen poems. The second stanza of "Cicada" (Cao chong 草蟲, #14) furnishes another example:

I climb that southern hill, / To pluck the fern shoots.
Before seeing the prince,
My anxious heart was **trot-trot* [distressed, tense].
But now having seen him, / Now having met him, / My heart is delighted.

陟彼南山，言采其蕨。未見君子，憂心惙惙。亦既見止，亦既覯止，我心則說。

Sima Qian inverts this formula in his eulogy. Like *Shi* personas who can't (yet) meet their loved ones, Sima Qian implicitly experiences an "anxiety" (*you* 憂) born of separation. But he takes solace in "the writings of Kongzi" as collected in his biography, which allow him "to imagine seeing" (*xiang jian* 想見) Kongzi in the flesh. In other words, Sima Qian's biography is a proxy for the long-dead Kongzi and thus a balm for our (*Shi*-inflected) longing.

As recorded in the *Zuo Tradition*, the *Grand Scribe's Records*, and the *Ritual Records*, another famous Kongzi eulogy belonged to Lord Ai of Lu 魯哀公 (r. 494–467 BCE):

① Merciful Heaven does not pity me, ② nor does it deign to leave me even one elder ③ to support me, the One Man, in my position. ④ **Gweŋ-gweŋ* [forlorn, alone] I am in trouble. ⑤ Woe is me! Alas, Father Ni! ⑥ I have no way of regulating [the realm] myself.

旻天不弔，不憖遺一老，俾屏余一人以在位。煢煢余在疚。嗚呼！哀哉尼父！無自律。(Ai 16/1698–1699)

It just so happens that every line of the eulogy has a close parallel in the *Shi*:

> Huangfu, so very wise; / You choose Xiang as your new city site.
> You select three ministers to serve,
> Truly plentiful are your stores and treasures.
> ② You do not design to leave even one elder / ③ To support our king.

> 皇父孔聖，作都于向。擇三有事，亶侯多藏。不憖遺一老，俾守我王。(193/6.1–6)

> Pity me, your child, / Inheritor of a house unfinished,
> ④ *Gweŋ-gweŋ* [forlorn, alone] and troubled / ⑤ Alas, august elders!

> 閔予小子，遭家不造。嬛嬛在疚，於乎皇考。(286/1.1–4)

> ① Unpitying is mighty Heaven, / The chaos is unending . . .
> ⑥ If [the king] himself does not govern,
> The hundred clans will long toil and suffer.

> 不弔昊天，亂靡有定 . . . 不自為政，卒勞百姓。(191/6.1–2,7–8)

There is also a hint of word play here. The first line of the sixth stanza of "Alignment in the Tenth Month" (Shi yue zhi jiao 十月之交, #193) refers to a person named "Huangfu" 皇父, who is described as "very wise" (*kong sheng* 孔聖). The word for "very" is *kong* 孔, that is, the "Kong" of "Kongzi." Stripped of its original context, the same line can be read as "August father, Kong[zi] the sage" (皇父孔聖).[43] The fact that Lord Ai refers to Kongzi as "Father Ni," the only such instance I'm aware of in the early literature, would seem to corroborate that possibility.

SHI POETICS BEYOND THE SHI

Extant Kongzi lore also owes a great debt to the *Shi*. To quote Jeffrey Riegel, "some of the literary remains of Confucius's life consist of bits and pieces of ancient poetry which in their origins had nothing to do with Confucius and even predated him."[44] As Riegel observes, the most widely attested Kongzi anecdote in early sources—the story of Kongzi's travails "between Chen and Cai" (*Chen Cai zhi jian* 陳蔡之間), wherein he and his followers are surrounded by hostile forces and left to starve in the wilds—shares a number of features with "How Few" (Shi wei 式微, #36) and "High Mound" (Mao qiu 旄丘, #37). These include the theme of "impoverishment" or "being in dire straits" (*qiong* 窮 or the loan character *gong* 躬), which features prominently in most versions of the anecdote as well as in the second stanza of "How Few":

> How few of us are left, how few! / Why do we not go home?
> Were our lord not in dire straits, / Why would we be here in the mud?

> 式微式微，胡不歸。微君之躬，胡為乎泥中。

Like the personas of "How Few," Kongzi's followers in most versions of the "between Chen and Cai" story ask Kongzi to explain their predicament. The description of the "followers" or "little brothers" (*dizi* 弟子) as exhausted and starving also echoes the plight of the "brethren" (*shu bo* 叔伯) of "High Mound." Here, too, the trigger for these associations may have been some accidental word play. Not only is Kongzi's given name (Qiu 丘) the second character of "High Mound" (Mao qiu 旄丘), the phrase "in the mud" (*ni zhong* 泥中; *nî-truŋ) is an inverted homophone for "Zhongni" 仲尼 (*druŋh-nîh), Kongzi's style name.

Sima Qian in his biography of Kongzi adapts the "between Chen and Cai" episode into a conversation about the same "What Plant Is Not Faded" couplet discussed in chapter 2: "We are not buffaloes, we are not tigers / To be led to these desolate wilds" 匪兕匪虎，率彼曠野 (234/3.1–2).[45] Kongzi quotes these lines to three of his closest followers to ask, "Is my Way wrong? How have I come to this?" 吾道非邪？吾何為於此, thus comparing himself to the suffering "men on the march" (*zhengfu* 征夫, 234/2–3.3) who "follow the Zhou roads" 行彼周道 (234/4.4) "day and night without rest" 朝夕不暇 (234/3.4). In other words, Kongzi wants to know if his plight is as hopeless as that of the campaigning soldiers of the *Shi*, to which Yan Hui responds with a *Shi* allusion of his own:

Sir, even if your Way is so great that the world can't contain it, how are you to blame for that? Only after not containing you [will the world come to] 'see the prince.'

夫子之道至大，故天下莫能容。雖然，夫子推而行之，不容何病，不容然後見君子！

Yan Hui enjoins Kongzi to think of himself not as a homesick soldier but as a prince à la the *Shi*, the exemplar whom personas throughout the anthology long to "see" (*jian* 見). Yan Hui's answer thus anticipates Sima Qian's invitation to meet Kongzi imaginatively through the text of his biography.

Our final example is an episode preserved in the *Ritual Records* and *Grand Scribe's Records* in which an ailing Kongzi sings a lament a week before his death: "Mount Tai tumbles down [*-ûi], / The tree beam decays [*-ûiʔ], / The wise man wilts away [*-oi]!" 泰山其頹乎，梁木其壞乎，哲人其萎乎.[46] In the *Grand Scribe's Records*, Kongzi goes on to complain to Zigong that "no one is capable of treating [him] as an ancestor" (莫能宗予; 47.1944). Although the correspondence is far from perfect, Kongzi's complaints echo a few stanzas from the *Shi*:

> I am like that decaying [*-ûiʔ] tree, / Diseased and limb-less.
> My heart is anxious indeed, / For no one understands me.
>
> 譬彼壞木，疾用無枝。心之憂矣，寧莫之知。(197/5)

> Zip, zip the valley winds, / The winds that turn to whirlwinds [*-ûi].
> In days of peril, in days of dread / You put me in your bosom. [*-ûi]
> In times of peace, of cheer, / You throw me away like slop water. [-i]
>
> Zip, zip the valley winds / Across the rocky hills. [*-ûi]
> There is no grass that is not dying, / No tree that is not wilting. [*-ʔoi]
> You forget my great merits / And remember only my small faults.
>
> 習習谷風，維風及頹。將恐將懼，寘予于懷。將安將樂，棄予如遺。

習習谷風，維山崔嵬。無草不死，無木不萎。忘我大德，思我小怨。(201/2-3)

Note the shared rhyme scheme of Kongzi's lament and "Valley Winds" (Gu feng 谷風, #201) and the parallel sequence in the third stanza from mountains to decaying trees to misrecognition. Kongzi's song and "Valley Winds" also share the words *tui* 頹 (whirlwind, tumble down), the homophones *huai* 壞 (decay) and *huai* 懷 (bosom), and *wei* 萎 (wilt). (In the *Grand Scribe's Records* version, the wooden beam is described as "breaking" *cui* 摧, a loan character for "rocky" *cui* 崔). The fifth stanza of "Wings Flapping" renders the metaphor of the decaying tree explicit while also providing a more direct parallel for Kongzi's complaint to Zigong that he has no one to treat him as an ancestor. As the word for "limb" or "branch" (*zhi* 枝) in the second line also refers to the collateral branches of a clan lineage,[47] Kongzi is literally "branchless" where the persona of "Wings Flapping" is only metaphorically so.

In short, the connection between Kongzi and the *Shi* runs even deeper than Kongzi's explicit endorsements of the *Shi* would suggest. Early Chinese authors invoked Kongzi as an authority on all manner of texts and traditions, especially the Five Classics. But the *Shi* were in Kongzi's bones in a way that other canonical traditions simply weren't, particularly in a pre-Han context.[48] To adapt the line from *Analects* 16/13, "If you don't learn the *Shi*, you'll have no way of talking about Kongzi (*不學詩，無以言孔子).

THE *LAOZI* AS THE ANTI-*SHI*

The *Laozi* 老子 or *Classic of the Way and Virtue* (*Dao De jing* 道德經) isn't just one of the most translated texts from ancient China in the modern era; it also had an unusually high profile in the early context. For starters, the *Laozi* is the only major Master text with an excavated manuscript counterpart from the Warring States period. The correspondence between transmitted versions of the *Laozi* and the manuscripts recovered from the tomb at Guodian and dated to about 300 BCE is far from perfect. However, the overlap is substantial enough to establish the existence of a *Laozi* tradition by the late fourth century BCE at the latest.[49] Two additional *Laozi* manuscripts on silk were discovered at Mawangdui 馬王堆 (Changsha 長沙, Hunan 湖南 province) within a tomb closed in 168 BCE.

The received literature also corroborates the *Laozi*'s specialness. Of all the Master texts catalogued in the Han imperial bibliography, the *Laozi* is the only one listed with multiple recensions and interpretive traditions.⁵⁰ It's the only Master text to receive a commentary in another Master text—the "Explaining *Laozi*" (Jie Lao 解老) and "Illustrating *Laozi*" (Yu Lao 喻老) chapters of the *Han Feizi* 韓非子. "Laozi said" (*Laozi yue* 老子曰) quotations also correspond with the text of the received *Laozi* at a much higher rate (at approximately 70 percent) than quotations of other Masters.⁵¹ A case in point is chapter 12 of the *Huainanzi* 淮南子, "Responses of the Way" ("Dao ying" 道應), which caps fifty-three of its fifty-six sections with "Laozi yue" 老子曰 quotations from the *Laozi*. The *Laozi* was also favored by political elites long before other Master texts. Decades before the first imperial princes started studying the *Analects*, Empress Dou 竇皇后 (d. 135 BCE), the consort of Emperor Wen 文帝 (r. 180–157 BCE) and the mother of Emperor Jing 景帝 (r. 157–141 BCE), "was fond of the sayings of the Yellow Emperor and Laozi" 好黃帝老子言.⁵² The postface to the *Annals of Lü Buwei* also alludes to *Laozi* section 12 and prominently features the concept of *wu wei* 無為 (forgoing action).⁵³

The nature of the relationship between the *Shijing* and the *Laozi* hasn't been a major focus of *Shijing* or *Laozi* studies. To the extent that the *Shijing* is deemed relevant to the *Laozi*, it's usually as a linguistic point of reference, as when Liu Xiaogan analyzes the rhyme categories, meter, and rhetoric of the *Laozi* against the *Shijing* to conclude (too optimistically, in my view) that the *Laozi* "was completed toward the end of Spring and Autumn period, when the *Book of Odes* was compiled and its rhyming styles were still dominant."⁵⁴ The lack of interest in the content of the *Shijing* vis-à-vis the *Laozi* is somewhat understandable given that the *Laozi* never quotes or mentions the *Shi* (or any other canonical tradition, for that matter). Under the influence of the standard typology of Warring States thought, the *Shi* is seen as the province of "Confucian" (*rujia* 儒家) thinkers like Kongzi, Mengzi, and Xunzi, not "Daoists" (*daojia* 道家) like Laozi and Zhuangzi.

The argument of this section is that the *Laozi*'s superficial disinterest in the *Shi* is misleading and that the poetics of the *Laozi* tradition developed in direct opposition to *Shi* poetics. With their dynamic descriptions of flora and fauna, busy peasants and toiling soldiers, multisensory rituals, and conspicuously awesome kings, the *Shi* are awash in movement, sight, and sound. They exhort us to see, to hear, to move, and to feel. In contrast, the

Laozi tradition prizes "darkness" and "obscurity" (*xuan* 玄), "silence" and "stillness" (*jing* 靜), and "not knowing" (*bu zhi* 不知) and "not speaking" (*bu yan* 不言). It tells us to eschew "the five colors [that] blind the eyes, the rushing and chasing [that] drive the mind wild, the rare goods [that] hinder one's movement, the five flavors [that] numb the taste buds, the five sounds [that] deafen the ears, the five flavors [that] numb the taste buds, 五色使人目明（盲），馳騁田臘（獵）使人〔心發狂〕，難得之賞（貨）使人之行方（妨），五味使人之口啪（爽），五音使人之耳聾 (section 12/273). Instead, we are exhorted to value that which is "looked for but unseen . . ., listened for but unheard" 視之而弗見 . . . 聽之而弗聞, the "formless form and thingless image" 无狀之狀，无物之〔象〕 (section 14/282–287). Where virtue in the *Shi* is a "conspicuous" (*xian* 顯) thing, in the *Laozi* it's "dark" and "obscure" (*xuan*). And if the *Shijing* reads like a literary inspection tour of the Zhou dynasty, then the *Laozi* is precisely the opposite:

> Don't go out the door / To know the world.
> Don't peer out the window / To know Heaven's Way.
> The farther out you go, / The less you know. / This is why the sage
> Knows without journeying, / Understands without seeing,
> Accomplishes without doing.
>
> 不出於戶，以知天下。不覞（窺）於牖，以知天道。其出也彌（彌）遠，其〔知彌少。是以聖人不行而知，不見而明，弗〕而〔成〕 (section 47/50–52)

As seen in the pivot from sagely knowing to sagely nondoing in the final line of this excerpt, the *Laozi*'s quietism isn't just a recipe for comprehending the mysteries of the cosmos. It's also a theory of political (in)action:

> The sage says, "I forgo action and the people transform themselves; I love stillness and the people correct themselves; I forgo assigning tasks and the people enrich themselves; I desire not to desire and the people simplify themselves."
>
> 〔是以聖人之言曰〕：我无為也而民自化，我好靜而民自正，我无事民〔自富，我欲不欲而民自樸〕。(section 57/106)

The *Laozi* has only contempt for the toiling, marching, conquering, try-hard kings of the "Greater Court Songs." "The most virtuous," it insists in a typical paradox, "do not [strive for] virtue, and thus have virtue" 〔上德不德，是以有德〕 (section 38/1). At almost every turn, the *Laozi* zags where the *Shi* zig.

For all of these differences, the *Laozi* agrees with the *Shi* that the path to political order, social harmony, and personal fulfillment is nothing but a "return" (*gui* 歸, *huan* 還, *fu* 復). In a text obsessed with stillness, return is the only permissible movement:

> Know your male aspect / But guard your female aspect;
> Be the world's ravine.
> Be the world's ravine, / Maintain your virtue—do not leave it.
> Maintain your virtue—do not leave it, / Return back to infancy.
> Know your honorable aspect / But guard your dishonorable aspect;
> Be the world's valley.
> Be the world's valley, / Maintain your virtue—it will be enough.
> Maintain your virtue—it will be enough, / Return back to simplicity.
> Know your white aspect, / But guard your black aspect;
> Be the pattern of the world.
> Be the pattern of the world, / Maintain your virtue—do not alter it,
> Return back to nonextremity.

> 知其雄，守其雌，為天下溪。為天下溪，恆德不雞（離）。恆德不雞（離），復歸嬰兒。知其日（榮），守其辱，為天下浴（谷）。為天下浴（谷），恆德乃〔足〕。恆德乃〔足，復歸於樸〕。知其白，守其黑，為天下式。為天下式。恆德不貣（忒）。恆德不貣（忒），復歸於无極。(section 28/369–371)

For a sage who never leaves home, the *gui* of the *Laozi* cannot be a literal homecoming. Instead, it's a home-*turning*, a reversion to a primal state of being; to quote *Laozi* section 40, "Turning back is the movement of the Way" 〔反也者〕，道之動也 (26). Where *gui* in the *Shi* is a movement across a physical (or social) distance, *gui* in the *Laozi* is a process of simplification or negation, a shedding of everything that distances us from our true nature:

> Cut off sagacity, throw out knowledge,
> And the people will benefit a hundredfold.
> Cut off benevolence, throw out propriety,
> And the people will return to filiality and compassion.
> Cut off cleverness, throw out sharpness,
> And thieves and brigands will have nothing.

絕聲（聖）棄知（智），而民利百負（倍）。絕仁棄義，民復畜（孝）茲（慈）。絕巧棄利，盜賊无有。 (section 19/311–312)

Chief among these distractions are the "patterns" (*wen* 文) and "accumulations" (*ji* 積) of culture: beautiful speech (*mei yan* 美言), fine clothing (*wen cai* 文綵), wealth (*cai huo* 財貨), learning (*xue* 學), and conventional moral precepts (*ren* 仁, *yi* 義, *li* 禮, etc.).

Although the manner of return in the *Laozi* is different, the political upshot is the same as in the *Shi*. A true king attracts the world through his virtue:

> The Way is ever nameless. / The simple is small
> Yet no one in the world dares to subjugate it.
> If a lord or king could guard it,
> The myriad creatures would lodge themselves with him.
> Heaven and Earth would harmonize
> And the sweet dews would rain down.
> Wholly unbidden the people would align themselves with him . . .
> The Way is to the world / As rivers and seas are to lesser streams.

道恆无名，握（樸）唯（雖）〔小，而天下弗敢臣。侯〕王若能守之，萬物將自賓。天地相谷（合），以俞（雨）甘洛（露），民莫之〔令而自均〕焉。. . . 卑（譬）道之在〔天下也，猶小〕浴（谷）之與江海也。 (section 32/397–401)

> The bringer of emptiness is the ridgepole,
> The guard of stillness is the overseer.
> The myriad living things arise together; / I observe their return.

Creatures *wən-wən [teem and seethe],
Each returning back to its root.
Returning to the root is called "being still,"
Being still is "returning [one's] command."
Returning [one's] command is constancy,
Knowing constancy is illumination.
Not knowing constancy is delusion, / Delusion gives rise to misfortune.
Know constancy to contain [the myriad creatures],
Contain them to become impartial,
Be impartial to become king, / Be king to become Heaven,
Be Heaven to become the Way,
Be the Way to endure, / Impervious unto death.

至（致）虛極也，守情（靜）表（篤）也。萬物旁（並）作，吾以觀其復也。天（夫）物雲雲，各復歸於其〔根。歸根曰靜〕。靜，是胃（謂）復命。復命常也，知常明也；不知常，芇（妄），芇（妄）作兇。知常容，容乃公，公乃王，王乃天，天乃道，〔道乃久〕。汋（沒）身不怠（殆）。(section 16/298–302)

Virtue in the *Laozi* exerts a familiar power at a grander scale. The sage-king is the "ridgepole," as in the *Shi* and *Documents* but of a much bigger tent; he oversees the human realm but also "Heaven and Earth" and the "myriad living things." More surprising from the perspective of the *Shi* is the idea that the sage-king isn't the "mate" or "Son of Heaven" but Heaven itself. Even the Zhou kings of the "Greater Court Songs" must be reminded that they serve at Heaven's pleasure, that "[Heaven's] command is not easy" 命之不易 (235/7.1), and thus that maintaining Heaven's support requires hard work.[55] Not so in the *Laozi*, in which the path of inaction gives the king a power equal, perhaps even superior, to Heaven: "The Way is great, Heaven is great, Earth is Great, and the [true] king is also great. There are four great things in the realm, and the king dwells first among them" 〔道大〕，天大，地大，王亦大。國中有四大，而王居一焉 (section 25/351).

For all of its implicit oppositionalism and one-upmanship, the *Laozi* embraces other lessons learned from the *Shi*. In chapter 2, I argued (following Assmann) that the idealized sociopolitical order of the *Shi* precludes the need for wisdom and thus that wisdom thrives when that order breaks down. In a society organized around the natural and inexorable movements of *gui*, people need only "follow" (*shun* 順), as Di tells King Wen in "Sovereign Might":

> Di said to King Wen: / "I long for your bright virtue.
> You have high renown but do not put on airs,
> You are great but without changing your former ways.
> Neither understanding nor knowing,
> You [merely] follow the precepts of Di."

> 帝謂文王，予懷明德。不大聲以色，不長夏以革。不識不知，順帝之則。(241/7)

The *Laozi* takes this idea one step further. Not only did the ancient sage-kings not require their subjects to be knowledgeable or wise, they actively promoted the people's ignorance so that they would naturally "follow" virtue's pull:

> Thus it is said that one practices the Way not to enlighten the people but to keep them ignorant. The reason why the people are hard to govern is because they have knowledge. Thus, ruling a state with knowledge is to be its scourge; ruling it with ignorance is to be [the source of] its virtue. Always know these two things—they are the model and the standard. Always know the model and the standard—this is called "dark virtue." Dark virtue is so deep, so distant. It turns back with [all] living things, and so brings about a great following.

> 故曰：為道者，非以明民也，將以愚之也。民之難〔治也，以其〕知（智）也。故以知（智）知（治）邦，邦之賊也；以不知（智）知（治）邦，〔邦之〕德也。恒知此兩者，亦稽式也。恒知稽式，是胃（謂）玄德。玄德深矣，遠矣，與物〔反〕矣，乃至大順。(section 65/pp. 140–145)[56]

By the same logic, any values or virtues that, like wisdom, depend on knowledge or effort are inimical to good order:

> When the great Way is abandoned, there is humaneness and propriety.
> When wisdom emerges, there is great hypocrisy.

SHI POETICS BEYOND THE SHI

When the six familial relationships are unharmonious, there are filial children and caring parents.

When the state and family are dark and disordered, there are loyal subjects.

大道廢，案有仁義。知（智）快（慧）出，安有大偽。六親不和，安有畜（孝）兹（慈）。邦家閽（昏）亂，安有貞臣。(section 18/310)

Like the *Shi*, the *Laozi* envisions a world in which those who follow the Way do so spontaneously and unthinkingly.[57]

Nowhere is the *Laozi*'s counterdependency on the *Shi* more evident than in section 20:

> Cut off learning and be without anxiety.[58]
> Agreement and flattery—/ How different are they?
> Approval and dislike—/ What is the difference?
> The one whom others fear / Cannot help but fear others.
> So distant, so limitless!
> The many are *hə-hə [joyful, jolly], / As if enjoying a great festival,
> As if climbing a terrace in spring.
> I am inert, inconspicuous, / Like an infant yet to smile,
> So exhausted, as if without a home to return to.
> The many all have more than enough; / I alone am lacking.
> My fool's mind / Is so *dûnʔ-dûnʔ [simple, stupid].
> Common folk are *tiao-tiao [light, bright];
> I alone am like the gloom.
> Common folk are *tshrêt-tshrêt [sharp, quick];
> I alone am *mân-mân [dull, slow],
> So hazy, like the ocean, / So distant, as if endless.
> The many all have the wherewithal;
> I alone am stubborn and contemptible.
> I wish to be alone and different from others,
> And to prize the mother who feeds [me].

【絕學无憂。】唯與訶，其相去幾何？美與惡，其相去何若？人之〔所畏〕，亦不〔可以不畏人。望呵，其未央哉〕！眾人巸（熙）巸（熙），若鄉（饗）於大牢，而春登臺。我泊焉未佻（兆），若〔嬰兒

SHI POETICS BEYOND THE SHI

未咳）。纍呵，如〔无所歸。眾人〕皆有餘，我獨遺（匱）。我愚人之心也，湷湷（沌沌）呵。鬻（俗）〔人昭昭，我獨若〕{門+月}（昏）呵。鬻（俗）人蔡（察）蔡（察），我獨閔（悶）閔（悶）呵。忽呵，其若〔海〕。朢（恍）呵，其若无所止。〔眾人皆有以，我獨頑〕以悝（俚）。我欲獨異於人，而貴食母。(315–327)

The language here is somewhat unusual compared to other *Laozi* sections. In keeping with its overall rejection of the senses, the *Laozi* tradition, unlike the *Shi* generally, avoids the use of sound-symbolic binomes—except in this excerpt, which features five reduplicating binomes in the Mawangdui manuscripts and six in the Wang Bi 王弼 (226–249 BCE) recension.[59] The explanation for this anomaly lies in the central rhetorical device of *Laozi* section 20, the contrast between the happy crowd and the lonely self, which derives from the elite laments of the *Shi*:

> *Ju-ju* [on and on] is my malady, / So very painful.
> [The people of] the four directions have more than enough;
> I alone dwell in anxiety.
> All people are at ease; / I alone dare not rest.

> 悠悠我里，亦孔之痗。四方有羨，我獨居憂。民莫不逸，我獨不敢休。(193/8.3–6)

> Wings flapping, those small crows,
> Flying homeward *di-di* [flock on flock].
> All people are nourished; / I alone am in distress.

> 弁彼鸒斯，歸飛提提。民莫不穀，我獨于罹。(197/1.3–4)

> My father begot me, / My mother fed me.
> Patted me, bred me, / Raised me, reared me,
> Watched me, tended me, / At every turn aided me.

SHI POETICS BEYOND THE SHI

Their good deeds I would requite.
[But] mighty Heaven['s cruelty] has no limit.

The southern hills *rat-rat [terrible, fell],
The storm-winds *pât-pât [fierce, piercing].
All people are nourished; / Why do I alone come to harm?

The southern hills *rut-rut [cragged, jagged],
The storm-winds *pət-pət [keen, extreme].
All people all nourished; / I alone can find no rest.

父兮生我，母兮鞠我。拊我畜我，長我育我。顧我復我，出入腹我。欲報之德，昊天罔極。
南山烈烈，飄風發發。民莫不穀，我獨何害。
南山律律，飄風弗弗。民莫不穀，我獨不卒。(202/4–6)

The winter winds *rat-rat [terrible, fell];
The storm winds *pât-pât [fierce, piercing].
All people are nourished; / Why do I alone come to harm?

冬日烈烈，飄風發發。民莫不穀，我獨何害。(204/3.3–4)

As we have seen, anxiety in the *Shi* is a symptom of one's separation from the collective. In these stanzas, the juxtaposition of the happy crowd with the suffering loner shows that "alone" (*du* 獨) is synonymous with unhappy. *Laozi* section 20 takes this device and turns it on its head. Its persona is dark where the crowd is bright, dull where they are sharp, and still where they are busy. The key difference is that isolation in the *Laozi* is a choice, not a symptom: the persona of *Laozi* section 20 "*wishes* to be alone and different from others" (emphasis added). Here, as elsewhere, the *Laozi* takes something undesirable from the perspective of the *Shi* and turns it into something attractive, even empowering.

What is isolation's payoff in *Laozi* section 20? The answer lies in the opening line: "Cut off learning and be without anxiety." *Laozi* section 20 is a prescription for immunizing oneself against the anxiety and alienation of the *Shi*. Those sorry complainers in the *Shi* are afraid of loneliness, the *Laozi* seems to say, but here in this text you can be alone and not experience anxiety. And whereas the estranged personas of the *Shi* lack the proper "nourishment" (*gu* 穀), the follower of the *Laozi* "prizes the mother who feeds [him];" that is, he finds a higher form of sustenance in the Way. (Note the focus on the mother in the fourth stanza of "Thick Tarragon" [Lu e 蓼莪, #202] quoted above, which may have inspired the closing line of *Laozi* section 20). The key to achieving this ideal state is rejecting "learning" (*xue* 學), which in the *Laozi* is a prime example of an effortful, desirous activity. And in the preimperial period, one of the most important objects of learning was the *Shi*. For those who wish to avoid alienation altogether, the *Laozi*'s message is simple: stop studying the *Shi* and start following this text.

YOU 憂 (ANXIETY) AND THE POTENT PERSONALITY

The very same Warring States and early Western Han tombs with *Laozi* manuscripts also introduced us to a previously unknown text with a very different take on the problem of "anxiety" (*you* 憂). What follows is the second section of the Mawangdui version of that text, the *Five Kinds of Conduct* (*Wu xing* 五行):

> If there is no anxiety within the heart of the prince, then there will be no wisdom within his heart. If there is no wisdom within his heart, then there will be no joy within his heart. If there is no joy within his heart, then he will not be at peace. If he is not at peace, then he will be unhappy. If he is unhappy, then he will lack virtue.

> 君子毋中［心］［之］憂，則亡中心之知（智）。亡中心之知（智）則亡中心之說。亡中心之說，則不安。不安則不樂。不樂則亡德。[60]

A treatise on the psychological and physiological dynamics of virtue, the *Five Kinds of Conduct* can be read as part of a wider effort to fill in the gaps in the *Shi* tradition's theory of "virtue" (*de* 德).[61] As we have seen, virtue is a key component of the *Shi* sociopolitical order. A well-regulated society has a good king at its center, and a good king is someone who radiates a quasi-magical power of attraction. For all their insistence on the power of virtue, however, the *Shi* have much less to say about its acquisition. How should a king or "prince" (*junzi* 君子) maximize his virtue? What does the process of virtue cultivation look like, and what are its psychological and physiological dynamics? The answers are unclear. The *Shi* are far more interested in demonstrating the power of virtue than analyzing it—and for good reason. In the *Shi*, the attraction of a virtuous ruler is supposed to be as natural as the attraction of one's home and family. To explain or rationalize ruler-centric *gui* is to acknowledge that it requires explanation, that it may not be as instinctive or intuitive as the *Shi* worldview needs it to be.

Into this conceptual vacuum steps *Five Kinds of Conduct*, which in the opening section defines virtue as the end result of a process of "harmonizing" (*he* 和) the five kinds of "virtuous conduct" or "movements of virtue" (*de zhi xing* 德之行), a phrase appearing five times across the *Shijing*.[62] These are "humaneness" (*ren* 仁), "wisdom" (*zhi* 智), "propriety" (*yi* 義), "ritual" (*li* 禮), and "sagacity" (*sheng* 聖), all of which are said to "take form within" (*xing yu nei* 形於內) the properly cultivated heart. The sorites of section 2 then expands upon the notion of "taking form within" by cataloging the preconditions of virtue.

For our purposes, the most striking feature of that catalog is that it opens with anxiety. Anxiety in the *Shi* is a natural response to separation or alienation—which is why the *Laozi*'s claim that virtue immunizes one against anxiety is so provocative. Remove *you* from the equation and the *Shi* lose a key proof of *gui*'s naturalness. *Five Kinds of Conduct* comes to the defense of the *Shi* with an argument that doubles down on anxiety's importance. Princely virtue seekers must actively cultivate anxiety as a precondition of wisdom, joy, peace of mind, happiness, and ultimately virtue. In this way, *Five Kinds of Conduct* links two of the *Shi* tradition's most central preoccupations within a single process of self-empowerment.

How do we know that the author(s) of *Five Kinds of Conduct* were thinking about and through the *Shi* in section 2? Consider section 5, which cites a close parallel of the second stanza of "Cicada":

> If you are not humane, then your thoughts cannot penetrate to the essential; if you are not wise, then your thoughts cannot be far-reaching. If you are neither humane nor wise, then "before seeing the prince your anxious heart" cannot be "**trot-trot* [distressed, tense]," and "having seen the prince your

heart" cannot be "delighted." The *Shi* say, "Before seeing the prince, / My anxious heart was **trot-trot* [distressed, tense]. / But now having seen him, / Now having met him, / My heart is delighted." This is what it means.

不仁思不能晴（精）。不知（智）思不能長。不仁不知（智），未見君子，憂心不能［惙惙。既見君子，心不能］說。•詩曰：未見君子，憂心殳（惙）殳（惙）。亦既見之，亦既鉤（覯）之，我［心則］說。［此之謂也。］⁶³

Here *Five Kinds of Conduct* adopts the notion of anxiety from the *Shi* but does something quite different with it. The "Cicada" citation is a simple description of its persona's emotional state before and after being reunited with the prince. But the authors of *Five Kinds of Conduct* instead read "Cicada" as a script or normative guide to virtue acquisition, with *Shi*-style anxiety only accessible to those who have already achieved wisdom, humaneness, and so on. Read as a rejoinder to *Laozi* section 20, the argument is that the *Laozi* persona lacks both the roadmap (the *Shi*) and the emotional depth to achieve virtue.

The problem with this argument from the perspective of *Shi* poetics is that it completely undermines the raison d'être of anxiety in the *Shi*. If anxiety is a learned response and not a simple emotional reflex, then the *Shi* vision of a naturalized sociopolitical order tied together by the universal impulse to *gui* comes apart at the seams. For a text more concerned with the training of elite "princes" or "princely men" (*junzi* 君子), this seems to have been an acceptable trade-off.

As seen in the contrast between the *Laozi* and *Five Kinds of Conduct*, early Chinese thinkers generally were of two minds about *you*, perhaps none more so than the Kongzi of the *Analects*:

[Kong]zi said, "Not cultivating my virtue, not practicing what I have learned, learning what is right but being incapable of moving toward it, not being able to reform my deficiencies—these are my anxieties."

子曰：德之不脩，學之不講，聞義不能徙，不善不能改，是吾憂也。(7/3)

Sima Niu asked about the princely man. [Kong]zi said, "A princely man is neither anxious nor fearful." "Is not being anxious or fearful all there is to being princely?" [Kong]zi said, "If he looks within himself and is without fault, then what does he have to be anxious or fearful about?"

司馬牛問君子。子曰：君子不憂不懼。曰：不憂不懼，斯謂之君子已乎？子曰：內省不疚，夫何憂何懼？(12/4)[64]

On one side of the divide are those like the authors of *Laozi* section 20 and *Analects* 12/4 who equated virtue with equanimity, thus treating *you* as a wholly undesirable state:

Sorrow and joy are twistings of virtue; delight and anger are transgressions of the Way; affection and aversion are the loss of virtue. Thus, a mind without anxiety or joy is the perfection of virtue; being singular and unchanging is the perfection of quiescence; resisting nothing is the perfection of emptiness; not conversing with things is the perfection of insipidity; lacking any contrariness is the perfection of purity.

悲樂者，德之邪；喜怒者，道之過；好惡者，德之失。故心不憂樂，德之至也；一而不變，靜之至也；無所於忤，虛之至也；不與物交，淡之至也；無所於逆，粹之至也。(*Zhuangzi* 15.542)

What all people live for is always their own happiness.
If anxious, they lose their guiding principles;
If angry, they lose their points of origin.
If anxious or sorrowful, joyful or angry,
Then the Way has no purchase [on them].
Affections and desires are to be quieted,
Foolishness and confusion are to be corrected.
Don't pull, don't push; / Good fortune will return of its own accord.

凡人之生也，必以其歡。憂則失紀，怒則失端。憂悲喜怒，道乃無處。愛欲靜之，遇亂正之，勿引勿推，福將自歸。(*Guanzi* 49.947, the "Inner Training" [Nei ye 內業])

Even the *Shijing* includes a hint of anti-*you* thinking in "Don't Push the Big Carriage" (Wu jiang da ju 無將大車, #206), the only *Shi* to advocate avoiding anxiety-inducing experiences:⁶⁵

> Don't push the big carriage, / You will only make yourself dusty.
> Don't think about the hundred sources of anxiety;
> You will only make yourself wretched.

無將大車，衹自塵兮。無思百憂，衹自疧兮。(206/1)

Note the parallel between "not pushing" (*wu tui* 勿推) in the *Guanzi* and "not pushing" (*wu jiang* 無將) the carriage of the poem.

On the other side are texts like *Five Kinds of Conduct* and *Analects* 7/3 that legitimize anxiety as a necessary component of virtue acquisition. In *Analects* 7/3, *you* isn't an acute feeling so much as an ongoing state of vigilance; what prompts Kongzi's anxiety is the distance between his current and perfected selves. The experience of *you* is negative but it is a productive, motivating negativity. As *Mengzi* 6B/15 argues, anxiety pushes one to "rise up" (*zuo* 作) to perform great deeds:

> Whenever Heaven was about to bestow a great responsibility on [the sages or superior men of old], it first tormented their minds and wills, burdened their bones and sinews, starved their bodies, impoverished their lives, and frustrated their actions as a way of rousing and fortifying their spirits and compensating for their inadequacies. Only after erring can a person change; only after his heart is hard-pressed and his thoughts are resisted does he rise up; only after visibly manifesting [his thoughts] and speaking them aloud does he make himself understood. Without law-abiding [great] families and advisers internally and enemies and other threats externally, a state will always fail—at which point one realizes that survival depends on anxiety and trouble and that death comes from contentment and joy.

天將降大任於是人也，必先苦其心志，勞其筋骨，餓其體膚，空乏其身，行拂亂其所為，所以動心忍性，曾益其所不能。人恆過，然後能改；困於心，衡於慮，而後作；徵於色，發於聲，而後喻。入則無法家拂士，出則無敵國外患者，國恆亡。然後知生於憂患而死於安樂也。⁶⁶

SHI POETICS BEYOND THE SHI

This passage doesn't spell out the psychology of anxiety as fully as *Five Kinds of Conduct*, nor does it explicitly tie it to virtue (*de*). Like *Five Kinds of Conduct*, however, it sees anxiety as a character-building force and not simply as an instinctive reaction to separation or estrangement. The "Commentary to the Appended Phrases" (Xici zhuan 繫辭傳) of the *Zhou Changes* (*Zhouyi* 周易) concurs:

> Didn't the *Changes* emerge in middle antiquity? Didn't the creator of the *Changes* [literally "the one who gave rise to the *Changes*"] experience anxiety and misery?
>
> 易之興也，其於中古乎。作易者，其有憂患乎。(8.368)[67]

The connection between creation and anxiety hinges on the intuition that creation is an individual act. In the context of *Shi* poetics, to be an individual is to suffer anxiety; thus, created works, institutions, practices, and so on, must be born of the anxieties of their creators. As the "Commentary to the Appended Phrases" elsewhere explains, the creator of the *Changes* was King Wen during the reign of the last Shang ruler, the infamous King Zhou 紂王.[68] Had King Wen not suffered at the hands of King Zhou, he would have had no reason to create the *Changes* in an effort to restore the sociopolitical order. As Wang Bi observes in his commentary to this line, "Without anxiety or misery, doing nothing would have been enough" 無憂患則不為而足也.

The widespread appeal of *Laozi*-style quiescence notwithstanding, on the imperial stage the pro-anxiety camp was the clear winner. Whether due to the authority of the *Shi* or because displays of effortful anxiety made for better political theater, early emperors routinely styled themselves as worriers-in-chief. Consider the following excerpts from the stele inscription erected by the Qin First Emperor on Mount Langye 琅邪 in 219 BCE, an edict issued by Emperor Wen 文帝 in 162 BCE, and another issued by Emperor Wu 武帝 in 122 BCE:

> Now, in his twenty-eighth year [219 BCE],
> The August Thearch created a beginning . . .
> He is anxious for and pities the black-haired people,
> From dawn to dusk he is never remiss.

維二十八年，皇帝作始。 . . . 憂恤黔首，朝夕不懈。⁶⁹

Being unenlightened, We cannot extend our Virtue far, with the result that certain domains beyond Our borders are not tranquil. When the lives of those beyond the border wilds are not peaceful, and when those within the fiefs and Our personal lands toil away without rest, the fault for both lies in the meagerness of Our virtue and its inability to extend far. For some years now, the Xiongnu acting in concert have ravaged the border regions and killed many of Our officers and people. Moreover, the subjects, soldiers, and officers of the borders have been unable to communicate Our true intentions, thus compounding Our lack of virtue. The central and outer domains have long been engaged in hostilities—how can We be content with this state of affairs? Now We rise early and go to bed late, laboring diligently on the world's behalf. We are anxious and pained for the myriad peoples; for their sake We are distressed and disturbed. Not for a single day have We forgotten [their plight] in Our heart.

朕既不明，不能遠德，是以使方外之國或不寧息。夫四荒之外不安其生，封畿之內勤勞不處，二者之咎，皆自於朕之德薄而不能遠達也。閒者累年，匈奴並暴邊境，多殺吏民，邊臣兵吏又不能諭吾內志，以重吾不德也。夫久結難連兵，中外之國將何以自寧？今朕夙興夜寐，勤勞天下，憂苦萬民，為之怛惕不安，未嘗一日忘於心。(*Shiji* 10.431)

The ruler is the heart, the people the body and limbs. If the body and limbs are harmed, then the heart is distressed. Of late [the kings of] Huainan and Hengshan were cultivating [men of] literature and learning and dispensing bribes. Their two domains being adjacent, [both kings] were tempted by pernicious doctrines, with the result that they fomented rebellion and assassination. This is because of Our lack of virtue. The *Shi* say, "My anxious heart is **tshâmʔ-tshâmʔ* [hurt, irked] / Thinking of the state's vicious ways." We have already granted an amnesty throughout the realm and washed away [the rebels] to give [the people] a renewal.

蓋君者心也，民猶支體，支體傷則心憯怛。日者淮南、衡山修文學，流貨賂，兩國接壤，怵於邪說，而造篡弒，此朕之不德。詩云：『憂心慘慘，念國之為虐。』已赦天下，滌除與之更始。(*Hanshu* 10.174)[70]

The influence of the *Shi* is most obvious in Emperor Wu's edict, which quotes the eleventh stanza of "First Month" (Zheng yue 正月, #192). But all three documents allude to the *Shi* in one way or another. The lines "from dawn to dusk never remiss" in the First Emperor's stele inscription and "rising early and going to bed late" in Emperor Wen's edict have multiple parallels in the *Shijing* and in *Shi* quotations generally.[71] In Han edicts in particular, emperors declare their anxieties in response to droughts, floods, incursions by foreigners, official corruption, unnecessarily harsh laws, and so on. These declarations allow emperors to claim such challenges as temporary glitches in the imperial virtue-engine as opposed to catastrophic breakdowns. Anxiety is the proof of their sincere and ongoing desire to return to a state of peace and prosperity, with the policy announcement at the conclusion of the edict effecting that return. For emperors, *Shi*-style anxiety was a powerful tool for maintaining moral authority in the face of disruptions to the social order.

SIMA QIAN'S TEXTUAL HOMECOMING

From a modern perspective, a remarkable feature of preimperial texts is their pervasive lack of named authors. Not until the Western Han period—most famously with the concluding chapter of Sima Qian's *Grand Scribe's Records*, the "Self-Narration" (Zi xu 自序)—do we begin to encounter authors who claimed ownership over their own texts in their own voices.[72] As befits a milieu in which authors were unaccustomed to asserting themselves in non-official contexts, Sima Qian's account of the genesis of the *Grand Scribe's Records* reads like a hodgepodge of apologistic arguments. But one way to make sense of the text is as a multistage study in movement and belonging à la the *Shi*, which are referenced more often in this chapter (eleven times) than in all but two chapters of Sima Qian's history.[73] In short, the "Self-Narration" can be read as the story of the Sima family's struggles to come home (*gui*).

Stage one—the history of the Sima clan. In the opening section, we learn the history of Sima clan from the time of the legendary emperor Zhuanxu

顓頊 down through the Han dynasty. Various verbs describe the movements of Sima Qian's ancestors: they "left Zhou and went to Jin" 去周適晉, they "entered Shaoliang" 入少梁, they "were split up and scattered" 分散, and so on. But in the wake of the Qin dynasty's collapse, the Sima clan ultimately "comes home" (*gui* 歸) to the Han, beginning with Sima Ang 司馬卬, a former general of Zhao 趙, who received a kingdom from Xiang Yu 項羽 only to turn it over to Gaozu.[74] From this point forward, the different branches of the Sima clan are reunited as faithful servants to the Han emperors. The lineage concludes with Sima Qian's father and initial author of the *Grand Scribe's Records*, Sima Tan 司馬談.

Stage two—the "Essentials of the Six Schools of Thought" (*Liu jia zhi yaozhi* 六家之要指). Here, the text transitions from family history to family intellectual biography. In response to the failures and fractiousness of contemporary scholars, Sima Tan composed an essay on the strengths and weaknesses of contemporary intellectual currents. That essay, which is included in its entirety, opens with a familiar movement:

> According to the "Great Commentary" to the *Changes*, "The world arrives at a single place but with a hundred different thoughts [along the way]; it returns to the same home but along different paths."
>
> 易大傳：天下一致而百慮，同歸而殊塗。(130.3288)

On one level, the essay is a performance of intellectual authority; on another, this *gui* mirrors the reunion of the splintered Sima clan under the Han. The implication is that the Han dynasty can align the world's intellectual currents in the right direction just as it brought the Simas home—provided, of course, that it heeds Sima Tan.

The bulk of the essay is devoted to showing that different intellectual lineages emphasize different facets of the Way, with practitioners of *Laozi*-style techniques (the "daoists" *daojia* 道家) having the best grasp of its dynamics. Most relevant for our purposes is the essay's concluding section on the preservation of "spirit" (*shen* 神) and "body" (*xing* 形):

> The spirit is what gives a person life and the body is what a person relies on. If the spirit is too exercised, it is used up; if the body is too exerted, it is worn out. If body and spirit become separated, then one dies. If dead, one cannot

come back to life. If [body and spirit are] separated, then they cannot return back to each other. Thus, the sage deems [the union of spirit and body] a weighty matter. Viewed from this perspective, the spirit is the root of life and the body is the tool of life. How could one say "I have the means to rule the world" without first settling one's spirit and body?

凡人所生者神也，所託者形也。神大用則竭，形大勞則敝，形神離則死。死者不可復生，離者不可復反，故聖人重之。由是觀之，神者生之本也，形者生之具也。不先定其神〔形〕，而曰「我有以治天下」，何由哉？(130.3292)

The verb "settle" or "fix" (*ding* 定) appears only once in the received *Laozi* (in section 37) but numerous times in the *Shijing* where it refers to the act of establishing a stable home, be it Heaven "protecting and settling" 保定 (166/1–3.1) its favorites, a lord settling his "residence" (*zhai* 宅; 259/2.6), ministers settling their king (e.g., 253/1.10), or ancestor spirits settling their "family" (*jia* 家; 294/1.7). On the flipside, to be unsettled in the *Shi* is to lack a home:

> My anxious heart is *ʔən-ʔən [pained, strained],
> Thinking of my old residence.
> I was born under a bad star, / Encountering Heaven's deep wrath.
> From the west and off to the east / There is nowhere to settle down.

> 憂心慇慇，念我土宇。我生不辰，逢天僤怒。自西徂東，靡所定處。(257/4.1–6)

Perhaps under the influence of the "Inner Training" or a text like it,[75] Sima Tan's treatise puts a psychological spin on the value of being settled: to be settled is to have no "separation" or "estrangement" (*li* 離) between body and spirit such that the spirit remains at home in the body.[76] In the context of what follows in the "Self-Narration," Sima Tan's discussion proves prophetic.

Stage three—Sima Qian's inspection tour. This section recounts Sima Qian's travels through the Han territories. First as a young man and then as an official, Sima Qian essentially performs his own inspection tour (*xun* 巡) of the Han dynasty, complete with mountain climbing, river following, a visit to Kongzi's temple in Lu 魯, and a "campaign" (*zheng* 征) to the far-flung reaches of the empire. At the conclusion of his travels, he "comes home" (*gui* 歸) and "returns and reports on his mission" 還報命. Like his father and ancestors before him, Sima Qian also has a home under the Han.

Stage four—Sima Tan's death. Things take a turn for the worse after Sima Tan is excluded from participating in Emperor Wu's revival of the hallowed (yet poorly understood) *feng* and *shan* sacrifices:[77]

> In this year [of Sima Qian's return from his official mission], the Son of Heaven [Emperor Wu] first established the *feng* sacrifices for the Han dynasty, and the Grand Scribe [Sima Tan] was left behind South-from-Zhou [in Luoyang 洛陽] and could not participate in the event. Consequently, he was riven with emotion and lay on the verge of death when his son Qian came back from his mission and saw his father between the [Yellow] River and the Luo [River].
>
> 是歲天子始建漢家之封，而太史公留滯周南，不得與從事，故發憤且卒，而子遷適使反，見父於河洛之間。(130.3295)

Describing Sima Tan as being "South-from-Zhou" (Zhou nan 周南), also the name of the opening subdivision of the "Airs of the States," is noteworthy given that Western Han sources overwhelmingly use the term in reference to the *Shi*.[78] More important, this is the first thwarted movement of the "Self-Narration." For some unspecified reason, Sima Tan is "left behind" when Emperor Wu travels to Mount Tai for the *feng* sacrifice and is "unable to follow after him." Denied the opportunity to return to his ruler's side, he is "riven with emotion" and seems to suffer the fate described in "The Essentials of the Six Schools of Thought": he dies of an unsettled spirit.

Before passing, Sima Tan instructs Sima Qian to finish the *Grand Scribe's Records* and "carry on from our ancestors" 續吾祖, a responsibility Sima Qian accepts: "[I am] a little child, unintelligent, but [I] fervently wish to arrange all the old reports of our ancestors, without daring to omit anything" 小子不敏，請悉論先人所次舊聞，弗敢闕 (130.3295). This scene is a crucial moment for Sima Qian's persona in the "Self-Narration." Prior to his father's death and his succession as the "little child," in other words, the head of the family, Sima Qian does not speak in his own voice. After this moment, he emerges as an "I" (*yu* 余) to defend the *Grand Scribe's*

Records from its detractors. In keeping with the analysis in chapter 2 of "Ritual Hymns" like "Pity Me, the Little Child" (Min yu xiaozi 閔予小子, #286), Sima Qian's bereavement is the first step in his emergence as a first-person author. In the "Self-Narration," the individuation of filial anxiety precedes that of political persecution.

Stage five—The debate with Hu Sui 壺遂. Here, Sima Qian counters objections from a high official named Hu Sui, who challenges Sima Qian on the affinities between his history and Kongzi's *Annals* (*Chunqiu* 春秋). If the *Grand Scribe's Records* is a latter-day *Annals*, Hu Sui argues, then Sima Qian must be criticizing the Han just as Kongzi criticized the rulers of his day. Sima Qian explicitly denies the equivalence ("Sir, for you to compare [my work] to the *Annals* is absurd" 君比之於春秋，謬矣; 130.3300). For our purposes, the key points are that (1) references to the *Shi* feature prominently throughout the exchange and (2) Kongzi establishes the second thwarted movement of the "Self-Narration" insofar as he composed the *Annals* after "the Way of Zhou was abandoned" 周道衰廢 and the "grandees [of Lu] obstructed him" 大夫壅之 (130.3297). Even as he rejects the criticism of the *Grand Scribe's Records* as a latter-day *Annals*, Sima Qian still needs Kongzi as an example of someone who turned to writing when stuck.[79]

Stage six—Sima Qian's tragedy and the list of exemplary authors. The influence of the *Shi* is most palpable in this section, where they bookend Sima Qian's reflections on the connection between "authorship" (*zuo*) and "misfortune" (*huo* 禍):

> Seven years later, the Grand Scribe encountered the misfortune of the Li Ling affair [in which he was condemned to death for defending a disgraced general but had his sentence commuted to castration] and was thrown into darkness in fetters. He then heaved a great sigh and said, "This is my fault! This is my fault! I am destroyed, useless." Withdrawing to reflect deeply on [his plight], he said, "Those vexed and constrained figures of the *Shi* and *Documents* wished to convey the thoughts at the forefront of their minds. In former times, the Earl of the West [King Wen] was confined [by the Shang] in Youli but expanded [beyond his confinement via] the *Zhou Changes*; Kongzi was hemmed in [between] Chen and Cai but rose up [through] the *Annals*; Qu Yuan was banished but [re]attached [himself via] *Parting's Sorrow*; Zuo Qiuming lost his eyesight but gained the *Discourses of the States*; Sunzi had his leg cut off at the knee but set forth the *Art of War*; Lü Buwei was sent

off to Shu but sent [back] his *Surveys* through the generations; Han Fei was impounded in Qin but expounded the *Difficulties of Persuasion* and the *Frustrations of Solitude*; and the bulk of the three hundred *Shi* were the creations of excellent and sagely men riven with emotion. All of these men had intentions that were **kît-ʔut* [choked, pent] because they could not open up their way home. Thus, they transmitted bygone affairs, thinking of those to come.

七年而太史公遭李陵之禍，幽於縲紲。乃喟然而歎曰：「是余之罪也夫！是余之罪也夫！身毀不用矣。」退而深惟曰：「夫詩書隱約者，欲遂其志之思也。昔西伯拘羑里，演周易；孔子厄陳蔡，作春秋；屈原放逐，著離騷；左丘失明，厥有國語；孫子臏腳，而論兵法；不韋遷蜀，世傳呂覽；韓非囚秦，說難、孤憤；詩三百篇，大抵賢聖發憤之所為作也。此人皆意有所鬱結，不得通其道也，故述往事，思來者。」(130.3300)

This is the third thwarted movement of the "Self-Narration." In yet another echo of Sima Tan's treatise, Sima Qian suffers the bodily torment of imprisonment and castration, presumably running the risk of dying from an unsettled spirit. Beyond the explicit *Shi* references, there are at least two *Shi* echoes in this passage. The first is "thrown into darkness" or "imprisoned" (*you* 幽; *ʔiu), which is both a synonym and a near homophone for "anxiety" (*you* 憂; *ʔu).[80] The second is the binome **kît-ʔut* (choked, pent; *yu jie* 鬱結), written *yu jie* 苑結 (also *kît-ʔut) in the third stanza of "Servitor of the City" (*Du ren shi* 都人士, #225):[81]

> That servitor of the city, / With ear-stops of precious stone;
> That lady, his daughter, / They call her Yin Ji.
> I do not see her! / My heart is **ʔut-kît [choked, pent].
>
> That servitor of the city, / Dangling a sash cut to hang.
> That lady his daughter, / With curled hair like a scorpion.
> I do not see her! / I will follow along after them.
>
> 彼都人士，充耳琇實。彼君子女，謂之尹吉。我不見兮，我心苑結。
> 彼都人士，垂帶而厲。彼君子女，卷髮如蠆。我不見兮，言從之邁。(225/3–4)

Note how the persona's frustration prompts him to follow along after the noble daughter just as the frustrations of Sima Qian's exemplars prompt a turn to authorship.

Much of the commentary on this passage from the "Self-Narration" has focused on the differences between Sima Qian's list of exemplary authors and accounts elsewhere in the *Grand Scribe's Records*.[82] In chapter 47, for example, Kongzi is said to have composed the *Annals* after returning home to the state of Lu, not while stuck between Chen and Cai; in chapter 63, Han Fei composes his treatises prior to his imprisonment by the future Qin First Emperor, not after. Reading the "Self-Narration" as a story of thwarted movement contextualizes these discrepancies. The key detail is that all of these figures were stuck and "could not open up a way home." King Wen was "detained," Kongzi "hemmed in," Qu Yuan and Lü Buwei "banished" and "sent off," and Han Fei "imprisoned." Zuo Qiuming's and Sunzi's movements are literally hampered due to blindness and amputation, respectively. As I have tried to capture in my translation, the act of authorship in each instance is a metaphorical movement out of each predicament. King Wen "expands [beyond]" (*yan* 演) his confinement by "expanding" (*yan* 演) the text of the *Zhou Changes*. Kongzi "rises up" (*zuo* 作) out of a siege by "creating" (*zuo* 作) the *Annals*. In "composing" (*zhu* 著) *Parting's Sorrow*, a banished Qu Yuan also "attaches" (*zhuo* 著) himself to his home state. Zuo Qiuming "loses" (*shi* 失) his eyesight but "gains" (*jue you* 厥有) something else. Lü Buwei maintains a line of "transmission" (*chuan* 傳) despite being "sent off" (*qian* 遷). And Han Fei's "expounding" (*shuo* 說) is also a "removal" (*tuo* 說, i.e., 脫) of his difficulties, a pun attested to in Sima Qian's biography of Han Fei.[83]

This is Sima Qian's solution to the problem first encountered in chapter 2 with "Northern Gate" and "Eastern Hills," and also arose with Jie Zhitui and Kongzi in this chapter: what becomes of the imperative to *gui* when one's loved ones—including one's lord—make homecoming impossible? What if the love for one's home goes unreciprocated? And how does one avoid the fate of Jie Zhitui (a lonely death) or Sima Tan (an unsettled spirit) in such circumstances? The answer for Sima Qian lies in writing. Through writing, the sundered or alienated can regain a virtual freedom of movement homeward. The only wrinkle is that their homecoming depends on the posthumous welcome of "those to come" (*lai zhe* 來者). Just as his biography of Kongzi allows one "to imagine seeing what [Kongzi] was like as a man," Sima Qian hopes that the *Grand Scribe's Records* will serve as his proxy for later generations. As he describes it in a concluding summary to the "Self-Narration," his text "completes the words of a single house" or "lineage" (*cheng yijia zhi yan* 成一家之言").[84] In other words, the *Grand Scribe's Records* creates the possibility of a future home for Sima Qian and his family.

Ultimately, the best reasons to take the thought of the *Shi* seriously are the insights gained from doing so. Whether or not my own theory of the *Shi* holds up to scrutiny, at the very least I hope to have demonstrated the value and possibilities of reading these sources through the *Shi* as opposed to the other way around. If the concept of *Dao* was "the *center* of Chinese philosophical discussion" and "the pivot of Chinese philosophy,"[85] if Kongzi was "civilization's greatest sage through the ages,"[86] if water was the foundational metaphor of early Chinese thought (Allan), if the *Laozi* was one of its most foundational texts, and if Sima Qian was China's most influential historian and "the first author of a truly autobiographical self-testimony in China,"[87] then the observations of this chapter make a strong case for the centrality of the *Shi* tradition from the Warring States into the early imperial period.

In the next chapter, we will see that a similar argument can be made about Qu Yuan 屈原, "the first author to be identified for an individual, poetic voice" and "the archetype for later Chinese poets."[88]

Chapter Four

THE *SHI* AND THE *VERSES OF CHU*
(*CHUCI* 楚辭)

This chapter extends the argument of chapter 3 to the second most important verse anthology from ancient China, the *Verses of Chu* (*Chuci* 楚茨). Amid the diversity of opinions regarding the origin and interpretation of these classics, most in the modern era have imagined *Shi*- and *Verses of Chu*–style verse as the products of two distinct cultures, one northern and one southern.[1] Where the *Shi* are set in the Zhou cultural sphere of the Yellow River Valley and North China Plain, the *Verses of Chu* is named for the southern state of Chu 楚, one of Qin's great rivals up until the loss of its capital in 278 BCE and its ultimate defeat in 223. The *Shi* are synonymous with the Zhou dynasty; the *Verses of Chu* was patronized by the Han dynasty's ruling Liu 劉 clan, whose founder was a southerner. The *Shi* are more quotidian; the "rhapsodies" or "poetic expositions" (*fu* 賦) of the *Verses of Chu* are more fantastical. The dominant religious practice of the *Shi* is ancestor worship; in the *Verses of Chu*, it's thought to be shamanism. The *Shi* are a communal, anonymous poetry; the *Verses of Chu* is strongly associated with a single poet—Qu Yuan 屈原, the Chu minister who supposedly composed "Parting's Sorrow" (Li sao 離騷), the first and most important piece in the collection, after being rejected by King Huai of Chu 楚懷王 (r. 328–299 BCE) and before drowning himself in the Miluo 汨羅 River. Add to this their different themes, imagery, and meters, and the anthologies appear as artifacts of two different literary milieus, albeit with some intermingling. Thus, Yuan Xingpei 袁行霈 in *An Outline of Chinese Literature* follows Wang Guowei 王國維 (1877–1927) in noting the "very pronounced regional characteristics" of the two anthologies, his foremost examples of the "regional nature of Chinese literature," while acknowledging that the *Verses of Chu* "absorbed some northern literary nourishment."[2] For David Hawkes, the *Shi* and *Verses of Chu* are the "dual ancest[ors]" of the Chinese poetic tradition:

> The Southern ancestor is less ancient than the Northern one and can, in a very roundabout sort of way, be derived from it; but the differences between them are so great that it is more convenient to think of them as two separate sources . . . The [*Verses of Chu*] poems, however popular, belonged to no canon, dealt in matters that were outlandish and unorthodox, and originated outside the area of sanctified Western Zhou tradition.[3]

Such is the prevailing view: the differences between the *Shi* and *Verses of Chu* are fundamental and regional in nature, their similarities superficial.[4]

This was not the consensus among ancient authorities on the *Verses of Chu*—or at least on "Parting's Sorrow" as its flagship text. Liu An 劉安 (ca. 179–122 BCE), the king of Huainan 淮南 and the text's earliest known commentator, wrote that it combined the edifying qualities of the "Airs of the States" and "Lesser Court Songs."[5] Sima Qian implicitly endorsed this view when he included Qu Yuan in his list of thwarted authors. Yang Xiong 揚雄 (53 BCE–18 CE) condemned it for endorsing suicide in response to political alienation and thus deviating from canonical norms.[6] Ban Gu 班固 (32–92) acknowledged the text's literary merit but criticized Liu An's commentary on similar grounds, arguing that the "Li sao" author was more interested in criticizing his king and showing off than in promoting good government.[7] The compiler of the received *Verses of Chu*, Wang Yi 王逸 (89–158) defended the text by arguing that it "relied on the *Shi* for its evocative imagery" 依詩取興 and was "composed in accordance with the principles of the *Shi* poets" 依詩人之義而作, which he then demonstrated by juxtaposing various lines from "Parting's Sorrow" with their *Shijing* counterparts.[8] But the question of regional identity was not a focus of these early debates.[9] All parties seem to have assumed that the *Shijing* and *Verses of Chu* were part of the same cultural milieu even as they associated "Parting's Sorrow" with the south.

THE *SHI* AND THE *VERSES OF CHU* (*CHUCI* 楚辭)

The argument of this chapter is that Wang Yi more or less got it right: the influence of the *Shi* on the *Verses of Chu* wasn't roundabout. Intertextual analysis reveals that *Verses of Chu* poetics (like *Laozi* poetics) developed in direct, even self-conscious opposition to *Shi* poetics.[10]

As we have seen, the one thing a person cannot do in the *Shi* is to turn one's back on the collective.[11] Sundered personas never abandon the hope for reunion with their loved ones, and disaffected elites never entirely forsake their lords. Like the mistreated wife of "Cypress Boat," they "cannot up and fly away" 不能奮飛. A poetry premised on separation, alienation, and departure, the *Verses of Chu* lets its personas do precisely that—to leave their homes behind forever. To quote (the *Shi*-inflected account of)[12] the *Grand Scribe's Records*,

> Despite his banishment, [Qu Yuan] looked back at Chu with affection, his heart knotted with concern for King Huai. He did not forget his desire to return, and hoped by some good fortune that his lord would realize his error and that [the state's] customs would be reformed entirely. In a single piece [i.e., "Parting's Sorrow"] he conveyed three intentions: to preserve his lord, to revive his state, and to reverse its fortunes. However, in the end there was nothing he could do. And so he was unable to return, and eventually came to see that King Huai would never realize his error.
>
> 雖放流，睠顧楚國，繫心懷王，不忘欲反，冀幸君之一悟，俗之一改也。其存君興國而欲反覆之，一篇之中三致志焉。然終無可奈何，故不可以反，卒以此見懷王之終不悟也。(84.2485)[13]

Even more so than Jie Zhitui, Kongzi, Sima Qian, or the personas of "Northern Gate" and "Eastern Hills" discussed in chapter 2, Qu Yuan was a locus of thinking about the limits of the *Shi* worldview. What if, like Qu Yuan, a person can't fulfill his sincere desire to *gui* à la the *Shi*? What happens when return becomes impossible? This is the ethical quandary at the heart of *Verses of Chu* poetics. Are such figures obligated to cling to the center, as they do in the *Shi*? Do they have the power and moral license to leave? And if they do, what is the value of a life lived beyond the margins? Or is suicide the only answer?

In the second half of the chapter, I read subsequent poems in the *Verses of Chu* and elsewhere as artifacts of a debate prompted by "Parting's

Sorrow." *Debate* is perhaps an odd label given that the debate of the *Verses of Chu* looks nothing like the debates typically featured in histories of early Chinese thought.[14] Its participants were early imperial authors writing in verse as opposed to Warring States Masters debating in person or writing in prose. What historians of early Chinese thought have failed to appreciate is that the *Verses of Chu* and related sources are among the earliest and richest records of an intellectual exchange conducted via written texts that have survived more or less intact to the present day. This isn't to say that the *Verses of Chu* represents the earliest debate from early China—far from it. The point is that earlier sources suggest all sorts of intellectual exchanges but offer precious few accounts of the mechanisms of those exchanges, most of which are one-sided—like the *Mengzi*'s account of the water-talking contest between Mengzi and Gaozi. Most so-called debates of the Warring States period are little more than reconstructions on the basis of contrasting positions or biased polemics. Not so with the *Verses of Chu*.

Looking ahead to the argument of chapter 5, the other remarkable thing about the debate of the *Verses of Chu* is that most of its participants were ventriloquists. Even when disagreeing with the Qu Yuan of "Parting's Sorrow," they expressed their disagreement in the voice of Qu Yuan or in the style of "Parting's Sorrow." For them, "Quzi" 屈子—as he is referred to in the *Verses of Chu* and elsewhere—was a historical figure but he was also a persona one could adopt to explore a specific moral dilemma in a particular discursive mode.[15] As a teaser for chapter 5's argument about the status of "The Masters," we might ask: what exactly is the difference between "Quzi" and "Kongzi," "Xunzi," "Zhuangzi," and so on? Might we also approach pre-Han Masters as voices through which the ventriloquist-authors of the Han debated the most pressing issues of the day? If the answer is yes, then the *Verses of Chu* emerge as an even more powerful tool in our ongoing efforts to understand the imperial construction of preimperial China.

OF HOMESICK DRIVERS AND ROAD-WEARY HORSES[16]

"Parting's Sorrow" opens with the dramatic "descent" (*jiang* 降) of an aristocratic hero who festoons himself with aromatic plants and sets out to woo/persuade a "Fair One" (*meiren* 美人, a term which also appears in the *Shi*),[17] only to be rebuffed when he heeds slanderers instead. Resolving to maintain his purity, the hero "withdraws" (*tui* 退; line 112) from society and embarks on a cosmic quest for a true mate. Along the way, he makes a series of failed love connections and encounters various interlocutors who criticize or applaud his high-mindedness. Ultimately encouraged by the last of these authorities, a Shaman Xian 巫咸, he travels into increasingly mythological territory and ascends higher and higher into the heavens with an expanding retinue of chariots and spirits. The entire poem is composed of 368 lines or ninety-two quatrains (plus a coda) in the sao style, consisting of rhymed couplets of five- or six-syllable lines separated by strong xi 兮 caesurae.

Our own point of departure is the final quatrain (lines 365–368) and coda of "Parting's Sorrow," when the hero begins his final ascent into the heavens. From his encounter with Shaman Xian up until the very end of the poem, the hero's flight is described in increasingly fantastic terms. Flying dragons pull him, phoenixes bear his banners, spirits act as his escorts, and a thousand chariots join his retinue. But the procession hits a snag:

> Ascending the heavens so dazzlingly brilliant,
> I look down suddenly and spy my old haunts
> My driver grieves, my horses long to return,
> Craning their necks back they go no further.
> *Coda:* Enough! / There is no one in the realm who recognizes me,
> So why long for my former capital?
> Since there is no one worthy of joining me in fine rule
> I will follow Peng and Xian where they reside.

陟陞皇之赫戲兮，忽臨睨夫舊鄉。僕夫悲余馬懷兮，蜷局顧而不行。

亂曰：已矣哉！國無人莫我知兮，又何懷乎故都。既莫足與為美政兮，吾將從彭咸之所居。[18]

With this, the hero declares his intent to cross over into the heavenly realm from which Shaman Xian and his retinue of spirits "descended" (*jiang* 降; line 279) earlier in the poem, thus capping his own "descent" from the opening quatrain.[19]

In the aristocratic and supernatural milieu of "Parting's Sorrow," a world peopled with spirits, shamans, sages, and "Fair Ones," the appearance of a lowly "driver" or "servant" (*pufu* 僕夫) in the final quatrain is surprising.

More surprising is the text's willingness to cede emotion and agency to such a figure. Throughout the poem, we are told that the hero is "singular" or "solitary" (*du* 獨), a raptor that "does not flock" (不群; line 97) with lesser birds.[20] Yet here he is a corporate entity who, like the ideal rulers of early didactic literature, must depend on others. Echoes elsewhere in the *Verses of Chu* show that this moment wasn't anomalous within the tradition, as when the hero of "Yuan you" 遠遊 (Distant Roaming) pauses before his final ascent: "My driver longs for home, my heart grieves; the outside horses look back and go no further" 僕夫懷余心悲兮，邊馬顧而不 (5.172).[21]

I suspect that the homesick driver and road-weary horses would have been familiar to early audiences as stock figures from the *Shi*. As noted in chapter 2, the "man on the march" (*zheng fu* 征夫) theme accounts for more than thirty poems across all four divisions and roughly 10 percent of all stanzas. Most of these pieces focus on a single stage (the departure, the march, or the return) of the campaign from a particular point of view (a general, his men, their loved ones at home) in a single mood (the homesickness of the men, the longing of the women, or the celebration of martial prowess); a handful narrate a complete campaign from beginning to end. The parallels between some of these *Shi* and the conclusion of "Parting's Sorrow" are striking.[22] Consider the campaigners of "Cocklebur" (Juan er 卷耳, #3) and "Bring out the Carts" (Chu ju 出車, #168):

> I am climbing that high ridge / My horses are sick and spent.
> I pause to drink from that horn cup / To still my heart's pain.
>
> I am climbing that shale, / My horses founder,
> My driver is stricken, / Oh, woe, oh, misery.
>
> 陟彼高岡，我馬玄黃。我姑酌彼兕觥，維以不永傷。
> 陟彼砠矣，我馬瘏矣。我僕痡矣，云何吁矣。(3/3–4)

> We bring out our carts / On to those outskirts.
> Here we set up the standards, / There we raise the oxtail banners,

The falcon banner and the standards / All *bâts-bâts* [flying, fluttering]
Anxious hearts *tshiau?-tshiau?* [mourning, sorrowing],
The drivers are worn out.
. . .
Long ago, when we started,
The ale millet and cooking millet were in flower.
Now that we are on the march again / Snow falls upon the mire.
The king's service brings many hardships,
We have no time to rest or bide.
We do indeed long to return / But we fear the written command.

我出我車，于彼郊矣。設此旐矣，建彼旄矣。彼旟旐斯，胡不斾
斾。憂心悄悄，僕夫況瘁。
昔我往矣，黍稷方華。今我來思，雨雪載塗。王事多難，不遑啟
居。豈不懷歸，畏此簡書。(168/2,4)

Like the protagonist of "Parting's Sorrow," the persona of "Cocklebur" attempts to "ascend" or "climb" (*chi* 陟) up high with a "driver" (*pu* 僕) and "horses" (*ma* 馬) who aren't up to the task. In all three pieces, the dominant theme is *huai gui* 懷歸, the unfulfilled "longing for return," with the associated "grief" of "Parting's Sorrow" and the "anxiety" (*you* 憂) of "Bring out the Carts."

These connections are amplified elsewhere in the *Verses of Chu*. In the "Nine Songs" (Jiu ge 九歌), the concluding couplet of "Lord of Yunzhong" (Yunzhong jun 雲中君) echoes the oft-repeated phrase "My anxious heart *thruŋ-thruŋ* [thronged with worry]" 憂心忡忡 from "Chu ju" and elsewhere: "I think of that lord and deeply sigh, / it pains my heart *thruŋ-thruŋ* [thronging with worry]" 思夫君兮太息，極勞心兮忡忡 (2.59).[23] In the "Nine Pieces" (Jiu zhang 九章), the hero's "chariot overturns and the horses founder" 車既覆而馬顛兮 (4.147); in "Lamenting My Lot" (Ai shi ming 哀時命), his "chariot breaks down and the horses are worn out" 車既弊而馬罷兮 (14.261). In Liu Xiang's 劉向 (77–6 BCE) "Nine Laments" (Jiu tan 九歎), the driver is described twice as *cui* 悴 (wan), a loan character for the *cui* 瘁 of "Bring Out the Carts" (16.296,302). Also in the "Nine Laments," three pieces lament the plight of "men on the march" (*zheng fu* 征夫), a term that appears very rarely in early sources outside *Shi* quotations.[24]

Writing in 1974, David Hawkes famously suggested that *Verses of Chu* poems could be analyzed in two parts: the "tristia," in which the protagonist vents his sorrows, and the "itineraria," in which he embarks on a quest.²⁵ Given his interest in the shamanistic origins of the *Verses of Chu*, Hawkes devoted more space to the latter than to the former without offering a convincing account of why the two parts were combined in the first place. His tentative suggestion was that the tristia "derives from the characteristic note of melancholy and frustration which shamanistic tradition prescribed for the hymns which they addressed to their fickle and elusive deities."²⁶ The present analysis suggests another explanation. Hawkes looked to Latin to label the hero's movement through "Parting's Sorrow" despite the poem's own terminology: *zheng* 征 (lines 143, 184). At the poem's conclusion, the movement that mattered wasn't a shamanistic spirit journey but a *Shi*-style campaign. In *Shi* poetics, separation occasions sadness.

A META-JOURNEY THROUGH THE *SHI*

Zooming out from the end of "Parting's Sorrow," the campaign theme first appears in the sixth quatrain and in almost half of all quatrains thereafter. As with so much of the poem, tracing the hero's movements is complicated by the many abrupt shifts in theme, mood, and voice. Unlike "Bring out the Carts," "Parting's Sorrow" doesn't follow a literal campaign from departure to homecoming.²⁷ Instead, its campaign is a metadiscursive movement through various roles associated with the "men on the march" theme of the *Shi*. As he struggles to rationalize his plight over the course of the poem, the hero assumes the roles of the driver, the lowly man on the march, the woman left behind, and the victorious king, only to abandon each in turn.

In this respect, "Parting's Sorrow" has a structure akin to that of the *Seven Stimuli* (Qi fa 七發). Both texts are framed as solutions to a problem: in *Seven Stimuli*, how to cure the prince's malaise; in "Parting's Sorrow," how to cure the hero's "alienated heart" (*li xin* 離心, line 339). The protagonists of both texts performatively embody culturally significant domains of experience: in *Seven Stimuli*, the pleasures appropriate to a ruler; in "Parting's Sorrow," various *Shi* archetypes. And in both texts, each successive performance fails until the very end, when the sufferer arises and leaves the source of his suffering behind: in *Seven Stimuli*, the prince "rises up" (*qi* 起) to follow the guest out of the inner palace; in "Parting's Sorrow," the hero turns his back on the world.

The Proem

The first *Shi* echoes come in the first six quatrains of "Parting's Sorrow," where the hero proclaims his quasi-divine ancestry from the god-king Gaoyang 高陽, the auspicious circumstances of his birth, his "descent" (*jiang* 降) into the world, the auspicious names (Upright Standard 正則 and Divine Balance 靈均) he received from his father, and his "inner beauty" (*nei mei* 內美), which he then complements by donning various aromatic botanicals. This sequence—the listing of auspicious omens, the descent, the botanical imagery, and the theme of moral rectitude—mirrors the structure of "Ding-Star in the Middle of the Sky" (Ding zhi fangzhong 定之方中, #50), one of only two pieces in the *Shijing* to refer to a locale named "Chu" 楚:[28]

> With the Ding-star is in the middle of the sky,
> We build the temple at Chu.
> Orienting it by the sun, / We build the house of Chu.
> Planting hazels and chestnuts / Catalpas, paulownias, lacquer-trees,
> That we may make zithers great and small
>
> We climb that hill / To look down upon Chu,
> To look down upon Chu and Tang / and the Jing hills and citadel.
> We descend and inspect the mulberry.
> We take omens; they are lucky, / All of them are truly good.
>
> A magical rain is falling. / We order the grooms
> By starlight, early, to yoke our steeds, / To rest in the mulberry orchards.
> Those are men indeed! / They hold hearts staunch and true,
> With their tall mares numbering three thousand.
>
> 定之方中，作于楚宮。揆之以日，作于楚室。樹之榛栗，椅桐梓漆，爰伐琴瑟。
> 升彼虛矣，以望楚矣。望楚與堂，景山與京。降觀于桑，卜云其吉，終然允臧。
> 靈雨既零，命彼倌人。星言夙駕，說于桑田。匪直也人，秉心塞淵，騋牝三千。

The astronomical omens of the first stanza recall the omens of "Parting's Sorrow," lines 1–4, just as "the house of Chu" recalls the hero's claim that he is descended from Gaoyang, the Chu progenitor. Both poems feature the "inspection" (*kui* 揆; line 5) of these omens together with additional verbs of "surveying" (*guan* 觀 and *wang* 望 in the *Shi*, *lan* 覽 in the "Parting's Sorrow"). Both poems feature a "descent" (*jiang* 降; line 4) and a "falling" (*ling* 零; line 19). Both include the word *ling* 靈 ("divine," "numinous"): the "magical" rain that falls in the *Shi* and the name "Divine Balance" (*ling jun* 靈均; line 8) that is bestowed on the descended hero. "Building" (*zuo* 作) gives way to "planting" (*shu* 樹) in the first stanza of the *Shi*, just as the arising (*zuo* 作) of the "Parting's Sorrow" hero in sections 1–2 gives way to the botanical imagery of lines 11–12. There is also some aural overlap: not only do both pieces open with rhymes on *-ung/-ong, the "auspicious names" (*jia ming* 嘉名; *krâi-meŋ) bestowed on the hero by his father echo the "command" (*ming* 命; *mreŋ) to "yoke" (*jia* 駕; *krâih) the horses. Finally, the third stanza of the *Shi* transitions to the faithful "grooms" or "drivers" (*guanren* 倌人, a synonym for *pufu*), just as "Parting's Sorrow" introduces the campaign theme with the horse and driver imagery of lines 23–24.

Role 1: The Driver

Although not explicitly labeled as such, at this point the hero takes on the role of the Fair One's "driver" (*pufu* 僕夫):

> Mount your piebald steeds, gallop away
> Come! I'll lead you in the forward chariot.

乘騏驥以馳騁兮，來吾道夫先路。 (lines 7–8)[29]

As the driver of the "forward chariot," the hero avoids "careening down twisted trails" 捷徑 (line 32), he "rushes ahead and behind" 奔走以先後 (line 37), and he plots a course in "the footsteps of former kings" 前王之踵武 (line 38). When expressing his "fear that the royal carriage might topple" 恐皇輿之敗績 (line 36) should the Fair One follow "a road dark and gloomy through dangerous passes" 路幽昧以險隘 (line 34), the hero echoes an admonishment from "First Month" (Zheng yue 正月, #192):

Do not toss your sideboards away / Or all will fall into your spokes.
If you take heed of your driver, / Your load will not tumble over
And you will pass by dangerous places—/ Have you not considered this?

無棄爾輔，員于爾輻。屢顧爾僕，不輸爾載。終踰絕險，曾是不意。(192/10)

Here we might also note the connection between the use of *xiu* 脩/修 ("prepare," "arrange;" "cultivate;" "fine;" "long") in the two anthologies. A key term appearing eighteen times in "Parting's Sorrow" and nearly fifty times in the *Verses of Chu*, *xiu* is often taken to refer to the "fine" or the "cultivation" of fine things. Of the ten appearances of *xiu* in the *Shijing*, all but three refer to the length of horses in campaigns or to the "preparation" of equipment prior to a campaign, as in "No Wraps (Wu yi 無衣, 133/1.3–5): "The king is raising an army; / I have made ready both spear and axe, / You shall share them with me as my comrade" 王于興師，脩我戈矛，與子同仇. Given the wealth of campaign imagery in "Parting's Sorrow," the militaristic connotations of *xiu* appear to be active in that poem as well.

Role 2: The Man on the March

After the Fair One "puts his faith in slanderers" (*xin chan* 信讒, line 40), another phrase from the *Shi*,[30] the driver fantasy bursts and the hero enters his first lament. Describing himself as a man of singular virtue, he becomes his own driver when he "turns his chariot around and retraces [his] path" 回朕車以復路兮 (line 107) away from the Fair One. In this section, the hero adopts the persona of a toiling "campaigner" or "man on the march" (*zhengfu* 征夫) who sheds the "tears" (*ti* 涕; line 77) and experiences the "loneliness" (*du* 獨; lines 94, 126), "sorrow" (*ai* 哀; line 78), "fear" (*kong* 恐 or *wei* 畏; line 64), and "many hardships" (*duo jian/duo nan* 多艱/多難; line 78) described in *Shi* like "Minor Bright" (Xiao ming" 小明, #207) and "High-Crested Southern Hills" (Jie nan shan" 節南山, #191):

Long ago when we set out, / The days and months were just becoming mild.
When shall I get back? / The year is drawing to a close.
When I think I am singlehanded / And my affairs very many,

Oh, the sadness of my heart! / Truly I cannot get leave.
Thinking of those that nurtured me
Kons-kons [craning] I look back longingly.
How could I not long for home?
But I am afraid of the wrath that would ensue.

昔我往矣，日月方除。曷云其還，歲聿云莫。念我獨兮，我事孔庶。心之憂矣，憚我不暇。念彼共人，睠睠懷顧。豈不懷歸，畏此譴怒。(207/2)

Driving forth those four steeds, / Four steeds with thick necks stretched.
I look out over the four quarters,
Tsiuk-tsiuk [fretting, stressing] I have no place to ride.

駕彼四牡，四牡項領。我瞻四方，蹙蹙靡所騁。(191/7)

Note the "looking back" (*gu* 顧) in "Minor Bright" and the "looking out" (*zhan* 瞻) in "High-Crested Southern Hills." In the *Shi*, these gestures are among the few outward signs of soldiers' distress (along with sighs and tears). The king's service doesn't permit them to return or rest, but nothing stops them from gazing in the direction of their loved ones. Lines 121–122 of "Parting's Sorrow" deploy both types of looking: "Suddenly I turned and looked back, let my eyes wander; I will go and survey the four reaches of the world" 忽反顧以遊目兮，將往觀乎四荒. But there is also a crucial difference here: whereas soldiers in the *Shi* experience homesickness because of their service to the king, in "Parting's Sorrow" the solo journey is prompted by "estrangement" (*li bie* 離別; line 47) from the Fair One.

Role 3: The Woman Left Behind

In the next section, the hero's aloofness earns him a scolding from Nüxu 女嬃 (the Sister), who introduces the next campaign-based role from the *Shi*: "Men of this era stand together and love their fellows / So why [act] so lonely [*gweŋ*] and childless? Why not hearken to me?" 世並舉而好朋兮，夫何煢獨而不予聽 (lines 139–140). As noted by Wang Yi, the words "lonely and childless" (*qiong du* 煢獨; *gweŋ–dôk) also appear in the thirteenth stanza of "First Month": "The rich are doing well indeed / but pity the lonely [*gweŋ] and childless" 哿矣富人，哀此惸獨 (192/13.5–6). The men-on-the-march poem "Wild geese" (Hong yan 鴻鴈, #181) includes a close parallel of the same line:

> The soldiers are on the march
> Painfully they struggle through the wilds.
> In dire extremity are the strong men / [But] pity the wives, left all alone.

> 之子于征，劬勞于野。爰及矜人，哀此鰥寡。(181/1.2–5)

Nüxu's question is thus a devastating criticism. Despite the hero's efforts to portray himself as a noble man who chooses to walk a lonely path, he is ultimately no more heroic than widowed wives or childless parents, the most vulnerable and pathetic victims of a king's campaigns. (Other early sources likewise identify the widowed and childless as the weakest members of society and thus the most requiring of a ruler's mercy.[31]) The message is something like: you are a wretched victim of circumstance, not a master of your own fate. This reading may also explain the choice of interlocutor. Who better to call the hero a forsaken wife than a woman whose name can be read as "Woman Waiting" (removing the radical from 嬃 to yield *xu* 須)?

Role 4: The King on the March

In rebuttal, the hero puffs himself up into a figure of royal stature. Professing to "rely on the former sage-kings for restraint and balance" 依前聖以節中兮 (line 141), he journeys southward to the sage-king Shun 舜 to "state his case" (*chen ci* 敶詞/陳辭, lines 144, 181), essentially a list of rulers who did and didn't "follow the plumb line without swerving" 循繩墨而不頗 (line 164). Prompted by the examples of ancient sage-kings, the hero proceeds to adopt the trappings of a triumphant king or general on the march. He creates a fabulous equipage ("I team jade dragons and mount phoenixes" 駟玉虯以桀鷖兮, lines 183–184) and acquires an increasingly fantastic entourage of gods and eventually an army of a thousand chariots:

I gather chariots, a thousand strong,
Line up jade axles, rush forward as one.
Yoke eight dragons, *ʔonʔ-ʔonʔ [wending, winding],
Fly cloud banners, twisting and snaking.

屯余車其千乘兮，齊玉軑而並馳，駕八龍之婉婉兮，載雲旗之委蛇。(lines 357–360)

This shift is accompanied by the first appearance of verbs of command: *wu ling* 吾令 ("I order," lines 189, 201, 207, 221, 224, 237), *shi* 使 ("make," lines 197–198, 300, 351–352, 354), *ming* 命 ("command," line 258), and *zhao* 詔 ("decree," line 352).

The correspondence with the kingly campaigns of the *Shi* is far from perfect. The entourages of the *Shi* don't include spirits or gods, nor do they travel to mythical locales. But the points of overlap are many: "dragon" (*long* 龍) and fantastic bird (*luan* 鸞) imagery;[32] opulent ornaments and fittings;[33] flags and banners (*qi* 旂 [*gəi], *qi* 旗 [*gə];[34] "flying" (*fei* 飛, lines 201, 337), "flowing" (*liu* 流, lines 332, 342), "galloping" (*chi* 馳, lines 358, 362) and "rushing" (*qu* 驅, line 197) movements;[35] "cloud" (*yun* 雲, lines 221, 343, 360) imagery;[36] and orderly hosts numbered in the thousands. Compare "Plucking White Millet" (Cai qi 采芑, #178) and "Always Mighty in War" (Chang wu 常武, #263):

With three thousand chariots
With banners *ʔraŋ-ʔraŋ [blazing, dazzling].
Yes, Fang-shu came / With leatherbound nave and metal-studded yoke,
His eight luan bells jingling, / Wearing his insignia,
The red greaves so splendid / The tinkling onion stones at his belt.

其車三千，旂旐央央。方叔率止，約軝錯衡，八鸞瑲瑲，服其命服，朱芾斯皇，有瑲蔥珩。(178/2.5–12)

The king's hosts *thân-thân [thronging, surging],
As if flying, as if winged,
Like the River, like the Han / Steady as a mountain,

Flowing onward like a stream,
Mên?-mên? [endless, ceaseless], *lək-lək* [ruly, orderly],
Immeasurable, unassailable, / Mightily they marched through Xu.

王旅嘽嘽，如飛如翰，如江如漢，如山之苞，如川之流，綿綿翼翼，不測不克，濯征徐國。(263/5)

There is no hint in these stanzas of the longing or hardship experienced by common soldiers. Kings on the march were to be celebrated, not lamented. So, too, in "Parting's Sorrow," the adoption of the royal persona precludes anxiety. Ultimately, however, the hero is no more successful as a king than as a driver or marching soldier. The first royal campaign (lines 181–206) ends when he approaches the gates of Heaven and finds the way barred: "I order the Lord's gatekeeper to open the barrier, / But he leans on the gate and looks down on me" 吾令帝閽開關兮，倚閶闔而望予. Ultimately, the royal persona isn't as empowering as the hero hoped.

Role 5: The Suitor

In classical Chinese thinking, a virtuous ruler requires a virtuous adviser. Perhaps that is why the failure of the kingly persona transitions in lines 213–216 to the search for a mate:

In the morning I set out to cross the White Water, / Climb Lofty Wind peak and tether the horses.
Suddenly I turn and look back, streaming tears, / Sad that this high hill has no woman for me.

朝吾將濟於白水兮，登閬風而繫馬。忽反顧以流涕兮，哀高丘之無女。

As the kings of the *Shi* didn't go on campaigns looking for love, the *Shi* allusions in this section shift away from campaign poems to poems of "seeking" (*qiu* 求) or wooing. The transformation from victorious king into hopeful lover also reopens a space for lamentation, hence the "looking back," "tears," "sadness," and hill-climbing of lines 213–216. The poem's debt to the wooing theme of the *Shi* is evident in the next stanza:

Straightaway I travel to this Spring Palace,
I break off sprays of garnet to add to my pendants.
While the blossoms' beauty has yet to fall,
I look for a woman below to whom gifts can be given.

溘吾遊此春宮兮，折瓊枝以繼佩。及榮華之未落兮，相下女之可詒。

Earlier in the poem (lines 11–12), the hero adorns himself with aromatic plants, but here the ornament changes to garnet. "Gifting" (*yi* 詒; lines 220, 243)[37] a friend or beloved with a (garnet) pendant is a stock gesture in the *Shi*, as in "Quince" (Mu gua 木瓜, 64/1):

She threw a quince to me / In requital I gave her a garnet pendant—
No, not just as requital, / But meaning I would love her forever.

投我以木瓜，報之以瓊瑤琚。匪報也，永以為好也。(134/2.3–4)[38]

Note the mixing of botanical and mineral imagery in both poems.

The most obvious point of overlap in this section is the figure of the "matchmaker" (*mei* 媒; lines 237, 240, 290), a role filled by multiple characters beginning in lines 224–249: Jianxiu 蹇脩, minister to the legendary Fuxi 宓羲, who approaches Lady Fu 宓妃, Fuxi's consort; the toxic bird (*zhen* 鴆) who approaches Jiandi 簡狄 of the Yousong 有娀 clan, the mother of the Shang 商 progenitor and a figure referenced in the *Shijing* (304/1.7); and the unnamed figure who approaches the two wives of Shaokang 少康, a king of the Xia 夏 dynasty.[39] All fail in one way or another: Lady Fu is proud and wanton, the toxic bird reports back (dishonestly?) that Jiandi doesn't care for the hero, and the third matchmaker is "weak" (*ruo* 弱) and "inept" (*zhuo* 拙). The failure prompts a minitriste in which the hero expresses his "doubts" (*yi* 疑) and laments the need for a matchmaker: "I wished to go myself but was not allowed" 欲自適而不可 (line 241).

In a poem that gives its hero the power to command the gods, who or what prevents him from acting as his own matchmaker? The answer lies in the *Shi*—specifically, in the fourth stanza of "Southern Hill" (Nan shan 南山, #101):

How do we cut firewood? / Without an axe it is impossible.
How does one take a wife?
Without a matchmaker he cannot get her.[40]

析薪如之何，匪斧不克。取妻如之何，匪媒不得。

Several early sources likewise caution against seeking a mate without a matchmaker, of which the *Shijing* is the most canonical and unequivocal.[41] The phrase "without a fine matchmaker" (*wu liang mei* 無良媒) from "A Simple Peasant" (Meng 氓, 58/1.8) also appears elsewhere in the *Verses of Chu*: "widowed, childless, alone / and without a fine matchmaker by my side" 既惸獨而不群兮，又無良媒在其側 (4.139).

The hero's failure to find a mate leads him to seek the advice of Divine Fen 靈氛 (lines 258–266) and Shaman Xian 巫咸 (lines 279–300) in the next section of the poem. The first encourages him to continue his search, while the second authorizes him to forgo a matchmaker altogether. To justify this break with tradition, Shaman Xian recites the examples of four rulers (Yu 禹, Wuding 武丁, King Wen 文王, Lord Huan of Qi 齊桓公) who found their own advisers.[42] If these rulers didn't require matchmakers, then neither does the hero—the petty morality of the *Shi* be damned.

Role 4 Redux: The King on the March

Like the first list of ancient exemplars (lines 145–162), the second list of sage-kings prompts a return to the kingly role in lines 337–340:

> For me are harnessed flying dragons,
> A chariot blended with jasper and ivory.
> How can an estranged heart ever be joined?
> I will go far away and keep myself apart.

為余駕飛龍兮，雜瑤象以為車。何離心之可同兮，吾將遠逝以自疏。

From here, the hero proceeds to the end of the poem, where the *zheng* once again sputters to a halt. Earlier his progress was thwarted by Heaven's gatekeeper, but in the final lines he is stopped by his driver and horses. To continue on, he must abandon his entourage and shed the trappings of a king on the march.

I opened this section with the suggestion that the hero's progress through "Parting's Sorrow" isn't a literal campaign but a movement through different roles associated with the *Shi*. After the descent of the opening quatrain, the hero offers to serve as the Fair One's driver, only to be slandered and rebuffed. Resolving to maintain his purity, he sets off as a wandering "man on the march." only for the Sister to flip the script and treat him as a wife left behind. He responds to her insult by adopting the role of a superempowered king but instead finds himself barred and mocked by Heaven's gatekeeper. Transitioning from a campaign to a suit, he seeks a mate but fails because of his reliance on flawed matchmakers, whom he is encouraged to abandon. He resumes the kingly campaign but is thwarted by the *Shi*-style homesickness of his driver and horses. The poem concludes with the hero turning away from his homeland once and for all.

Where does he go at the end of the poem? Much ink has been spilled on the question of the identity of Peng and Xian (or Pengxian) and whether Qu Yuan commits suicide.[43] However, the poem itself is mostly uninterested in such questions. What matters isn't where the hero ends up but what he leaves behind. Beginning with the bursting of the driver fantasy in line 39 and ending with the abandonment of the homesick drivers at the very end, the poem takes up these *Shi* archetypes in order to move beyond them. The coda begins with the hero exclaiming, "Enough!" 已矣哉. A threshold is crossed, and it feels momentous. The entirety of "Parting's Sorrow" up until this moment is an accumulation of rationales for escaping the gravitational pull of *Shi* poetics. Those people in the *Shi* are always yearning for home and companionship, the hero of "Parting's Sorrow" seems to say, but I'm not like those people. I don't need a Fair One, a ruler, a mate, a matchmaker, a driver, or any other stock roles from the *Shi*. Here, in this poem, I can say goodbye and leave the world (of the *Shi*) behind forever.

THE QU YUAN DEBATE

But can the hero really leave the world of the *Shi* forever? Even if he can, should he? And even if he should, what does it mean to leave the world behind? Beginning with the "Nine Pieces" (Jiu zhang 九章) and continuing with "Distant Roaming" (Yuan you 遠遊), "Lament for [a Broken] Oath" (Xi shi 惜誓), "Seven Remonstrations" (Qi jian" 七諫), "Lamenting My

Lot" (Ai shi ming 哀時命), Wang Bao's 王褒 (84–53 BCE) "Nine Longings" (Jiu huai 九懷), Liu Xiang's "Nine Laments" (Jiu tan 九歎), and Wang Yi's 王逸 (89–158 CE) "Nine Pinings" (Jiu si 九思), most *Verses of Chu* sections take up the Qu Yuan conundrum and the "Parting's Sorrow" template in one form or another. They feature personas who fail to woo the objects of their affections, suffer estrangement, and/or embark on a journey. However, following the script of "Parting's Sorrow" didn't necessarily entail an endorsement of a final departure. *Verses of Chu* poems are profoundly ambivalent about the possibility and propriety of saying goodbye, and thus about the power of the imperative to *gui*.

Qu Yuan the Hero

Like "Parting's Sorrow" itself, some pieces portray the Qu Yuan persona in a more heroic light. They celebrate a figure who preserved his purity, exercised his moral agency, and emerged unscathed. Or in the words of Liu An,

> [Qu Yuan] sloughed off his cicada-shell in the grime and went floating off and wandering beyond the dust, escaping the burgeoning filth of the world. Gleaming he went through the muck to emerge unsullied. With such [purity of] intention, his radiance rivaled that of the sun and moon.

> 蟬蛻於濁穢，以浮游塵埃之外，不獲世之滋垢，皭然泥而不滓。推此志，雖與日月爭光可也。[44]

In the heroic reading, alienation is ultimately a test of Qu Yuan's ability to transcend his circumstances, to purge those parts of himself (the "cicada-shell") that tied him to the "dust" and "filth" of the world.[45]

The most celebratory treatment of the Qu Yuan persona belongs to "Distant Roaming" (Yuan you 遠遊), which reads like a cross between "Parting's Sorrow" and the *Laozi*. As we saw in the last chapter's discussion of *Laozi* section 20, the *Laozi* rejects the equation of individuation with alienation. *Laozi*-style "isolation" or "solitude" (*du* 獨) is a mark of empowerment and inoculation against *Shi*-style anxiety. This stance makes the *Laozi* a complicated resource for authors working with the Qu Yuan persona. On the one hand, the *Laozi* sage's imperviousness to alienation undercuts the pathos at the heart of "Parting's Sorrow"; on the other, some authors found in *Laozi*-style equanimity a solution to the Qu Yuan predicament. Alienation is just a test of the *Laozi* hero's ability to transcend his circumstances.

Early in "Distant Roaming," the persona experiences the typical "grief" (*bei* 悲; line 1), "solitude" (*du* 獨; line 6), and "sadness" (*ai* 哀; line 20). But the torment doesn't last long:

> The spirit leaves abruptly and doesn't return,
> The body withers, left all alone.
> I ponder and reflect within to strengthen my resolve:
> I seek the source of the purest *qi*.
> In silence, emptiness, and stillness I find peace and contentment,
> Tranquil and effortless, I am at ease in myself.
> I have heard that Red Pine brought purity to the dust—
> Would that I might receive the influence of his example.
> I value the magnificent virtue of realized men,
> I marvel at the transcendents of bygone eras.
> They left [the world of] transformation never to be seen again,
> Their names renowned and growing by the day.

> 神儵忽而不反兮，形枯槁而獨留。內惟省以端操兮，求正氣之所由。
> 漠虛靜以恬愉兮，澹無為而自得。聞赤松之清塵兮，願承風乎遺則。
> 貴真人之休德兮，美往世之登仙。與化去而不見兮，名聲著而日延。(lines 17–28/5.164–165)

As befits the more heroic and empowered tone of "Distant Roaming," its persona begins his royal procession much earlier in the poem when he assembles an entourage ten times larger than that of "Parting's Sorrow." When the time comes to "command Heaven's gatekeeper to unbar the gates" 命天閽其開關兮 (line 87), he encounters no resistance as he "enters the palace of Di" (入帝宮; line 91). Here, we might also note the many parallels between "Distant Roaming" and Sima Xiangru's 司馬相如 (d. 117 BCE) "Rhapsody on the Great Man" (Daren fu 大人賦), which, when presented to Emperor Wu, reportedly made him feel "**phiau-phiau* [airy, breezy] with the *qi* of soaring clouds, as if he had a mind to roam idly between Heaven and earth" 飄飄有淩雲之氣，似游天地之閒意.[46]

THE *SHI* AND THE *VERSES OF CHU* (*CHUCI* 楚辭)

What makes the journey of "Distant Roaming" possible is the persona's abandonment of his corporeal self: his spirit "leaves abruptly and doesn't return" as his body "withers" away. This is a neat solution to the Qu Yuan conundrum. By splitting him in two, authors allowed his body to remain in the human world (of the *Shi*) so that his spirit could move beyond it. (Although not often invoked in discussions of the mind-body problem in the Chinese context, the *Verses of Chu* offer unequivocal evidence of the dualist position.[47]) As revealed in the poem's conclusion, that movement is essentially a *gui*:

> Below is an immensity, without an earth;
> Above is a vastness, without a Heaven.
> My eyes are dizzy, without sight; / My ears are confused, without acuity.
> I surpass the effortless and arrive at purity
> To join the neighborhood of the Great Beginning.

> 下崢嶸而無地兮，上寥廓而無天，視儵忽而無見兮，聽惝怳而無聞，超無為以至清兮，與泰初而為鄰。(lines 167–172/5.174–175)

In tracing a path back to the beginning, "Distant Roaming" brings about a metaphysical homecoming.

The "Nine Laments" of Liu Xiang, the first confirmed compiler of the *Verses of Chu* collection, offers a less triumphant version of the heroic Qu Yuan. In the coda to the first piece of the suite, "Encountering Troubles" (Feng fen 逢紛), Liu Xiang likens Qu Yuan to water that violently smashes against "obstructions" or "blockages" (*zu* 阻) but that ultimately finds an outlet in textual composition:

> I compare him to flowing water: roaring with the crash of boulders,
> Waves sweeping up and surging, rapids boiling and racing,
> Whipped to wild frenzy, plunging in foaming flood, dashing on jagged rocks,
> Swirling and circling, whirling and eddying, hurling against obstructions.
> Meeting with many misfortunes, falling on dire disgrace,
> Pouring out his wondrous words in writing, leaving them for those to come.

譬彼流水，紛揚磕兮，波逢洶涌，濆滂沛兮，揄揚滌盪，漂流隕往，觸崟石兮，龍邛脟圈，繚戾宛轉，阻相薄兮，遭紛逢凶，塞離尤兮，垂文揚采，遺將來兮。(16.284–285)[48]

The comparison of Qu Yuan to "flowing water" (*liu shui* 流水) is noteworthy given the last chapter's discussion of water as a foundational metaphor in early Chinese thought. By assimilating Qu Yuan within a much older tradition of performative water viewing, Liu Xiang positions him as an object of contemplation while also flaunting his own intellectual credentials. And like Sima Qian in the "Self-Narration, Liu Xiang presents Qu Yuan as a figure who sought to regain his freedom of movement through writing. By the middle of the suite, however, the turn to writing fails:

> By unfolding my feelings and reciting this *shi* / I had hoped to free myself.
> [Instead] I fall to ruin / And become more distant by the day.

> 舒情陳詩，冀以自免兮。頹流下隕，身日遠兮。(16.295)

In the final piece, also called "Distant Roaming" (Yuan you" 遠遊), Qu Yuan remains mired in grief as he declares his intent to "drown [his] body in the Yuan and Xiang [rivers]" 殞余躬於沅湘 (16.311). But the final coda to the "Nine Laments" suggests a different fate, one more in keeping with the other "Distant Journey":

> I compare [Qu Yuan] to the flood-dragon: floating in watery vapors, like a dense mist;
> Billowing formlessly, with thunder roll and lightning flash, high aloft he races;
> Mounting the void, treading the dark sky, spurning the turbid vapors, swimming in the clear ones, he enters the House of Di;
> Shaking his wings and beating with his pinions, racing the wind, driving the rain, he wanders without end.

> 譬彼蛟龍，乘雲浮兮，汎淫澒溶，紛若霧兮，潺湲轇轕，雷動電發，駁高舉兮，升虛凌冥，沛濁浮清，入帝宮兮，搖翹奮羽，馳風騁雨，遊無窮兮。(16.312)[49]

The flowing water of the first coda is vaporized into something airier and more magical, a dragon that transcends the world to go "wandering without end." Liu Xiang ultimately embraces the dualist solution to the Qu Yuan conundrum: he drowns Qu Yuan's body in order to free his spirit.

"Sorrowful Plaint" (Xi song 惜誦), the first of the "Nine Pieces," offers a very different version of the heroic Qu Yuan. After the persona professes his loyalty to his lord and endures "blame" (*you* 尤) and "slander" (*bang* 謗), he faces a "vexatious perplexity" (*fan huo* 煩惑):

> Shall I tarry, shall I try to stay?
> I fear doubling my misfortune and incurring a[n even greater] blame.
> Shall I fly up high and roost far away?
> My lord will slander me and say, "Where are you going?"
>
> Shall I run counter [to what is right], shall I lose my path?
> My will is too firm and will not endure it.
> My back and breast are riven with anguish,
> My heart is stifled and knotted [with indecision].
>
> 欲儃佪以干傺兮，恐重患而離尤。欲高飛而遠集兮，君罔謂汝何之。欲橫奔而失路兮，堅志而不忍。背膺牉以交痛兮，心鬱結而紆軫。(4.127)

But perplexity isn't paralyzing for this particular persona. In the poem's final lines, he finds solace both in his own beauty and in the possibility of a life lived apart:

> I pound magnolia to mix with orchid
> And grind the flowering pepper for my fare.
> I seed gracilaria and grow chrysanthemum,
> Hoping for a spring day when they might flavor my food.
>
> Afraid that my disposition and character will not be trusted,
> I have recited [these words] to make myself understood.
> I will uphold my loveliness to live a life all my own,
> Hoping to deepen my thoughts and take myself far away.

> 檮木蘭以矯蕙兮，鑿申椒以為糧。播江離與滋菊兮，願春日以為糗芳。
>
> 恐情質之不信兮，故重著以自明。矯茲媚以私處兮，願曾思而遠身。(4.127)

The preparation, wearing, and consumption of aromatics is a key motif across the *Verses of Chu*. In "Parting's Sorrow," the protagonist adorns himself with aromatics, only to criticize them for their inconstancy later in the poem: "How have the fragrant botanicals of yesteryear / Now become this [toxic] mugwort? 何昔日之芳草兮，今直為此蕭艾也 (lines 309–310). But the hero of "Sorrowful Plaint" maintains his faith in aromatics and his own "loveliness," which ultimately justifies his decision to "live a life all his own" (*si chu* 私處). Here, we might also note the use of *si* 私 in reference to the domain of the personal or private. Many early sources (including the *Shijing*) define *si* in opposition to *gong* 公, which refers literally to a "lord" and by extension to the "impartial" concern for the common good of all within the lord's domain.[50] This dichotomy offers another way of framing the conundrum of "Parting's Sorrow": is the pull of the *gong* truly inescapable, or is it possible to carve out a life for the *si* beyond it? In "Sorrowful Plaint" at least, the answer is clear.

The conclusion to the "Nine Changes" (Jiu bian 九變) gives precisely the opposite answer. After saying that he will leave and fly off into the clouds, its protagonist declares his real intention:

> With plans **ton-ton* [fast and fixed], unchangeable—
> I wish to press forward and do good.
> Relying on august Heaven's great virtue,
> I will return to my lord in good health.
>
> 計專專之不可化兮，願遂推而為臧。賴皇天之厚德兮，還及君之無恙。(8.196)

From the perspective of these four lines at least, alienation turns out not to be so existential after all. The Qu Yuan conundrum is really just a test of his commitment to his lord. This is a hero that the architects of the *Shi* tradition would have approved of.

Qu Yuan the Stuck

Numerous other poems in the *Verses of Chu* anthology paint Qu Yuan as a much more pathetic figure who never succeeded in transcending his circumstances:

> For three years I have thought of him, amassing these thoughts,
> Wishing to see [my lord] just once more to state my case.
> If, not meeting him, I were to let my apology run loose,
> Who in this age would it enlighten?
> My emotions are sunken and checked, unexpressed.
> There is no one among the masses to be my interlocutor;
> I grieve that my spirit has no way out.

念三年之積思兮，願壹見而陳詞。不及君而騁說兮，世孰可為明之。情沈抑而不揚。眾人莫可與論道兮，悲精神之不通。("Seven Remonstrances" no. 7, "Foolish Remonstrance" [Miu jian" 謬諫], 13.256)

> With my hands on the railing, I gaze into the distance,
> I think of my lord—I will not forget him.
> Miserable, with nothing to say, / Endlessly longing and tormented within.

撫檻兮遠望，念君兮不忘，怫鬱兮莫陳，永懷兮內傷。("Nine Longings" no. 1, "Straightening the Doorstop" [Kuang ji 匡機],15.269)

> Melancholic and gloomy / I pine for my lord, listless.
> My body has departed but my thoughts remain, / Despairing I long for him.

荔蘊兮黴黧，思君兮無聊。身去兮意存，愴恨兮懷愁。("Nine Longings" no. 6, "Gathered Blossoms" [Xu ying" 蓄英],)15.276)

All are *hən-hən [glad and gleeful], drunk with joy,
I am *kons-kons [pining], grieving alone.
I look back at Zhanghua [Palace] and heave a great sigh,
My thoughts *rons-rons [filled with longing] and *ʔəi-ʔəi [woe].

咸欣欣兮酣樂，余眷眷兮獨悲。顧章華兮太息，志戀戀兮依依。("Nine Pinings" no. 7, "Pained by the Times" [Shang shi 傷時],17.325)

In this last excerpt from Wang Yi's "Nine Pinings," note the variation on the "the many are happy/I alone am not" pattern from the *Shi*. The allusion is fitting given that these pieces are essentially *Shi* in *Verses of Chu* clothing. All deny the persona the autonomy to reject his lord à la "Parting's Sorrow" and only reluctantly acknowledge the possibility of suicide, as the standard version of the Qu Yuan legend would have it. Elsewhere in the *Verses of Chu*, we find the Qu Yuan persona declaring that he will "drown [himself] and never turn back" 遂沒身而不反 (13.252).[51] In these passages, however, even a posthumous escape is impossible.

Qu Yuan the "Entangled One"

For other authors, the Qu Yuan legend wasn't a story of self-empowerment or powerlessness at all. The problem wasn't that Qu Yuan lacked autonomy but that he didn't exercise it correctly. One of Qu Yuan's greatest critics in the Han period was Yang Xiong 揚雄 (54 BCE–18 CE), the famed scholar-official and author whose career spanned the end of the Western Han dynasty and Wang Mang's 王莽 founding of the Xin 新 dynasty (r. 9–23 CE). As recounted in his *History of the Han* (*Hanshu* 漢書) (auto-)biography,[52] Yang Xiong criticized Qu Yuan's decision to drown himself because "he believed that if a princely man comes by the right time he proceeds grandly, but if he doesn't he [hides away like a] dragon or snake. Whether one meets with the right time is a matter of fate—why did [Qu Yuan] have to drown himself?!" 以為君子得時則大行，不得時則龍蛇，遇不遇 命也，何必湛身哉.[53] Yang Xiong's solution to the Qu Yuan conundrum introduces a new variable: timeliness" (*shi* 時). If a ruler cannot draw superior men to him with his virtue, then they simply withdraw from the world until a truly virtuous ruler arises. One can ignore the imperative to *gui* in the present as long as one promises to obey it in the future.

THE *SHI* AND THE *VERSES OF CHU* (*CHUCI* 楚辭)

To develop this argument, Yang Xiong composed a poem in the style of "Parting's Sorrow" called *Against "Parting's Sorrow"* (*Fan Lisao* 反離騷), in which he refers to Qu Yuan as "The Entangled" or "Bound One" (*lei* 纍).[54] A meaning attested in the *Shi* (e.g., 4/1.1–2), "entanglement" cuts to the heart of Yang Xiong's critique. The noble Qu Yuan allowed himself to become unnecessarily bound to an ignoble ruler:

> To dense thickets of thorny orange and prickly brambles
> Even the gibbon and monkey hesitate to descend.
> The Divine Beauty trusted the false flattery of Pepper and Thoroughwort,
> But our Entangled One was careless and took heed too late.
> He was garbed in a green coat of water chestnut and lotus leaves,
> Clothed in a vermeil skirt of lotus blossoms.
> His fragrance was pungent and strong, but no one smelled it;
> He should have folded his clothes and hidden them in a separate room . . .
> Best for a divine dragon to hide deep in a pool
> And await an auspicious cloud to take him up.

> 枳棘之榛榛兮，蝯狖擬而不敢下。靈修既信椒蘭之唼佞兮，吾纍忽焉而不蚤睹？衿芰茄之綠衣兮，被夫容之朱裳。芳酷烈而莫聞兮，（固）不如襞而幽之離房。. . . 懿神龍之淵潛，俟慶雲而將舉。(*Hanshu* 87a.3517–3518)

> The failure of the sage and wise / Certainly is bound up with time and destiny.
> Even though he repeatedly sighed in despair,
> I fear the Divine Beauty would not change for the Entangled.
> In the past, when Kongzi left the state of Lu,
> Lingering and loitering, taking his time, he journeyed far and wide.
> In the end he returned to his home city;
> Why should he have [thrown himself] in the pools and billowy rapids of the Xiang?

> 夫聖哲之（不）遭兮，固時命之所有；雖增欷以於邑兮，吾恐靈修之不纍改。昔仲尼之去魯兮，斐斐遲遲而周邁，終回復於舊都兮，何必湘淵與濤瀨？ (*Hanshu* 87a.3521)[55]

Kongzi's example shows that Qu Yuan might have traveled elsewhere instead of committing suicide. Instead, Qu Yuan thwarted his own movement and squandered his excellence.

A similar critique can be found in Jia Yi's 賈誼 (d. 169 CE) *Lament for Qu Yuan* (*Diao Qu Yuan* 弔屈原), which, like Yang Xiong's poem, criticizes Qu Yuan in the style of the Qu Yuan persona:

> You encountered these troubles, one after the other,
> And it was your fault!
> You could have looked through the Nine Regions for a lord to serve,
> So why pine for this your capital?
> The [auspicious] *feng-huang* birds soar a thousand meters up
> And look for virtue's gleam before alighting.
> If they see signs of meager virtue, / They flap their wings and fly away.
> How could a ditch just a few feet across / Hold a boat-gulping fish?
> Even a river- or lake-clogging leviathan
> Will bow to crickets and ants [on land].

> 般紛紛其離此尤兮，亦夫子之辜也！瞻九州而相君兮，何必懷此都也？鳳皇翔于千仞之上兮，覽德煇而下之；見細德之險（微）〔徵〕兮，搖增翮逝而去之。彼尋常之汙瀆兮，豈能容吞舟之魚！橫江湖之鱣鱏兮，固將制於蟻螻。(*Shiji* 84.2494–2495)[56]

The *feng-huang* 鳳凰 (often translated as "phoenix") here is an allusion to "Bend in the Hillside" (*Juan a* 卷阿, #252):

> The *feng-huang* is in flight, / *Hwâts-hwâts [flap, flap] its wings;
> Here it alights.
> *Ɂâts-Ɂâts [thickly thronging] the king's many good men;
> But it is our prince who is chosen to serve,
> For by the Son of Heaven he is loved.

> 鳳皇于飛，翽翽其羽。亦集爰止，藹藹王多吉士。維君子使，媚于天子。(252/7)

What seems to be a standard example of flying bird imagery in the *Shi* becomes a sign of virtue in Jia Yi's poem. Just as the *feng-huang* chooses to roost or not depending on the presence of virtue, Qu Yuan had a choice to stay or leave. Qu Yuan's decision not to look for another lord from across the Warring States seems to have been especially galling for Jia Yi as a subject of empire with its laws against "absconding" (*wang* 亡) from imperial authority.[57]

This chapter's analysis of *Shi–Verses of Chu* intertextuality suggests a new way of framing the latter's place in Chinese literary history—new from a modern but not an ancient perspective. For all its differences, "Parting's Sorrow" is a text steeped in the *Shi* tradition. From the opening quatrains to the failed ascent of the homesick driver at the very end, the poem unfolds as a series of confrontations with various *Shi* archetypes. Can a noble man alienated from his ruler and society find solace in the conventional roles of the *Shi*? Can he be a driver? A soldier? An abandoned wife? A suitor? A king? Again and again, the answer is no. Having exhausted the menu of *Shi*-based social options, the hero does in the end what no one in the *Shi* ever could: he says goodbye.

In short, the *Verses of Chu* are distinct from the *Shi* but not in the way most have imagined. On the literary map of early China, the *Shijing* and *Verses of Chu* aren't disconnected territories but contiguous domains whose boundaries are mutually constitutive—think Virginia and West Virginia more than New York and Alabama. Like Attic tragedy and comedy, they're two sides of the same cultural coin, not different currencies. By challenging the view of the *Verses of Chu* as an artifact of a distinctly southern culture, this chapter makes a literary contribution to debates among archaeologists and historians regarding Chu cultural identity.[58] In the realm of literature no less than in ritual or politics or material culture, the Zhou system was the framework within and against which Chu identity was articulated. As the literary linchpin of that system, the *Shi* made the *Verses of Chu* possible.

Chapter Five

COMPARING CANONS

The *Shi* Versus the Masters

Thus far I have argued that the thought of the *Shi* is accessible (chapter 1), interesting (chapter 2), and influential (chapters 3 and 4). In this chapter and the conclusion, I explore the implications of these conclusions for the study of early Chinese thought, the most obvious of which is that there is a very large *Shi*-sized hole in the modern study of the subject. To understand how ancient Chinese thinkers made sense of the world, we have to think about and through the *Shi* as much as they did. The minds behind the *Shi*—whoever they were, whenever they lived—deserve a seat at the table at least as much as Kongzi, Laozi, and other more famous figures.

But what if taking the *Shi* seriously isn't simply a matter of reading them alongside the Masters? What if it entails a different way of conceptualizing the subject? As I argued in the introduction, the biggest factor in the *Shi* tradition's marginalization as a source of early Chinese thought is the dominance of the Masters Narrative. Framed as a dialectical sequence of singular philosophers primarily within a Warring States context, the study of early Chinese thought leaves little room for the anonymous nonargumentative verse of the *Shi*. Every canon is a trade-off. Insofar as we have allowed the Masters to overshadow the *Shi*, we have to ask ourselves if this particular trade-off is worth it.

What should we want out of a basic model or canon of early Chinese thought? At a bare minimum, it should (1) be true to the historical milieu it purports to represent, (2) capture that milieu's most central dynamics, and (3) facilitate the kinds of connection and comparison making that are vital to its study. Just as crucially, the special claims made on behalf of the Masters, the *Shi*, or any other canon come with a special burden of proof. If we are going to define a subject according to a particular corpus then we should (4) have good evidence for doing so. On all four counts, a *Shi*-centric model succeeds where the Masters Narrative fails.

CHRONOLOGY

In light of its variability and that fact that its best and most comprehensive source is still the received anthology of the Han-era *Mao Shi*, determining the absolute chronology of the *Shi* with any degree of certainty or precision is impossible. Fortunately, the argument of this section doesn't depend on a stable, maximally elaborated timeline of *Shi* verse. For our purposes, it's enough that excavated and transmitted sources from the Warring States period through the early empire testify to the *Shi* tradition's existence and importance. In source after source, early authors quote, reference, and discuss a *Shi* tradition that more or less resembles the received *Shijing*.

How do we know that the Masters circulated in the Warring States context? Chronological arguments typically proceed in two steps: first, develop a dating criterion from a corpus of texts whose chronology is known; second, apply that criterion to a text of uncertain dating. Step one is the real hurdle in the early Chinese context. How does one build a sufficiently representative corpus of reliably dated texts from thousands of years ago? Throwing the Masters and other transmitted texts of uncertain provenance into the mix only begs the question. Dating a text requires a stable point of reference, somewhere to plant one's feet. But in the long history of "authentication studies" (*bianwei xue* 辨偽學) and the Masters, most efforts to date a particular text or section have assumed the overall legitimacy of the Masters Narrative framework.[1] A study might consider the dating of a chapter within a text but not the text as a whole, or it might date a text by comparing it to other Masters texts whose chronology is just as problematic.[2]

The single exception is the *Laozi* 老子 or *Classic of the Way and Virtue* (*Dao De jing* 道德經), the only text with a scientifically excavated (as opposed to looted) manuscript counterpart dated to the Warring States period. If any Masters text deserves its own chapter within a survey of

Warring States thought, it's the *Laozi*. For present purposes, the *Laozi* together with the *Shi* establish a baseline standard for assessing the chronology of other texts traditionally dated to the Warring States period. How many other Masters texts meet that standard? Restricting our focus to the most famous—the *Analects, Mozi, Mengzi, Xunzi, Zhuangzi,* and *Han Feizi,* which typify "Confucianism" (ru jia 儒家), "Mohism" (Mo jia 墨家), "Daoism" (dao jia 道家), and "Legalism" (fa jia 法家)—the answer is none.

After the Laozi, the Masters text with the most robust manuscript record is the *Analects,* partial versions of which were recovered from the tomb of Liu Xiu 劉脩, or King Huai of Zhongshan 中山懷王 (d. 55 BCE), in the village of Bajiaolang 八角廊 near Dingzhou 定州, Hebei province, and the tomb of a magistrate of Lelang commandery 樂浪郡 (d. 45 BCE) in the suburbs of P'yŏngyang, North Korea.[3] Note that both finds postdate the earliest references to an *Analects* text and the earliest evidence of its patronage by Han imperial elites during the reign of Emperor Wu 武帝 (r. 141–87 BCE). The sudden burst of interest in the *Analects* beginning in the mid-Western Han and the absence of *Analects* quotations prior to that moment have led me to argue elsewhere that the text is best read not as an authentic source of the historical Kongzi's teachings but as a Western Han selection, adaptation, and compilation of material from preexisting Kongzi traditions[4]

Elsewhere, there are few mentions of the Masters (Kongzi, Laozi, and Mozi, excepted) in received or excavated sources dated to the Warring States and Western Han, fewer quotations, and even fewer quotations that correspond with transmitted Masters texts.

Mozi. Although multiple early sources connect Mozi with mottos known from the received *Mozi,* including "indiscriminate care" (*jian ai* 兼愛), "against music" (*fei yue* 非樂), "frugality" (e.g., *jian* 儉), and "against offensive warfare" (*fei gong* 非攻), they generally don't associate these mottos with quotations that might be checked against the *Mozi* text.[5] The treatise "On Music" (Yue lun 樂論) from the *Xunzi* repeatedly attacks Mozi for his criticism of music but includes only a single Mozi quotation.[6] That saying is consistent with the ideas of *Mozi* chapter 32, "Against Music, part one" (Fei yue shang" 非樂上), but otherwise lacks any verbal parallel in the *Mozi.* The only stand-alone Mozi quotation in any pre-Han or Western Han source with a direct parallel in the *Mozi* appears in the *Annals of Lü Buwei* 2/4, "Appropriate Dyeing" (Dang ran" 當染), which also appears in

Mozi, chapter 3, "What Is Dyed" (Suo ran" 所染).⁷ The only quotation of Mozi in the whole of the *Zhuangzi* has no parallel in the *Mozi*, and the only direct quotation of Mozi or Mohists in Sima Qian's *Grand Scribe's Records* has a close parallel in the *Han Feizi* but not the *Mozi*.⁸

Mengzi. Aside from the two-character motto "human nature is good" (*xing shan* 性善), none of the *Xunzi*'s four quotations of Mengzi have direct verbal parallels in the *Mengzi*. (For the *Xunzi*'s famous "Human Nature Is Bad" [Xing e 性惡] polemic, see below.) The *Grand Scribe's Records* includes multiple versions of *Mengzi* 1A/1 but also includes Mengzi quotations without parallel in the *Mengzi*.⁹

A handful of verbal and thematic parallels between the received *Mengzi* and the *Five Kinds of Conduct* manuscript from Guodian and Mawangdui would seem to corroborate the *Xunzi*'s (polemical) association of Meng Ke 孟軻 with a "five kinds of conduct" (*wu xing* 五行) theory.¹⁰ However, Mark Csikszentmihalyi has rightly cautioned that "[t]he actual chronological relationship between [*Five Kinds of Conduct*] and the *Mengzi* may remain impossible to characterize."¹¹ At best, the manuscript confirms the Warring States origins of certain ideas and passages in the received *Mengzi* but without illuminating the chronology of the *Mengzi* compilation or even—absent confirmation of the *Xunzi*'s Warring States provenance—the association between Mengzi and a "five kinds of conduct" doctrine.

Xunzi. There's only a single stand-alone Xunzi quotation in any source prior to Liu Xiang's *Garden of Persuasions*, a four-character saying ("With material things one must prohibit excessive prosperity" 物禁大盛) in Sima Qian's biography of Li Si 李斯 that doesn't appear in the received *Xunzi*.¹²

Zhuangzi. The earliest source to quote Zhuangzi is the *Annals of Lü Buwei*, which includes an anecdote with a parallel at *Zhuangzi*, chapter 20, "Shan lin" 山林 (Mountains and Trees), and a "Zhuangzi says" (*Zhuangzi yue* 莊子曰) saying that *Zhuangzi*, chapter 19, "Da sheng" 達生 (Comprehending Life), attributes to Kongzi.¹³ Sima Qian's biography of Zhuang Zhou describes an oeuvre of "hundreds of thousands of words" (十餘萬言) but lists only a handful of titles—"The Fisherman" ("Yu fu" 漁父, chapter 31), "Robber Zhi" ("Dao Zhi" 盜跖, chapter 29), "Ransacking Luggage" ("Qu Qie" 胠篋, chapter 10)—with possible allusions to "Gengsang Chu" 庚桑楚 (chapter 23), and "Imputing Words" ("Yu yan" 寓言, chapter 27).¹⁴ There is little evidence for the circulation of the so-called Inner Chapters (*nei pian* 內篇) in the Warring States context, as Esther Klein has shown.¹⁵ Manuscript finds from the early Western Han have revealed several dozen fragmentary bamboo strips with parallels in the *Zhuangzi*.¹⁶

Han Feizi. The *Grand Scribe's Records* includes a complete version of "The Difficulties of Persuasion" (Shui nan 說難, chapter 12), references a number of other *Han Feizi* chapters, including "The Five Vermin" (Wu du 五蠹, chapter 49) and "Conspicuous in Learning" (Xian xue 顯學, chapter 50), and also quotes Han Feizi with sayings found in those two chapters.[17] Thus, evidence for the circulation of certain *Han Feizi* and *Zhuangzi* chapters in the early Western Han is significantly stronger than it is for the *Mengzi*, *Xunzi*, and *Mozi*.

Is it possible that the most famous Masters texts date to the Warring States period? Yes. Do we have solid corroborating evidence for that conclusion? And is that evidence anything like what we have for the *Shi* and the *Laozi*? No and no.

CENTRALITY

How do we know the *Shi* were important? Here, too, the answer is straightforward: in source after source, early Chinese authors tell us so. They discussed the *Shi*, extoled the virtues of the *Shi*, quoted the *Shi*, and organized entire texts around the *Shi*.

For proponents of the Masters Narrative, the importance of the Warring States Masters is similarly self-evident. We are told that the Masters were "philosophers"[18] (*zhexuejia* 哲學家) and "thinkers" (*sixiangjia* 思想家),[19] "scholars who responded to an apparent crisis of civilization."[20] They were the founders of "schools" and the teachers of "disciples."[21] Many have emphasized the Masters' independence from the state: they were "schoolmen" or "private individuals who often sought, but rarely achieved political influence."[22] The opening sentence of one recent monograph declares that " 'Masters' refers to the different academic schools, thinkers, social activists, educators, scholars, and their works during the Zhou, Qin, Han, and Wei periods of Chinese history, and the Zhou-Qin and Qin-Han periods in particular."[23] Even when disagreeing about the particulars, most scholars would seem to agree that " 'Master' was an important concept around which textual production was organized during the Warring States" and that "there can be little doubt that Masters literature was regarded in its day as constituting a coherent subject."[24]

My view is that the answers to the "Why were the Masters important?" question aren't at all straightforward, nor is the subject at all coherent. Were we to survey the meaning of, say, *philosopher* in the Greco-Roman context, we would have a wealth of sources to work with, beginning with the writings of Plato and Isocrates as the first self-identifying *philosophoi* in the fourth century BCE.²⁵ But that isn't true of *zhuzi* 諸子, the term conventionally translated as "Masters." Not until two centuries after the close of the Warring States period did anyone begin using the term in reference to wise figures or their texts, let alone discussing his own or anyone else's *zhuzi* membership.²⁶ For the Han bibliographers who gave us the term, *zhuzi* was an inherently miscellaneous, if not debased, category—which is why "Masters" is far too flattering a translation.

"The Misters" (*zhuzi* 諸子)

In 27 BCE, Liu Yu 劉宇, the vassal king of Dongping 東平 in modern-day Shandong province, was on a mandated visit to the imperial court in Chang'an 長安 when he submitted a request for "writings of the *zhuzi*" 諸子書 and a copy of Sima Qian's history.²⁷ Apparently this wasn't something that kings did because the request prompted Emperor Cheng 成帝 (r. 33–7 BCE) to seek the advice of General-in-Chief (*da jiangjun* 大將軍) Wang Feng 王鳳. Wang Feng responded by criticizing Liu Yu for a breach of protocol and for concerning himself more with texts than with his own moral education, at which point he turned his attention to "writings of the *zhuzi*":

> Some *zhuzi* writings go against the methods of the classics and [even] criticize the sages, while others take up ghosts and spirits and foster belief in oddities . . . None of this is fit for circulation among the vassal kings.
>
> 諸子書或反經術，非聖人，或明鬼神，信物怪 . . . 皆不宜在諸侯王。(*Hanshu* 80.3324–3325)

Wang Feng went on to recommend ordering Liu Yu to abandon the pursuit of "lesser Ways" (*xiao dao* 小道) and to rededicate himself to the study of the Five Classics. In the end, Liu Yu returned home empty-handed.

What texts did Liu Yu have in mind when he requested these "writings of the *zhuzi*" from the imperial archives? And who were these *zhuzi* whose ideas were too dangerous for impressionable imperial scions? It's hard to say because Liu Yu's request is the earliest documented use of "*zhuzi*" 諸子

in reference to texts or the people responsible for texts (as opposed to the term's literal meaning, "the many sons").[28]

Given that the *zhu* 諸 of *zhuzi* indicates a group or class of people, one obvious solution is to induce a definition from known -*zi* individuals. The problem is that the telltale "-*zi*" 子 of "Kongzi," "Laozi," "Mozi," and so on, was never used consistently or exclusively enough to serve as a badge of group membership.[29] According to several early commentators, including Zhao Qi 趙岐 (d. 201 CE) in a gloss on the name Mengzi, it was simply a "generic way of referring to a man" 丈夫之通稱.[30] In other words, So-and-So-*zi* was a mild honorific or courtesy not unlike Mister So-and-So in the contemporary American context. It was the sort of thing that might have been rude not to say in certain situations but that ultimately didn't signify much about the person it was applied to. Compiling a list of Masters in the early context is about as useful as a list of Misters would be for us.

With a core meaning of "son" or "child," -*zi* also referred to the political rank of prince.[31] The logic of the association between childhood and political authority is connected to the ancestral cult and the practice of calling a clan's oldest living male the "little child" (*xiaozi* 小子) to indicate his relationship to the dead and thus his authority over the living. Just like the English Master and its derivative Mister, this usage seems to have fed the use of -*zi* as a more generic honorific.

The cavalier way in which early authors used -*zi* is telling. Consider the teacher-student lineages sketched in the *Annals of Lü Buwei*:

> Kongzi learned from Lao Dan [Laozi], Meng Sukui, and Jing Shu. Lord Hui of Lu sent Steward Rang to request instruction from the Son of Heaven [in Zhou 周] concerning the rituals of the suburban altar and ancestral temple. King Huan [of Zhou] sent Shi Que, and Lord Hui kept him so that his descendants lived in Lu. Mozi learned from them . . . Zigong, Zixia, and Zengzi learned from Kongzi; Tian Zifang learned from Zigong, Duangan Mu learned from Zixia, and Wu Qi learned from Zengzi. Qin Guli learned from Mozi, Xu Fan learned from Qin Guli, and Tian Xi learned from Xu Fan.
>
> 孔子學於老聃、孟蘇夔、靖叔。魯惠公使宰讓請郊廟之禮於天子，桓王使史角往，惠公止之，其後在於魯，墨子學焉。. . . 子貢、子夏、曾子學於孔子，田子方學於子貢，段干木學於子夏，吳起學於曾子。禽滑釐學於墨子，許犯學於禽滑釐，田繫學於許犯。(2.4/98)

Of the fifteen figures listed here, only three are identified as *-zi*. Not even Kongzi's teachers make the cut. Another example is the list of wise figures in the final section of Mei Cheng's *Seven Stimuli*. Why is Mengzi the only figure graced with a *-zi*? And why would Mei Cheng so disrespect Kongzi and Laozi, who were far more famous than Mengzi, by removing the *-zi* from their names and mashing them together ("KongLao")? I have no idea. The *Seven Stimuli* doesn't advance an obviously Mengzian program nor does it show any hostility toward Kongzi or Laozi. But such questions become much less interesting when "Mengzi" is read as "Mister Meng" as opposed to "Master Meng."

"The Contenders" (*zhuzi* 諸子)

Returning to the Liu Yu affair of 27 BCE, the decision to deny the king his books probably had as much to do with the requester as with the request. This was someone who nearly lost his kingship after strangling a consort.[32] But in light of Wang Feng's concerns about what was fit for circulation among the vassal kings, and given the policy initiative announced the very next year, Liu Yu's request might have alerted the imperial court to a real problem: there was a body of heterodox writings in high demand by the very people who couldn't be trusted with heterodox writings—imperial princes and kings like Liu Yu with the status and bloodline to make their own claims on the throne.

Perhaps that is why Emperor Cheng in 26 BCE ordered imperial cousin and noted scholar-official Liu Xiang to oversee the cataloguing of the imperial archives and the collation of texts therein.[33] Within that larger remit, Liu Xiang was instructed to "collate classics and commentaries, *zhuzi*, and poems and rhapsodies" 校經傳諸子詩賦, with other officials overseeing more technical genres. Unfortunately, only fragments remain of Liu Xiang's *Separate Listings* (*Bielu* 別錄), the piecemeal bibliographic summaries produced in the course of his project. The *Seven Surveys* (*Qilüe* 七略), the synoptic overview prepared by his son and collaborator, Liu Xin 劉歆 (50 BCE–23 CE), survives in redacted form as the "Record of Arts and Letters" (*Yiwen zhi* 藝文志) bibliographic treatise, the thirtieth chapter of Ban Gu's 班固 (32–92 CE) *History of the Han* (*Hanshu* 漢書). That text is our earliest *zhuzi* inventory and the earliest extant bibliography in the Chinese tradition.[34]

What do the 185 titles and more than 160 named individuals of the *zhuzi* division have in common? Not much. For starters, the Han bibliographers clearly didn't conceive of *zhuzi* as a particular social group or role. There are "teachers" (*shi* 師, five times), "students" (*dizi* 弟子, twelve times), "ministers" (*xiang* 相, ten times), "scribes" (*shi* 史, five times), "princes" (*gongzi* 公子, three times), "marquises" (*hou* 侯, twice), "generals (*jiang* 將, twice), "kings" (*wang* 王, twice), and even "emperors" (*di* 帝), with one petty "officer" (*li* 吏) and another "hidden man" or "hermit" (*yinshi* 隱士). Fewer than half of these figures are identified as -*zi*.

The chronology of *zhuzi* is much more complex than the notion of "the Warring States Masters" would suggest. Roughly half of the texts are associated with figures who lived from the time of Kongzi through the end of the Warring States period.[35] But there are also more than fifty entries pegged to the Qin and Han empires, with another dozen or so dated to the time of the Yellow Emperor 黃帝, the Xia 夏, Shang 商, or Western Zhou 西周 dynasties, or the Spring and Autumn 春秋 period.

Based on their titles alone, *zhuzi* texts comprise an impressive array of genres. There are "persuasions" (*shui* 說), "remonstrations" (*jian* 諫), "discussions" (*lun* 論), "annals" (*chunqiu* 春秋), collections of "sayings" (*yan* 言) and "dialogues" (*yu* 語), transcripts of "conferences" (*yi* 議), "responses" (*dui* 對) to emperors' questions, one "rhapsody" (*fu* 賦), constitutional texts like the "Laws of Zhou" (Zhou fa" 周法), and emperors' "edicts" (*zhao* 詔). The bibliographers' notations describe texts that "criticize" (*nan* 難), texts that "explain" (*shuo* 說), and texts that "expound" (*chen* 陳). Modes of textual composition are similarly varied: there are texts described as acts of "arrangement" (*xu* 序), "transmission" (*shu* 述), and "collection" (*ji* 輯).

Descriptions of *zhuzi* in the "Record of Arts and Letters" only deepen the confusion. Both in the preface and in a prose summary appended to the *zhuzi* division, *zhuzi* are defined more by division and discord than by any shared identity:

> Formerly when Zhongni [Kongzi] passed away his subtle words were cut off, and when the seventy students died his great principles were split. Thus, the *Annals* was divided into five traditions, the *Shi* into four, and the *Changes* into several textual lineages. Amid the strategic scheming of the Warring States and the struggle between the true and the false, the words of the *zhuzi* were chaotic and confused.

COMPARING CANONS

昔仲尼沒而微言絕，七十子喪而大義乖。故春秋分為五，詩分為四，易有數家之傳。戰國從衡，真偽分爭，諸子之言紛然殽亂。(30.1701)

[The *zhuzi*] all arose after the Kingly Way had declined, when the vassal lords governed through force and the rulers of the day pursued their own likes and dislikes. It was at this point that the techniques of the nine streams emerged, each drawing from a single aspect [of the Way] and honoring [only] that which it excelled at. And so [the *zhuzi*] spread their doctrines and ingratiated themselves with the vassal lords. Although their words are distinctive, [ultimately] they are like fire and water—mutually negating and mutually generating.

皆起於王道既微，諸侯力政，時君世主，好惡殊方，是以九家之（說）〔術〕蠭出並作，各引一端，崇其所善，以此馳說，取合諸侯。其言雖殊，辟猶水火，相滅亦相生也。(30.1746)

Clearly, Wang Feng wasn't the only one with a low opinion of *zhuzi*. Other Han sources offer similarly bleak assessments. Yang Xiong implies in the *Model Sayings* (*Fayan* 法言) that the *zhuzi* are unworthy of study when he defines them in opposition to sages like Kongzi: "*zhuzi* are those whose knowledge differs from Kongzi's" 諸子者，以其知異於孔子者也.[36] Ying Shao 應劭 (140–206) paraphrases the "Record of Arts and Letters" when he describes the *zhuzi* as "chaotic, confused, and all ignorant of what to follow" 紛然殽亂，莫知所從.[37] A rare pro-*zhuzi* voice was Wang Chong 王充 (27–100 CE), who in the *Balanced Discourses* (*Lunheng* 論衡) describes Kongzi as "pre-eminent among the *zhuzi*" 諸子之中最卓者 (13.137) and advocates reading *zhuzi* alongside the classics.[38]

The relationship between Kongzi and *zhuzi* suggests another way of understanding the term's use in the "Record of Arts and Letters" preface. In accounts of royal succession across the early literature, *zhuzi* are also candidates for the position of crown prince or king. The *Zuo Tradition* and *Grand Scribe's Records* tell the story of Lord Jing of Qi 齊景公 (r. 547–490 BCE), who ignored his officials' advice "to select an older man of excellence from among the *zhuzi* to be crown prince" 擇諸子長賢者為太子 and instead elevated the underage son of a favored concubine. Within a year of Lord Jing's death, his successor was deposed and killed.[39] The biography of the Lord of Mengchang 孟嘗君 (d. 279 BCE) in the *Grand Scribe's Records* relates that his "*zhuzi* vied for the throne" 諸子爭立 (75.2358) after their father's death and ended up losing their lands to neighboring powers. In his advice to the future King Zhuangxiang 莊襄 (r. 250–247 BCE) and father to the First Emperor, Lü Buwei warned that he "had no hope of vying for [the position of] Crown Prince with the oldest son or the *zhuzi* who spend their days and nights before [the king]" 毋幾得與長子及諸子旦暮在前者爭為太子矣.⁴⁰

The "Record of Arts and Letters" also associates *zhuzi* with succession, albeit a nonpolitical version of it. A true sage, Kongzi expounded upon the "Kingly Way" (*wang dao* 王道) and the "great principles" (*dayi* 大義) of the classics. But after his death and the deaths of his closest followers, his sapiential inheritance was "split" (*guai* 乖) and diluted, eventually resulting in the "chaos" (*luan* 亂) of the Warring States. In that brief intellectual history, the *zhuzi* aren't just assorted "misters." They are "contenders" or "candidates" for sagehood in a post-Kongzi world. And like the Lord of Mengchang's sons, they succeeded only in fracturing Kongzi's great estate into smaller and smaller holdings.

If *zhuzi* were such a motley crew, then why bother listing them in the first place? Rhetorically, there is a clear payoff to *zhuzi*-bashing: the greater their unruliness, the greater the glory of the Han imperium in putting Humpty Dumpty back together again. The bibliography divides *zhuzi* into the "ten streams" (*shi liu* 十流) of the Ru 儒, *dao*-ists 道, *yin-yang* 陰陽 cosmologists, legalists (*fa* 法), terminologists (*ming* 名), Mohists (*Mo* 墨), political strategists or "vertical and horizontal [alliance makers]" (*zongheng* 從橫), "syncretists" (*za* 雜), "agriculturalists" (*nong* 農), and "storytellers" (*xiaoshuo* 小說). In a series of prose summaries appended to these subdivisions, it also traces the origin of each stream to a particular "office" (*guan* 官) within the bureaucracy of the Zhou 周 dynasty. Ruist texts are said to have arisen from the office of the Overseer of the Masses (*situ* 司徒), daoist texts from "scribal offices" (*shi guan* 史官), and so on. The "Record of Arts and Letters" thus "surveys" (*lüe* 略, in the sense of demarcating territory) and domesticates the *zhuzi* as a manageable domain within the Han imperium's panoptic purview.

The *zhuzi* category had a practical utility, too. At minimum, it seems that each *zhuzi* text in the bibliography was deemed worthy of inclusion because (1) it was associated with a famous individual and/or spoke to fundamental matters of governance;⁴¹ (2) it was distinct enough to deserve its own entry as opposed to being absorbed within another collection; and (3) it was unsuited for inclusion within the other, more clearly defined divisions of the "Record of Arts and Letters."[42] The *zhuzi* were less authoritative than the texts of the "Six Classics" (*liu yi* 六藝); less obviously poetic or performative than "songs and performance texts" (*shi fu* 詩賦); and less obviously technical than writings on military strategy, numerology, divination, materia medica, and so on. The category primarily served as a convenient catch-all for all sorts of texts and individuals with a reputation for wisdom—from a Han perspective. (Prior to the late Western Han, the preferred term for these people was *baijia*, the "hundred personages" or "figures."[43]) Insofar as figures like Kongzi and Laozi were important in the Warring States context, their status had nothing to do with their *zhuzi* membership.

CONNECTIVITY

How do we know that the *Shi* were integral to the Warring States intellectual milieu? Not only are extant sources lousy with *Shi* quotations, most of which have parallels in the *Shijing*, the lesson of chapter 3 is that early thinkers did a lot of thinking about and through the *Shi*. Knowledge of the *Shi* and of *Shi* poetics established a terrifically productive framework for the development of the early intellectual tradition.

Can we say the same about the Masters? According to many scholars, the answer is an unequivocal yes. To take one spectacular example (see figure 5.1), sociologist Randall Collins, in his book *The Sociology of Philosophies: A Global Theory of Intellectual Change* (1998), diagrams the network of Warring States thinkers from Kongzi (upper left) down to Li Si 李斯 (bottom right; d. 208 BCE), the prime minister to the Qin First Emperor 秦始皇 (259–210 BCE). Showing roughly a hundred figures (from "major philosophers" to "minor philosophers" to "incidental persons") and twice as many connections, Collins offers these diagrams as evidence that "[i]ntellectual creativity is driven by opposition," which he calls "a principle of worldwide application."[44]

Collins paints an appealing picture of a diverse yet interconnected intellectual milieu. But look more closely and one finds more than a little bubblegum and duct tape holding it all together.[45] To take just a few examples: he draws a "probable tie" between Mengzi and Hui Shi 惠施, even though no early source (including the *Mengzi*) places the two together or has the

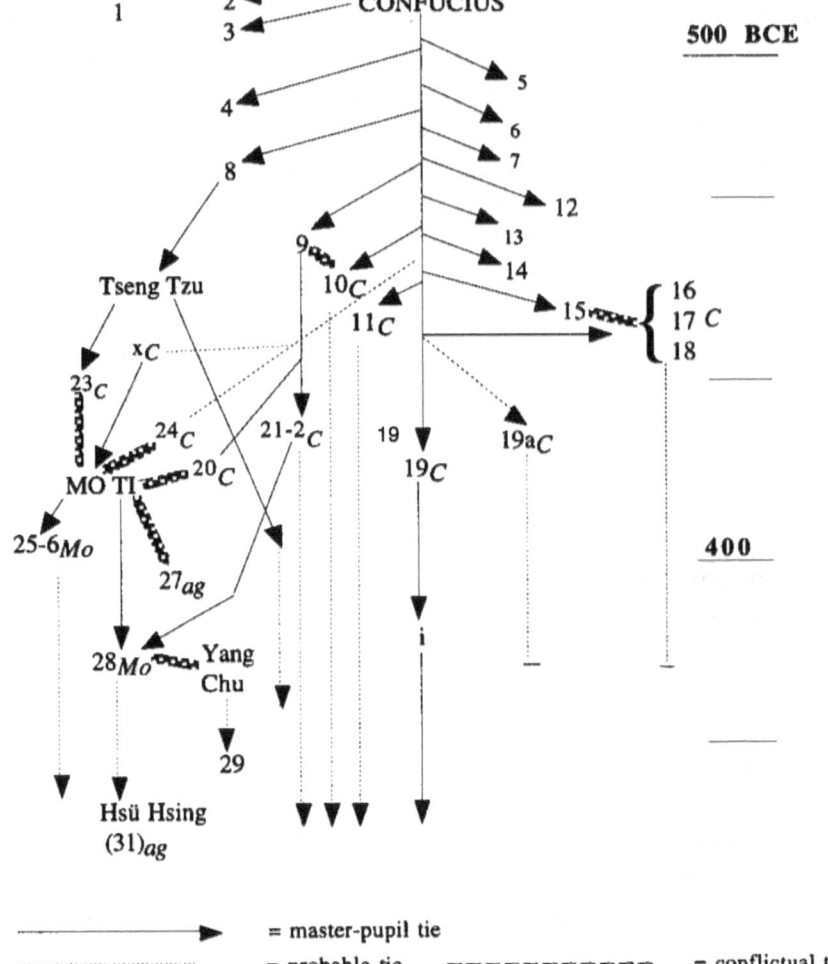

FIGURE 5.1 The Warring States intellectual network according to Randall Collins
Source: Collins 1998, 139, 144 (with his diagram keys on 893–894).

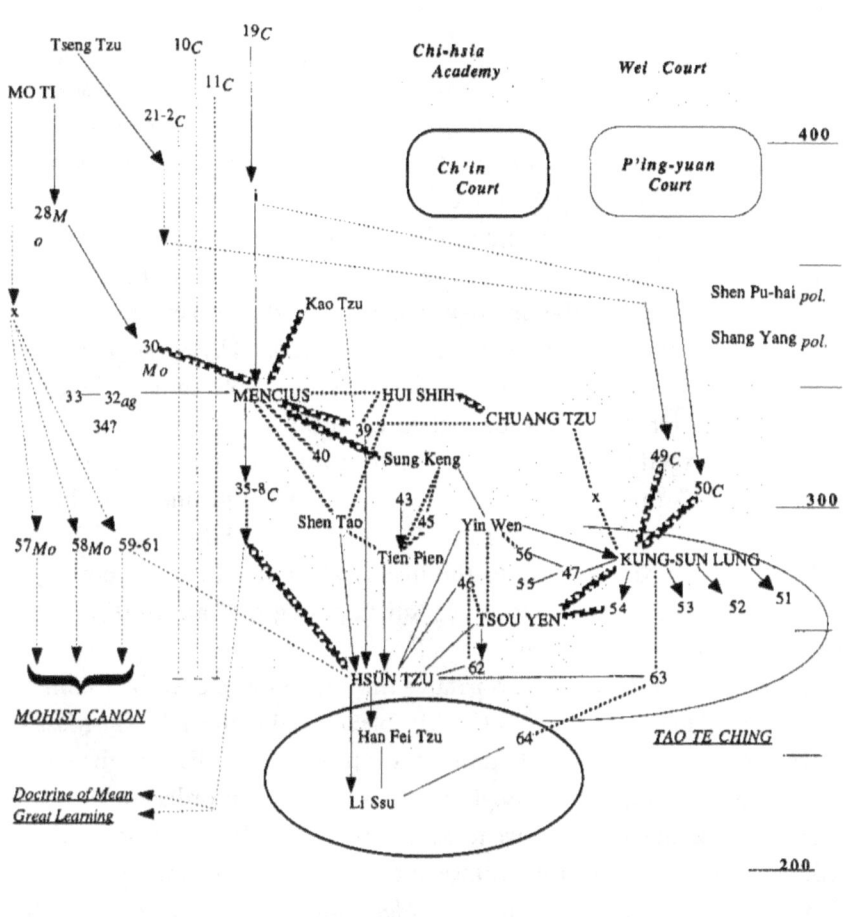

FIGURE 5.1 (continued)

one comment on the other. Likewise, his squiggly "conflictual ties" connect thinkers like Zengzi and Mozi, who are never represented in direct opposition. Collins also assumes the historical reality of a Jixia 稷下 "academy," where the Qi 齊 court supposedly gathered the best minds of the mid– to late Warring States period, despite Nathan Sivin's persuasive debunking of that notion as a "myth" perpetuated by those who "wishfully imposed [a] medley of Chinese imperial and modern Western institutions on a chaotic, creative set of circumstances."[46] Never mind the fact that so many of Collins's connections, like the one between Xunzi and Han Fei, are based on the testimony of post–Warring States informants, usually Sima Qian.

Of course, it isn't just the connections that are problematic. If the chronology of Masters texts is suspect, then we also have to wonder about the dots. What exactly does "Confucius" refer to in the graph on the left in figure 5.1? If it's the Kongzi of the *Analects*, then what justifies that choice? What about other famous Masters (Collins's "major philosophers")? Does "HSUN TZU" [Xunzi] refer to the historical Xunzi, Xunzi as portrayed in the *Xunzi*, Sima Qian's version of Xunzi, passages about Xunzi in other sources, or some combination thereof?

Proponents of the Masters Narrative (including those cited by Collins)[47] likewise tend to downplay the difficulties of connecting the dots. The Masters Narrative is a timeline, but it's ultimately a program for charting the development of Warring States thought via Masters texts. In order for that program to work, the Masters have to be meaningfully relatable to one another. We read the *Mozi* against the *Analects*; the *Mengzi* against the *Analects* and *Mozi*; the *Xunzi* against the *Analects*, *Mozi*, and *Mengzi*; and so on, on the assumption that successive authors (1) knew and (2) cared about the content of those earlier works as much as we do. In the process, Warring States thought emerges as a single continuous conversation to which Masters texts provide direct access. To quote Philip J. Ivanhoe and Bryan W. Van Norden,

> The thinkers of the hundred schools period not only disagreed in theory, they disagreed with each other. That is to say, their views were not only in conflict but they themselves often argued with one another. Such exchanges led to greater philosophical sophistication, with thinkers responding to and often adapting each other's views in order to enhance their own positions. The careful reader [of *Readings in Classical Chinese Philosophy*, which consists of selections from the *Analects*, *Mozi*, *Mengzi*, *Laozi*, *Zhuangzi*, *Xunzi*, and *Han Feizi*] will be able to see numerous examples of such disagreement

and mutual borrowing in the selections presented here, and understanding this aspect of philosophical life during this period is important for a full appreciation of the lively and creative spirit of the time.[48]

A common refrain is that classical Chinese philosophy is essentially dialectical. As they declare in the opening sentence of their introduction, "[p]hilosophy—in the sense of self-conscious reflection upon, modification, and defense of one's views—begins with the debate between Kongzi and Mozi."[49]

For the reasons outlined above, I am less sanguine about connecting the dots of Warring States thought via the Masters. If the chronologies of Masters texts are doubtful and if the very concept of "The Masters" dates to the Han period, then using Masters texts to reconstruct the intellectual exchanges of the Warring States period is bound to be problematic.

But let us set those problems aside for the moment. Do Masters texts give different answers to the fundamental questions confronting early Chinese thinkers? Of course. Were the authors of the Masters texts aware of that fact? Absolutely. Masters texts reveal a fiercely competitive milieu in which thinkers vigorously defended themselves from critics and criticized others in turn. But do they also reveal an awareness of other Masters texts? In other words, did the texts of the Masters as we know them drive the debates of the period? As a rule, no. Extant Masters texts (minus the *Laozi*) didn't control talk about the Masters until the late Western Han at the earliest. Our Masters texts were peripheral to the conversation, if they were involved at all.

Critiquing Mengzi Versus Critiquing the *Mengzi*

Consider *Xunzi* chapter 23, "Human Nature Is Bad" ("Xing e" 性惡), that classic example of early Chinese debate. One of the most unapologetically polemical sections of any Masters text, the text argues for the inherent badness of human nature against the view that human nature is good, which it thrice ascribes to Mengzi:

Mengzi said, "That people learn is due to their nature being good."

孟子曰：人之學者，其性善。(23.435)

Mengzi said, "Now, since people's nature is good, being bad is in all cases a result of losing one's nature."

孟子曰：今人之性善，將皆失喪其性故〔惡〕也。(23.436)⁵⁰

Mengzi said, "People's nature is good."

孟子曰：人之性善。(23.439,441)

"Human Nature Is Bad" has prompted a lively debate in the secondary literature over the difference (if any) between Mengzi and Xunzi on human nature and the place of this chapter within the *Xunzi* anthology, questions complicated by doubts about its integrity.⁵¹

The curious thing about these quotations is that they don't appear in the received *Mengzi*. Even more strangely, the *Mengzi* generally seems reluctant to ascribe the "human nature is good" (*xing shan* 性善) idea to Mengzi, instead having others say it for him:

> When Lord Wen of Teng went to Chu as crown prince, he passed through Song and met with Mengzi. Mengzi discoursed on the goodness of human nature and praised Yao and Shun whenever he spoke.
>
> 滕文公為世子，將之楚，過宋而見孟子。孟子道性善，言必稱堯舜。(3A/1)

> Gongduzi said, "... Now you say that human nature is good, so are all those others [with different views of human nature] wrong?"
>
> 公都子曰：...今曰性善，然則彼皆非歟？(6A/6)

Only in the third person does the Mengzi of the *Mengzi* "discourse on the goodness of human nature"—which is to say, introduce his teachings to an uninitiated audience. In all other passages, as in 6A/6, he responds to interlocutors who are already familiar with the theory. The closest Mengzi himself comes to saying "human nature is good" is the water-talking contest with Gaozi from *Mengzi* 6A/2. There we find the lines, "The goodness of human nature is like the downward flow of water. All people are good; all water flows downward" 人性之善也，猶水之就下也。人無有不善，水無有不下.

There are other, more direct formulations of the "human nature is good" idea elsewhere in the *Mengzi*. One such passage is *Mengzi* 2A/6, which opens with the idea that all people have "a heart that can't endure [the suffering of] others" 不忍人之心; illustrates it with the thought experiment of seeing a child about to fall down a well; and amplifies it with a discussion of the "four sprouts" (*si duan* 四端), the innate moral sentiments undergirding humaneness, propriety, ritual, and wisdom. However, no other extant source from the early period associates these ideas with Mengzi.

For A. C. Graham, who also notes the disconnect between "Human Nature Is Bad" and the *Mengzi*, the latter's reluctance to place the "human nature is good" slogan in Mengzi's mouth is evidence of the *Mengzi* authors' discomfort with sloganeering: "[S]ince they use their respective slogans only as convenient labels and pivots of debate, one may suspect that they had some inkling that the formulae unduly simplify what they have to say."[52] A very different possibility is revealed by Zhao Qi's 趙岐 (d. 201 CE) preface to his *Mengzi* commentary, the basis of the received version, in which he describes excising four sections of "outer writings" (*wai shu* 外書) that "seemed to be the wrongly attributed imitations of later generations, not the true and original [teachings of] Mengzi 似非孟子本眞，後世依放而托之者也. According to Zhao Qi, one of these sections was entitled "Human Nature is Good" (Xing shan 性善).[53] Without that text, however, we have no way of determining whether it is the missing link between the received *Mengzi* and *Xunzi*.

Contrast the *Xunzi*'s critique of Mengzi with chapter 30 of Wang Chong's *Balanced Discussions* (*Lunheng* 論衡), entitled "Needling Mengzi" (*Ci Meng* 刺孟). What follows is a quotation of *Mengzi* 7A/2, followed by Wang Chong's rejoinder:

> Mengzi said, "There's nothing that isn't mandated [by Heaven]; those who comply receive their proper due. Thus, one who understands his mandate doesn't stand under a teetering wall. Dying after following the Way to the

very end is adhering to one's mandate; dying shackled isn't adhering to one's mandate."

孟子曰：莫非命也，順受其正；是故知命者不立乎巖墙之下。盡其道而死者，正命也；桎梏死者，非正命也。

Ⓐ Mengzi said, "There's nothing that isn't mandated by Heaven; those who comply receive their proper due. Thus, one who understands his mandate doesn't stand under a teetering wall. Dying after following the Way to the very end is adhering to one's mandate; dying shackled isn't adhering to one's mandate."
Ⓑ According to Mengzi's saying, a person shouldn't go against his mandate. One who conducts himself compliantly adheres to his mandate; one who acts rashly and negligently doesn't adhere to his mandate. This is because [according to Mengzi] Heaven's mandate depends on one's conduct.
Ⓒ [However,] Kongzi didn't become king, Yan Yuan died young, Zixia lost his eyesight, and Boniu had leprosy—did these four men not comply [with their mandate]? How could they not have received their proper due? Bigan was eviscerated, Zixu was boiled, Zilu was pickled. These men suffered the most extreme tortures in the world; they weren't merely "shackled." But if we must take "shackles" as proof of "not adhering to one's mandate," then [we are forced to conclude that] the conduct of Bigan and Zixu wasn't compliant.
Ⓓ A person is endowed with a nature and a mandate but he could be crushed to death, drowned, killed in battle, or incinerated. Even if he is careful in his dealings and refined in his conduct, what good does it do him?

孟子曰：莫非天命也，順受其正。是故知命者，不立乎巖牆之下。盡其道而死者，為正命也；桎梏而死者，非正命也。
夫孟子之言，是謂人無觸值之命也。順操行者得正命，妄行苟為得非正〔命〕，是天命於操行也。
夫子不王，顏淵早夭，子夏失明，伯牛為癘，四者行不順與？何以不受正命？比干剖，子胥烹，子路葅，天下極戮，非徒桎梏也。必以桎梏效非正命，則比干、子胥行不順也。
人稟性命，或當壓溺兵燒，雖或慎操脩行，其何益哉？(*Lunheng* 30.467–468)

This is a direct rebuttal of a text closely resembling the received *Mengzi*. Not only does "Needling Mengzi" quote Mengzi 7A/2 in its entirety Ⓐ, it offers a summary Ⓑ, an extension of its logic in the form of a *reductio ad absurdum* Ⓒ, and a counterstatement Ⓓ. Each section reinforces the connection to a written *Mengzi* text by lifting vocabulary and concepts from the original passage.

"Human Nature Is Bad" and Wang Chong's essay thus present two very different Mengzis. The first is shallower and more nebulous, a figure remembered primarily for the two-character "human nature is good" (*xing shan* 性善) slogan; the second inspired a written text closely resembling the received *Mengzi*. If Wang Chong's *Balanced Discussions* dated to the Warring States period as opposed to the first century CE, we would have much better evidence for reading the received *Mengzi* (or at least 7A/2) as a vector of intellectual exchange in a Warring States context.

Of course, this discussion of "Human Nature Is Bad" and "Needling Mengzi" is but one (oft-discussed) demonstration of the problem of connecting received Masters texts. We might just as easily have examined the *Xunzi*'s quotation of Mozi in its "On Music" (Yue lun 樂論) treatise, the *Mengzi*'s treatment of Mozi, or the absence of *Analects* quotations amid the wealth of pre-Han Kongzi material. The conclusion in all of these cases is the same: our Masters texts (again, minus the *Laozi*) left few marks on the intellectual exchanges of the period.

To sum up, the argument of this chapter isn't that the Masters are unimportant, uninteresting, or otherwise unworthy of study. If we were to choose a canon based on philosophical merit or perennial relevance, we could do far worse than Masters. The question is whether the Masters Narrative should continue to dominate the modern imagination of early Chinese thought given (1) its tendency to minimize the *Shi* (and all sorts of other sources) and (2) the lack of evidence for the Masters' canonicity in the Warring States context.

This chapter focuses on the "Masters" half of the Masters Narrative. But this critique has implications for the "Narrative" bit as well. Masters-centrism aside, is a narrative model really the best way of organizing our thinking about the subject? Should telling the *story* of Warring States thought be our overarching goal?[54]

Consider the basic elements of a narrative, beginning with plot. How do we sequence ("and then . . . and then . . ."), let alone narrate ("and so . . . and so . . ."), Warring States thought given the quagmire that is textual chronology? Excavated (as opposed to looted) manuscripts offer one path forward—or they would if we had a larger sample of excavated manuscripts to go by. And who are the main characters, the most interesting or influential "thinkers" of our story? The tradition casts various figures in starring roles, from wise men like Kongzi to ministers like Guanzi, to rulers like the First Emperor. However, extant accounts of such figures are as didactic and literary as they are historiographical, and the dogged anonymity of preimperial sources makes connecting extant texts with known thinkers exceedingly difficult. The same problems apply to setting because preimperial texts preserve almost as little information about the circumstances of their creation as they do about their authors. There's even a sense that this occasion- or placelessness was baked into Warring States textual culture.[55]

The greatest failing of the Masters Narrative isn't that it gets Warring States thought wrong but that it misrepresents the challenges of telling its story. The historian who sets out to tell the story of Warring States thought, or the student tasked with tracing the historical development of a particular concept from the *Analects* through the *Mozi*, *Mengzi*, and so on, risks asking more of our sources than they can reasonably provide.

Is it possible to weave our sources into a grand narrative of Warring States thought? I'm not sure. In the meantime, narrative isn't our only option. In the conclusion, I propose reconceptualizing early Chinese thought as a network anchored to the *Shi*.

CONCLUSION
A Classic of N/Odes

This book has two goals, the first of which is rediscovering the thought of the *Shi*. I have argued that the *Shi* worldview is obsessed with movement and flow, and the movement of homecoming (*gui* 歸) in particular. I have suggested that the purpose of *Shi* poetics is to naturalize the flow of people to the Zhou kings as a manifestation of the universal impulse to *gui*. I have traced the influence of that worldview on subsequent texts from the Warring States and early empire, including the *Laozi* and the *Verses of Chu*. The takeaway, to poach a line from Alfred North Whitehead, is that the classical philosophical tradition in China is best characterized as a series of footnotes to the *Shi*.[1]

The second goal is exploring how the study of early Chinese thought or philosophy might change to accommodate these conclusions. I have proposed making space for the *Shi* by demoting the Masters as the protagonists of Warring States thought. To that end, I have argued that the evidentiary basis for the Masters Narrative is much flimsier than for a *Shi*-centric approach. And in the remaining pages, I offer a few tentative suggestions for what that approach might look like, beginning with my proposal to reconceptualize early Chinese thought as a network anchored to the *Shi*.

A few words of caution are in order. Network theory emerged in the twentieth century (out of earlier antecedents) as a way of analyzing complex technological, biological, social, and semantic systems. A network model is a tool for parsing systemic complexity. By reducing a system to a bundle of connections or edges among discrete nodes or vertices, a network model filters out less essential information to reveal the underlying structure. Network theory then offers various tools for analyzing that structure and even predicting the behavior of a system, be it a North Atlantic fishery, a school for girls in New York, or the internet.[2]

In theory, the intellectual scene in early China is also amenable to network analysis. Even if the details are murky, early sources describe a milieu in which ideas, their purveyors, their textual carriers, and their consumers mixed, clashed, and flowed. In practice, however, mapping a network of ancient thinkers is very different from collecting data about cod or teenagers or internet traffic. (This is what Randall Collins failed to appreciate with his byzantine diagrams of Warring States philosophers; see figure 5.1). We have the scattered written remnants of a system but precious little information about the people who produced those remnants, let alone those who participated in the system but left no written traces. And even if we set the people aside to focus on textual and material remains, devising a workable network ontology is a major challenge. Do we treat the *Shijing* as a single node, a subnetwork of 305 nodes for each piece in the collection, or 305 different subnetworks?[3] And what counts as an edge? An explicit citation of one text by another is a relatively clear-cut case, but what about allusions, thematic parallels, and other more nebulous connections?

The singular advantage of a network model is that it allows us to draw and analyze connections without prejudging a system's structure.[4] We can grow our model organically, node-by-node and edge-by-edge, without worrying about beginnings, middles, or endings—be it the birth of Kongzi or the Qin unification or the canonization of the Five Classics. Even if the contemporary researcher resorts to a network model because of a surfeit of data, the student of ancient thought because of its dearth, the methodological rationale is the same: we venture a peek at the macro only after grappling with a multiplicity of micros.

So how do we build a network of early Chinese thought? The question has no one answer because there are as many ways of wiring a network model as there are paths through it. But one way to summarize the conclusions of this study is that one very good, if not the very best, starting point is the *Shi* tradition. More than other corpora, the *Shi* set the terms of early thinkers' engagement with the intellectual tradition and with one another.

CONCLUSION

To restate the argument in network theoretical terms: the *Shi* tradition is the most central node (or bundle of nodes) in the network of early Chinese thought from the Warring States through the early empire. A key concept within graph theory and network analysis, centrality is the measure of a node's importance within a network, with the definition of *importance* hinging on the type of network and the questions put to it.[5] For our purposes, I define *centrality* in structural terms as the measure of "a node's involvement in or contribution to the cohesiveness of the network."[6] Thus, to call the *Shi* tradition the most central node is to argue that it, more than other corpora, bound early thinkers together to create the possibility of a shared intellectual tradition.

One consequence of the focus on connectivity is a corresponding deemphasis on debate, competition, or conflict, which is the central plot device of the Masters Narrative. As we have seen, proponents of the Masters Narrative tend to take debate or competition as the fundamental dynamic of the Warring States intellectual scene. However, in casting Warring States thinkers as "Disputers of the Tao" (to borrow A. C. Graham's memorable label), many sidestep the problem of determining whether and how those thinkers were connected in the first place. We learn of "the debate between Kongzi and Mozi" (see chapter 5) without being told that no version of Kongzi in any early source ever mentions Mozi, or that the Mozi of the *Mozi* never quotes the *Analects*. Like a narrative, a debate comes with certain preconditions. Did the debaters know each other? Were they familiar with their opponents' ideas? Was there a plausible mechanism or occasion for their exchange? Do extant sources of a particular "debate" choose sides (as the *Mengzi* clearly does in the water-talking contest between Mengzi and Gaozi), or do they represent the debate objectively?

If the advantage of a network model is that it foregrounds the problem of connecting extant texts and thinkers, then the advantage of a *Shi*-centric network model is that it offers the greatest number of pathways for making those connections. Even if we can't draw a direct line between, say, the *Analects* and the *Mozi*, we can still connect them via the *Shi*. Once those connections are mapped, we will be in a much better position to understand the debates, polemics, and competition that made the early Chinese intellectual scene so vibrant.

The focus on connectivity prompts new questions at the microlevel, too. How did individual authors become nodes in the network? How did they plug in? The wealth of extant *Shi* quotations is evidence that, in a *Shi*-centric network, tying one's text to the *Shi* was a common strategy. But which *Shi* couplets? Which poems? Which key themes and concepts? And when an author plugged in via the *Shi*, how did that change the content, presentation, or reception of his text? Did tying a text to the *Shi* entail an acceptance or reproduction of the *Shi* worldview? How much wiggle room did authors have to modify or reject its ideology?

The *Laozi* is a fascinating case study in this regard. The *Laozi* never quotes or mentions the *Shi*, instead evincing its familiarity with *Shi* poetics in the breach (see chapter 3). But for all its oppositionalism, the *Laozi* still embraces lessons learned from *Shi* poetics, including the homeward orientation of the *dao*. Would the *Laozi* have become so popular had its authors not shaped it in response to the *Shi*? I suspect not.

Of course, not plugging into the *Shi* was also a live option for early authors. The striking absence of *Shi* quotations in the *Zhuangzi* (aside from the obvious parody quotation uttered by two grave-robbing *Shi* reciters in chapter 26)[7] isn't accidental. In a collection named for a figure who preferred "dragging his tail in the mud" 曳尾於塗中 (17.603–604) to serving at court, the centralizing ideology of the *Shi* held little appeal. However, not even the *Zhuangzi* entirely escapes the pull of *Shi* poetics. What is the image of the metamorphosizing leviathan-bird from the opening of chapter 1, "Free and Easy Wandering" (Xiaoyao you 逍遙遊), if not a funhouse-mirror version of a *Shi* prompt image? Where the *Shi* juxtapose nature imagery (including birds and fish) with human scenes to naturalize the latter, the *Zhuangzi* uses the mind-bendingly gargantuan fish-bird to destabilize the human.

What might a fully elaborated network model of early Chinese thought look like? What is its structure? What sorts of emergent phenomena might it reveal?[8] *Shi* centrality aside, I'm still not sure. But there is an appealing symmetry to modeling early Chinese thought as a *Shi*-centric network. As cultural touchstone, the *Shi* tradition exemplifies the etic concept of network centrality. As intellectual historical artifacts, they also inculcated a centralizing ideology that was a cornerstone of classical thought. The *Shi* taught early thinkers to go home to the center, and early thinkers obliged by anchoring their texts to the *Shi*. Ideology sustained social function as social function reinforced ideology. The remarkable power of the *Shi* in the early period and beyond is an artifact of that dynamic.

NOTES

INTRODUCTION

1. See, for example, Schaberg 1999, 305–307, Assmann 1992, 56–57, Owen 1996a, xxxix.
2. Egyptologist Barry Kemp's (1989, introduction) reflections on the study of ancient thought are indispensable in this context, for example, on page 5: "Because of the common and oceanic character of mind, as well as the similarity of the situations in which individuals and societies find themselves, the aim of studying past societies should really be the same as that of studying present societies which are different from our own. Because time has destroyed so much of the evidence from the distant past historians and archaeologists must spend much more time on technical matters just to establish basic facts that in contemporary societies can be observed directly . . . But interest in the methods of research must not blind us to the fact that the passage of time makes no difference to the ultimate goal: that of studying the variations of mental pattern and behavioural response which man has created to come to terms with the reality around him."
3. Indispensable introductions to the *Shi* in English include Owen (1996b), Allen (1996), Nylan (2001, chapter 2), and Kern (2011, 17–39). Chen and Williams (2018) is a good recent introduction to the formal features of the *Shijing* anthology, Li (2018) to its themes and settings.
4. 192/8.7 and 194/2.1 (for this *Shijing* citation style, see the concluding section of the introduction).
5. The identity of this figure is mysterious. The earliest account is that of the *Hanshu* 漢書 (30.1708–1709, 88.3614), which identifies "Excellency Mao" (Mao gong 毛公) as as an Erudite (*boshi* 博士) at the court of King Xian of Hejian 河間獻王 (171–130 BCE). Zheng Xuan 鄭玄 (127–200 CE) later stated that there were two Excellencies Mao—an "Elder Mao" 大毛 from the state of Lu 魯 who composed the commentary, and a "Younger Mao" 小毛 who served at King Xian's court (*Mao Shi* 1.2). Not until

INTRODUCTION

the third century did Lu Ji 陸機 (261–303 CE) identify them as Mao Heng 毛亨 and Mao Chang 毛萇, whom he claimed were part of a scholarly lineage stretching back to Kongzi (cited in *Fengsu tongyi jiaozhu* 512).

6. *Hanshu* 30.1708–1709: "The reason why [the *Shi*] survived the [bibliocaust of the] Qin dynasty [221–206 BCE] intact was because they were recited [from memory] and didn't depend solely on bamboo and silk" 遭秦而全者，以其諷誦，不獨在竹帛故也. For caveats to the notion of the *Shi* as an oral tradition, see Shaughnessy (2015).
7. Kern 2019, 16–36.
8. Rusk 2012, especially chapter 1.
9. *Shiji* 47.1936.
10. Beecroft (2010, 51–52) cautions against taking the preimperial *Shi* as "a canonical anthology with defined contents and fixed interpretations," and instead takes "*Shi*" as "the notional total of the poetic production of the era." I offer a speculative theory of the *Shi* tradition's origins in the conclusion to chapter 2.
11. Beecroft 2010, 9, especially n17. Following Gregory Nagy's (1990) notion of the "Panhellenic," Beecroft defines the Panhuaxia as "the dimension of early Chinese literature that aims at speaking to the entire Chinese political and cultural world of the Spring and Autumn and Warring States eras." He also characterizes it as "a universal system of ritual and discourse that both facilitates interaction among peer polities of the Huaxia world and marks as outsiders those who do not know the correct practices" (205).
12. Nylan 2001, 74, 84. See also Lewis 1999, 158.
13. Kern 2011, 19. See also Kern 2018, 41–42.
14. *Shangshu* 3.95.
15. Owen 1992, 27–28.
16. Fuller 1993, 21. Saussy 1997a, 24: "A rhetoric whose job is to ground the categories of art in those of nature is by the terms of its own argument committed to not recognizing its handiwork in some of its objects."
17. Yu 1987, 76ff.
18. Lee 2005, 36.
19. Schneider 1971, chapter 5.
20. Xie 1931; translated in Lee 2005, 56.
21. Saussy 1993, 17–23. See also Kern 2010, 38, on the persistence of this line of thinking in more recent scholarship on the *Shi*.
22. Giles 1901, 13–14; also quoted in Saussy 1993, 19–20. See also Karlgren 1942, 73–74.
23. Granet 1932, 86.
24. Granet 1932, 86–87.
25. Saussy 2016, 31.
26. Owen 1996b, xv.
27. Waley 1996, 239. See also Saussy (1997a, 6): "the primitive man is the benchmark of perceptual accuracy because he sees naïvely, sees things as they are without the fog of culture, theology, or artifice."
28. These are *Mao Shi* numbers 191–199, 243–254, 257–258, and 264–265, which Joseph Allen translates in a 1996 reprint of Waley's translation.
29. Nylan 2001, 82, citing Karlgren (1964, 75–76), and Gu (1931). As documented in Schneider (1971, 177–178, including nn61–63), Gu Jiegang "found it technically much

INTRODUCTION

easier to demonstrate that the *Odes* contained no folksongs than to show that the crafted songs were folksong derivatives."
30. See especially Wang 1988 (discussed in Allen 1996, 337).
31. Gibson 2015, 7. See, for example, the opening sentence of Nylan (2001, chapter 2), which describes the *Shijing* as a collection of "polished folk songs." Ivanhoe and Van Norden (2001, 355) define the *Shi* as "[a] collection of rhymed poems derived from early folk songs and ceremonial incantations.... The message of the *Odes* was thought to be more allusive and allegorical in nature and interpreting the poems has been a pre-occupation of thinkers from Kongzi on down to contemporary times."
32. Owen 1996b, xiv. I am not accusing Owen of naiveté on this point (see, for example, the notion of the "artifice of simplicity" in Owen 1981, chapter 4). I simply find his framing unhelpful for my own purposes.
33. Kern 2007b, 792–793. See also Kern 2010. The distinction Kern draws between hermeneutically problematic "Airs" and other *Shi* isn't so clear-cut. Various pieces in the "Lesser Court Songs" and even the "Major Court Songs" and "Hymns" are just as opaque. A case in point is "Stout" (Jiong 駉, #297), which Saussy (1993, 67–73) reads in parallel with the "Airs."
34. Kern 2005, 179–180.
35. Kern 2007b, 792. See also Kern 2010, 39–40, echoed in Beecroft 2010, 50–51.
36. Kern 2007b. See also Kern 2019, 36.
37. Saussy 1993, 195, n19: "[T]he *Odes* shorn of their commentaries (the form in which they're usually taught today) make up a 'classic' whose very presence in many centuries of Chinese literature is disputable." See also pages 22–23, where Saussy writes of "The Wolf" (Lang ba 狼跋, #160) that it "needs putting together," hermeneutically speaking.
38. Saussy 1993, 60.
39. Compare Christopher Nugent's (2010, 10) comments on the "intensely alienating" nature of the "new medievalism" that focuses on "margins, erasures, and multiple meanings."
40. See, for example, Goldin 2020; Puett and Gross-Loh 2016; Van Norden 2011; Denecke 2010; Bo 2009, which opens with a chapter on the *Classic of Changes* [*Zhouyi* 周易]); Lai 2008; Liu 2006; Ivanhoe and Van Norden 2001; Nivison 1999; Hansen 1992; Graham 1989; Schwartz 1985; and the "Dao Companions to Chinese Philosophy" series (Dordrecht: Springer), ed. Yong Huang. See also Ge Zhaoguang's (2014, 7–11) diagnosis and critique of a "narrow concentration on a small number of elite thinkers and classic texts and a disregard for the larger life and general knowledge of the past" (9). However, Ge's focus on the "general knowledge, thought and belief [that] genuinely functioned in people's decisions, interpretations and dealings with the world around them" (9) is meant to supplement the Masters Narrative, not replace it (10). Zhang (2009) also critiques the tendency to relegate the *Shijing* to the "background" (*beijing* 背景) of the Masters but still reads the *Shijing* primarily through the texts of the Masters.
41. Puett and Gross-Loh 2016, chapter 2.
42. For "radiant originality and variety," see Graham 1989, 313. For "Axial Age" (articulated in Jaspers 1953), see, for example, Puett and Gross-Loh 2016, chapter 2; Ge 2014, 120–121; Schwartz 1985, 1–3. For "Golden Age," see, for example, Guo and Wu 2015, 3; Feng 1997, xiv. The same notion is implied in accounts of the stultifying impact

INTRODUCTION

of empire, for example, Hansen (1992, 15), on "China's philosophical dark age" or Collins (1998, 137): "It is when the oppositions come to an end, when Chinese philosophy settles into a period of hegemonic consensus, that creativity freezes."

43. Makeham 2012, 77, 93. See also Nylan 2016a, 102–103.
44. Makeham 2012, 78.
45. Makeham 2012, 90–91, quoting Dirlik 2009.
46. Jaspers 1953, 4–6.
47. See, for example, Goldin 2011, 22; Shen 2013; Hall and Ames 1987, 63 ("Viewing the *Book of Songs* in terms of Confucius' curriculum . . ."). A noteworthy exception is Lewis 1999, chapter 4.
48. Schwartz 1985, 41.
49. Slingerland 2003, 39. On "religious thought" before Kongzi, see also Ivanhoe and Van Norden 2001, xii.
50. Ivanhoe and Van Norden 2001, xi.
51. Hu 2013, 85: "[The *Book of Poetry*] taught the people how to speak and sing, but it also taught them how to think." However, Hu Shih also posited a sharp distinction between "the age of the poets" and "the age of the philosophers," which I reject.
52. *Republic* 607b5–6.
53. Kern (2019) also applies the word *repertoire* to the preimperial *Shi* tradition to argue that we should think of it as "a living poetic tradition, with the interaction of writing and performance in multiple, mutually independent strands continuing over many centuries beyond the Western Zhou, and possibly all the way through the Warring States." See also Fu 2004 and Cook (Gu Shikao) 2014 for the reading of the "Major Court Songs" as selections from an earlier liturgical repertoire.
54. For the term *distant reading*, see Moretti 2000, 56–58; for its demonstration, see Moretti 2005.
55. Miller 1994, 1.
56. On the problem of early intellectual typologies, see especially Peterson 1988. Peterson's approach is a major inspiration for this study.
57. Knechtges 1987, 1–13.
58. Goldin 2013, Barbieri-Low 2017.

1. READING THE *SHI*

1. All *Lunyu* citations refer to the *Lunyu zhuzi suoyin*. For a similar conversation between Kongzi and Zigong, see *Lunyu* 1/15; for another between Kongzi and Zixia, see *Hanshi waizhuan* 3.15/98–99.
2. Saussy 1993, 60; Kern 2007b.
3. The *Mao Shi* was first "established" (*li* 立) by Han Emperor Ping 漢平帝 (r. 1 BCE–6 CE), who came to the throne as an eight-year-old child under the regency of Wang Mang 王莽 (45 BCE–23 CE). Tellingly, the bibliographic treatise of the *Hanshu* (30.1707–1708) lists the *Mao Shi* after all other *Shi* recensions and also seems to describe it with some incredulity: "There is also the learning of Excellency Mao, who himself claimed that it was passed down from Zixia" 又有毛公之學，自謂子夏所傳.
4. For an overview of this history, see Kern 2007a.

1. READING THE *SHI*

5. The most comprehensive effort to reconstruct the text and commentary of the other three *Shi* recensions is Wang Xianqian's 王先謙 *Shi sanjia yi jishu* 詩三家義集疏 (Wang 1987). With regard to "A Splendid Woman," Wang argued that the missing *Analects* line came from the Lu 魯 recension of the *Shi* on the basis of a very loose parallel in Liu Xiang's 劉向 (77–6 BCE) *Lienü zhuan* 列女傳 (*Biographies of Exemplary Women*), which he supposed (without much evidence) made use of the Lu recension (283).
6. Kern 2005, 181–182.
7. *Hanshu* 30.1708–1709.
8. See especially Galambos 2006 for the conclusion that "variability was an integral part of Warring States writing" (145). Pan 2015 is a succinct overview of early rebus writing.
9. Kern 2005.
10. Kern 2002, 155–156.
11. See Kern 2019 and Shaughnessy 2015, 344–347, for side-by-side translations of two pieces appearing in the *Mao Shi* and the looted Qinghua Museum manuscripts. Shaughnessy's study focuses on variations indicative of written as opposed to oral textual transmission.
12. See Kern 2019, 25, for a parallel point about "Cuckoo" (Shi jiu 鳲鳩, #152).
13. See also "Furs of Lamb's Wool" (Gao qiu 羔裘, #80, 120, and 146).
14. Still other *Shi* were lost such that only their titles remain. The anomalous Mao preface to "Sixth Month" (Liu yue 六月, #177) describes the deleterious consequences of "abandoning" (*fei* 廢) a series of twenty-two "Lesser Court Songs," a list that includes a number of orphaned titles: "Southern Ridge" (Nan gai 南陔), "White Flower" (Bai hua 白華), "Flowering Millet" (Hua shu 華黍), "Following the Road" (You geng 由庚), "High Hill" (Chong qiu 崇丘), and "Following the Rites" (You yi 由儀). See *Mao Shi* 10.738.
15. *Zuozhuan* Xuan 12/744–746. Wang 1988, 8–25. The first to note the possibility of longer Western Zhou liturgies being broken down and rearranged was Fu Sinian (2004, 15–34). See also Kern 2019, 26–27. Another relevant example discussed by Shaughnessy (2006, chapter 2, and 2015, 350–355) is the first stanza of "Servitor of the City" (Duren shi 都人士, #225), which is quoted by the "Black Robes" (Zi yi 緇衣) chapter of the *Liji*. In his commentary on that quotation, Zheng Xuan states that "the Mao Shi has this *Shi* but the three [other *Shi*] lineages don't" 此詩，毛氏有之，三家則亡 (*Liji* 33.1757). Observing that the first stanza of #225 differs significantly from the other four, Wang Xianqian hypothesized that it's a fragment of a lost poem later added to "Servitor of the City." Shaughnessy (2015, 355, n48) notes another example identified by Li Xueqin (2008, 20–21).
16. Translation after Durrant et al. 2016, 534–535.
17. See Schaberg 1999, 328–331, on "song as coded communication;" on *Shi* citations in the *Zuozhuan* more generally, see Schaberg 2001; on the "cultural roles" of the *Shi*, see Schaberg 2018.
18. *Xunzi* 8.134, *Mengzi* 7B/3. Admittedly, such instances are quite rare.
19. Translation adapted from Durrant et al. 2016, 1039.
20. For a parallel argument, see Kern 2019.
21. Kern 2010. Wang 1987 is an excellent source for this diversity in a Han context; for "Ospreys Cry," see 4–16.

1. READING THE *SHI*

22. *Mao Shi zhengyi* 1.5, 22–32.
23. Followng Zheng Xuan's emendation of 哀 to 衷.
24. The "Great Preface" (Da xu 大序), a 459-character discussion of the significance of the *Shi* as a whole, begins from here.
25. Kern 2007b and 2010.
26. Schuessler 2009, 199, indicates that this reconstruction is uncertain.
27. For an overview, see Boltz 2015, which distinguishes three types of sound-symbolic or "*Gestalt* binomes": reduplicative, alliterative, and riming.
28. Csikszentmihalyi 2004, 363–367. In the same section, "Ospreys Cry" is cited as an example of "using sex to illustrate ritual propriety" 由色諭於禮, that is, re-creating the experience of sexual longing in order to inculcate a sense of its proper limits.
29. This observation was first made by Ma Ruichen 馬瑞辰 (1782–1835); see Ma 1989, 417–418.
30. Kern 2007b, 792. Elsewhere, Kern 2010, 39–40, puts the point even more pointedly: "The wholesale rejection of the Mao prefaces and other early readings altogether [is] a fallacy born out of ignorance and arrogance. It is simplistic to believe that we have direct access to the 'original meaning' of any of the 'Airs' when our earliest sources—that is, before Mao—indicate that the true meaning of a song rested in its proper application and hence was generated in ever new ways through the flexible adaptation to various contexts . . . To claim that somehow, we understand the songs better than the ancients who were actively engaged with them is a folly."
31. Culler, 1997, 61–62: "Poetics does not require that we know the meaning of a work; its task is to account for whatever effects we can attest to."
32. For a parallel approach, see Owen 2006, chapter 2 ("A 'Grammar' of Early Poetry"). See also Saussy 1997a, 26, for his "syntactic reading."
33. Owen 2006, 73.
34. Of particular interest are a series of stone drum inscriptions from the state of Qin, translated in Mattos 1988.
35. For Chen Zhi (2007, 18), it clearly isn't. Chen criticizes the synchronic or "planimetric" approach to *Shijing* studies, whereby "the three-hundred-some poems in the compilation are treated as an anthology of works of the same era, despite the fact that they actually were written and collected from the early 11th century B.C., during the transformation from the Shang to the Zhou dynasties, until the 6th century B.C., when Jizha attended the performance at the Lu Court and Confucius claimed to have read the current version of the *Shijing*." In my view, however, we have far too little evidence to say when *Shi* poems "actually were written and collected."
36. Richter 2013, 19: "No other text figures as prominently in the newly discovered early Chinese manuscripts as the *Odes*."
37. A useful starting point is Ho and Chan 2004 (*Citations from the* Shijing *to Be Found in Pre-Han and Han Texts*); this resource is also limited because it (1) excludes evidence from excavated manuscripts; (2) includes too few implicit quotations of the *Shi*; and (3) aggregates all citations regardless of source or time period, for example, by listing *Shi* citations in Eastern Han and later commentaries alongside citations in the texts that are the objects of those commentaries.
38. For the *Shijing*, see Ho and Chan 2004, 307–310; for the *Shangshu*, see Chan and Ho 2003, 290–320. Note that the base text of the *Shijing* is larger (approximately 30,000 characters) than that of the *Shangshu* (approximately 26,000 characters).

39. For a discussion of the use of regular expressions to search digitized corpora, see Hunter 2017b, 25–31.
40. This is line 11 of the "Rhapsody on Literature" (Wen fu 文賦). See *Wenxuan* 17.763, translated at Knechtges 1996, 213.
41. Fifty-six stanzas across twenty-eight *Shi* feature flying, roosting, and/or or calling birds. Forty stanzas across twenty-six *Shi* feature bells, drums, and string instruments. Images of streams and rivers pervade the *Shijing* (as discussed in chapter 2), appearing in roughly 10 percent of all stanzas.
42. Waley 1996, 333–334, lists seventy *Shi* under "courtship" and forty-seven under "marriage." His next largest category is "warriors and battles," with thirty-six *Shi*.
43. Note that this discussion assumes Zheng Xuan's arrangement of the text (five stanzas of four lines each), which differs somewhat from the earlier *Mao Shi* arrangement (three stanzas total, with four lines in the first and eight lines in the second and third). See *Mao Shi zheng yi* 1.32–33; for corroborating evidence of Zheng Xuan's arrangement, see Li 2008, 25–26.
44. In the "Greater Court Songs," see 235/3 and /3–7, 236/3 and /5 and /7, 243/2–3 and /5–6, 245/6–7, 247/3–8, 249/4, 257/3, 260/2–3, and 263/5. Other examples in the "Airs" and "Court Songs" are 82/2, 107/2, 203/6, and 223/2.
45. For the reading of *tu* 兔 (rabbit) as the *tu* 菟 of *wutu* 於菟 (tiger), see Yuan et al. 2018, 30.
46. Despite being the second-most cited title of any *Shi*, "Ospreys Cry" isn't among the most quoted *Shi*. The Guodian *Black Robes* (*Zi yi* 緇衣) manuscript quotes only a single line without mentioning "Ospreys Cry" by title; see Cook 2012, 414–415. The Mawangdui *Five Kinds of Conduct* manuscript quotes a few more lines but, again, without a title; see Csikszentmihalyi 2004, 363–367.

2. A POETRY OF RETURN

1. Bao Xian's 包咸 (7–65 CE) gloss on this slogan (*Lunyu zhushu* 2.15) is noteworthy given the argument of this chapter: "[the *Shi*] return to the correct" 歸於正.
2. Kern 2000b, 18–19.
3. Owen 1996b, xvi.
4. On gates as "liminal space[s] [where] things often happened and stories began," see Waley 1996, 107.
5. Here, I follow the reconstruction and translation in Kern 2009, 173–177.
6. For Zheng Xuan's gloss of *huang* 皇 (*wâŋ) as *wang* 往 (waŋʔ), see *Liji* 35.1198.
7. On the meaning of formal repetition in the *Shi* (and for a more dedicated reading of repetition and rhyme in "Drooping Boughs"), see Saussy 1997b; for repetition in a ritual context, see Owen 2001 and Kern 2009, 195–197.
8. *Mao Shi* 1.116.
9. Waley 1996, 20.
10. See especially Yu 1987, chapters 1–2. A useful summary is Saussy 1997a, 7–11 ("All Chinese Poems Are True").
11. Yu 1987, 35; echoed in Sun 2011, 1–10, and quoted in Saussy 1997a, 8.
12. Saussy 1997b, 532.
13. For an overview and critique of the idea that Chinese thinkers made no distinction between the human and the natural, see especially Puett 2001.

14. Richardson 2019, chapter 1, is a useful recent review of the theoretical literature on home (in which Despres 1991 features prominently). Matt 2011 corrects the tendency in modern American culture to dismiss the significance of homesickness.
15. See 59/1.3, 73/1-2.3, 89/2.3, 146/1-3.3, 162/1-2.3 and /5.3, 168/4.7, and 207/1-3.11.
16. For "father and mother to the people," see also 172/3.4.
17. See, for example, 3/1.3, 30/4.4, 76/1-3.5, 162/1-2.3, 207/1-3.11.
18. Translation adapted from Kern 2000a.
19. *Zuozhuan* Zhao 7/1291–1292; translation adapted from Durrant et al. 2016, 1425.
20. This line is obscure. The Mao commentary suggests that the mulberry and catalpa trees of the third stanza "were planted by the [persona's] father" 父之所樹, and thus that the inner and outer garments represent the father and mother, respectively. Compare *Mengzi* 6B/3, which says that this poem is about "a great wrongdoing by the parents" 親之過大.
21. On the ambiguity of *Zhou dao* 周道 (or *Zhou hang* 周行 or *Zhou lu* 周路), see chapter 3 of this book.
22. Given that personal pronouns in literary Chinese are often ambiguous with respect to number, the distinction between "I" and "we" isn't always clear-cut. In some cases, as with soldiers on the march, it may be more accurate to say that a smaller suffering "we" desires to rejoin a bigger collective. Another exception is the king, for whom the "I" is somewhat less problematic; see, for example, 261/1.7.
23. For a parallel discussion, see Lewis 1999, 153–155.
24. For background, see Cook 2009 and 2017.
25. 163/1.3, 169/1–4.7, 234/2–3.3, 260/7.3.
26. See *Mao Shi* numbers 3, 19, 31, 36, 40, 66, 68, 73, 110, 121, 156–157, 162–163, 167–169, 177–179, 181–182, 203–205, 207, 227, 230, 232, 234, 260, 262–263, and 299.
27. See also 9/2–3.5–8 for the image of uncrossable rivers juxtaposed with "this girl going to her new home" 之子于歸.
28. See also 70/3.5–6: "I have met these hundred griefs. / Would that I might sleep and wake no more" 逢此百憂，尚寐無覺.
29. See also 257/4: "From west to east / There is no place to make our homes" 自西徂東，靡所定處.
30. See, for example, *Zhouli zhushu* 3.85 (for *gao*), 3.72 (for *song*), and 14.415 (for *jian*).
31. The few quasi-exceptions are all passing mentions of wise or sagely kings; see 243/1.2, 282/1.9, 304/1.1, and 282/1.9.
32. Hunter 2017a.
33. See also 254/4.3–4: "Old men are **kwâns-kwâns* [sincere, true], / Young men are **gauk-gauk* [proud, pompous]" 老夫灌灌，小子蹻蹻.
34. See, for example, 40/1.4, 58/5.7, 65/1–3.5–8, 109/1–2.5–11. On this theme see also Nylan 2001, 104–119.
35. Lewis 1999, 151–152.
36. Assmann 1994, 194.
37. See also 181/3, 205/4–6.
38. For "sage," see also 198/4.4; for "wise man," see 181/3.3, 256/1.7, and 256/9.5; for "fool," see also 181/3.6 and 256/9.8. The use of *sheng* 聖 in the *Shi* is mostly restricted to elite laments; see 32/2.3, 192/5.7, 193/6.1, 195/5.2, 196/2.1, 198/4.1, 254/1.5, 257/10.1, and 304/3.4.
39. Hall and Ames 1987, 15.

3. SHI POETICS BEYOND THE SHI

40. See also Kemp, 1989, 7: "The history of man is the record of his slow subjugation to polities of increasing size, ambition, and complexity."
41. This isn't a novel suggestion. The traditional account of Kongzi's compilation of the *Shijing* assumes a post-Western Zhou context; see *Shiji* 47.1936–1937.
42. Scott 2017; for the quotation, see page 7.
43. Scott 2017, 88ff.

3. SHI POETICS BEYOND THE SHI

1. Deleuze and Guattari 1987, 8.
2. For "connectivity" in a network theoretical context, see Newman 2010, 145ff.
3. On the "problem of categoriz[ing]" the noncanonical songs of the Warring States and Han periods, see Schaberg 1999, 321–328.
4. Also discussed in Schaberg 2018, 186–187.
5. Translation after Durrant, Li, and Schaberg 2016, 1, 13.
6. *Zuozhuan* Xi 24/417–419.
7. *Shiji* 39.1662 includes another, rather different version of the poem. At *Shuiyuan* 6.118–122, the snake cuts meat from his thigh to feed the starving dragon.
8. For "in flight," see 33/1–2.1, 181/1–3.1, 252/7–8.1, and 278/1.1.
9. The rare exception is "Big Rat" (Shuo shu 碩鼠, #113): "Big rat, big rat, / Do not gobble our millet! / Three years we have slaved for you, / Yet you take no notice of us. / At last we are going to leave you / And go to that happy land; / Happy land, happy land, / Where we shall have our place" 碩鼠碩鼠．無食我黍．三歲貫女．莫我肯顧．逝將去女．適彼樂土．樂土樂土．爰得我所．
10. Yang 1984; on Zhou roads generally, see Lei 2011.
11. See also *Mao Shi* 270/1: "Heaven made a high hill; / The Great King laid hand upon it. / He felled the trees; / King Wen strengthened it, / He cleared the bush. / Mount Qi has level ways, / May sons and grandsons keep them! 天作高山，大王荒之。彼作矣，文王康之，彼徂矣。岐有夷之行，子孫保之。
12. Compare *Lüshi chunqiu* 3.1/124 (trans. adapted from Knoblock and Riegel 2000, 96): "In this [the third] month, [the Son of Heaven] orders the Overseer of Works as follows: 'The seasonable rains are about to fall, so the groundwater will be rising. Make tours of inspection through the capital and walled cities, comprehensively examining the plains and fields. Put dams and dikes in good repair; channel the ditches and trenches; clear the thoroughfares and roadways, allowing no obstacle or obstruction to remain'" 是月也，命司空曰：時雨將降，下水上騰；循行國邑，周視原野；修利隄防，導達溝瀆，開通道路，無有障塞。
13. See *Mao Shi* 3/1.4, 149/1–2.3, 161/1.8, 162/1.2, 203/1.3, 203/2.6, and 234/4.4.
14. As detailed in Lei 2011, 3–9, Zhu Xi was the first to understand *Zhou dao* as an actual road, a reading later confirmed by Qu Wanli 1952 and Gu Jiegang 1977, 121–124, among others.
15. See also *Mao Shi* 194/3.3–8: "Like those who walk along / With no place in the end to go, / All the hundred princes / Take special care only of themselves. / Why do they not fear the others, / Or hold no fear of Heaven?" 如彼行邁，則靡所臻。凡百君子，各敬爾身。胡不相畏，不畏于天。

16. This and all subsequent *Laozi* citations in this chapter are of the Mawangdui *Laozi* A (甲) manuscript as transcribed by Gao Ming in his *Boshu Laozi jiaozhu* (1996). Section numbers refer to the order in the Wang Bi recension. For this passage in the Guodian *Laozi* materials, see Cook 2012, 256–259.
17. Translation adapted from Knoblock and Riegel 2000, 111.
18. *Mozi* 16.124.
19. See also "Nutgrass Grows on the Southern Hills" (Nan shan you tai 南山有臺, 172/3): "On the southern hills the aspen; / On the northern hills the plum tree. / Rejoice in this prince, / Father and mother of his people. / Rejoice in this prince, / His virtuous reputation unending" 南山有杞，北山有李。樂只君子，民之父母。樂只君子，德音不已.
20. For a partial list, see He and Chan 2004, 235. The most cited *Shi* couplet is "*Ji-ji* [splendid] were those many knights / Who gave comfort to King Wen" 濟濟多士，文王以寧 (235/3.7–8).
21. For this text and its manuscript counterpart in the Shanghai Museum corpus, see Richter 2013.
22. See also *Lüshi chunqiu* 18.6/1207 and *Liji* 54.1731.
23. See, for example, *Mao Shi* 257/8.1, 258/8.10, 264/1.2, 269/1.3.
24. Parallels include the *Six Virtues* (*Liu de* 六德) manuscript from Guodian (夫夫，婦婦，父父，子子，君君，臣臣; *Guodian Chu mu zhujian* 188) and the *jiaren* 家人 hexagram (父父，子子，兄兄，弟弟，夫夫，婦婦，而家道正；正家，而天下定矣; *Zhouyi zhengyi* 4.185).
25. For "fathers and mothers" (*fumu* 父母) as objects of longing, see *Mao Shi* 2/3.6, 39/2.4, 51/1–2.4, 59/2.4, 169/3.4, 205/1.6, and 258/4.9.
26. This is Zheng Xuan's reading; see *Mao Shi zhengyi* 17.1330.
27. Allan 1997, 95. See also page 125: "Many of the most fundamental concepts of early Chinese philosophy are grounded in the imagery of water and the plant life that water nourishes." On the connection between *gui* and water, see pages 42–46.
28. For the Guodian version (section 2 in of the *Laozi* A bundle), see Cook 2012, 230–233.
29. For the translation and normalized transcription (minus Cook's suggested reconstructions for the missing sections), see Cook 2012, 343–348.
30. Cook 2012 argues that the missing word is "sagacity" (*sheng* 聖), which fits the rhyme scheme of the section.
31. On the connection between the cult of the Great Unity or Great One (*tai yi* 太一) and cosmograph (*shi* 式) divination, and for the argument that "water" here is the "river" (also *shui* 水) of the Milky Way, see Allan 2003.
32. *Analects* 9/17, *Shuiyuan* 13.312–313, 17.434–437, *Da Dai Liji* 64.135–136, *Kongzi jiayu* 9.101, and *Mengzi* 4B/18 and 7A/24.
33. Translation (with minor modifications) by Knechtges and Swanson 1970–1971, 115–116.
34. For this and the next quotation, see Knechtges and Swanson 1970–1971, 114, 116.
35. Waley 1939. A recent summary of this debate is Jones 2016, 193–195.
36. Allan 1997, 43. However, I disagree with Allan that Mengzi's victory means that "Mencius' argument is both powerful and logical." In my view, "logic" has little to do with it.
37. Reading *bi* 毖 as *bi* 眵 (look directly at) in parallel with the line from "Fourth Month" (204/5.1) below; see Yuan, Xu, and Cheng 2018, 141.

3. SHI POETICS BEYOND THE SHI

38. See, for example, *Shiji* 28.1357.
39. *Hanshi waizhuan* 3.25/110–111.
40. Hunter 2017b, 159.
41. For additional discussion, see Hunter 2017b, chapter 2.
42. A recent overview is Shen 2013.
43. For "Kong[zi] the sage" (孔聖), see, for example, *Hou Hanshu* 33.1144.
44. Riegel 1986, 14; see also Hunter 2017b, 81–83.
45. *Shiji* 47.1931–1932.
46. *Liji* 7.241.
47. See, for example, *Shijing* 235/2.6.
48. From the Western Han onward, the classic most often referenced in conjunction with Kongzi was the *Annals* (*Chunqiu* 春秋) thanks to the perception that it was the one classic wholly authored by Kongzi. As noted at Hunter 2017b, 73, n118, however, references to Kongzi's authorship of the *Annals* don't seem to predate the Han period.
49. For a summary of the debate over the relationship of Guodian *Laozi* materials to the received *Laozi*, see Cook 2012, volume 1, 195–209.
50. *Hanshu* 30.1729. The three recensions are "the canon and explanations of the Mr. Lin *Laozi*, in four fascicles" 老子鄰氏經傳四篇, "the canon and explanations of the Mr. Fu *Laozi* in 37 fascicles" 老子傅氏經說三十七篇, and "the canon and explanations of the Mr. Xu *Laozi* in six fascicles" 老子徐氏經說六篇.
51. Hunter 2017b, 92–94.
52. *Shiji* 49.1975
53. Cook 2002, 318–323.
54. Liu 2015, 39.
55. On *wuwei* 無為 in the *Shi*, see Slingerland 2003, 39–42. See especially the opening stanza "A Hare Slowly" (Tu yuan 兔爰, #70): "A hare moves slowly, / But the pheasant is caught in the snare. / Would that I had nothing to do as when I was first born! / In my latter days / I have met these hundred woes. / Would that I might sleep and never stir! 有兔爰爰，雉離于羅。我生之初尚無為。我生之後，逢此百罹，尚寐無吡.
56. See also Chan 1963, 216, for the connection between *Laozi* section 65 and the lines from "Sovereign Might" quoted earlier in this chapter.
57. Slingerland, 2003, 42.
58. This line has been lost in *Laozi* A but is present in *Laozi* B. Commentators have long suspected that it belongs at the end of section 19, which advocates "cutting off sageliness" 絕聖, "cutting off humaneness" 絕仁, and "cutting off cleverness" 絕巧; see *Laozi jiaozhu* 76–77. However, the two sections aren't contiguous in the Guodian *Laozi* B manuscript, which groups the "cut off learning" line with section 20 as shown here; see Cook 2012, 288–291 (especially n30). Note that only the first seven lines of this question are present in the Guodian materials.
59. I count only seventeen reduplicating sound-symbolic binomes in the Wang Bi recension, at sections 6, 14, 16, 39 (two times), 49, 58 (four times), and 73.
60. For the transcription, see Csikszentmihalyi 2004, 313.
61. On the "moral psychology" of the text, see Csikszentmihalyi 2004, chapter 2.
62. *Mao Shi* 33/4.2, 236/2.6, 256/2.3 and 9.7, and 288/1.12.
63. For the transcription, see Csikszentmihalyi 2004, 315–316.

64. Other *Analects* passages that endorse eliminating anxiety include 7/19, 9/29, and 14/28; passages that embrace anxiety include 2/6 and 15/32. See also the contrast between the Kongzi saying at *Hanshi waizhuan* 1.18/18 ("A prince has three kinds of anxiety" 君子有三憂) and *Shuiyuan* 17.429 ("Zilu asked Kongzi, 'Does a prince have anxiety?' Kongzi said, 'He does not'" 子路問孔子曰：君子亦有憂乎？孔子曰：無也).
65. For a parallel theme and an injunction against "laboring one's heart" (*lao xin* 勞心), see "Too Big a Field" (Fu tian 甫田, #102).
66. On the connection between the *Mengzi* and *Five Kinds of Conduct*, see Csikszentmihalyi 2004, 103–113. For the explicit association of Mengzi (and Zisi 子思) with a doctrine called "the five kinds of conduct" (*wu xing* 五行), see *Xunzi* 6.94.
67. See also *Lüshi chunqiu* 17.2/1061: "Creators are anxious, reliers are equanimous" 作者憂，因者平. For a discussion of the "Commentary to the Appended Phrases" passage in the larger context of the "ambivalence of creation," see Puett 2001, 86–90. Here Puett focuses on how acts of creation model natural processes but does not comment on their affect.
68. *Zhouyi zhengyi* 8.375.
69. Translation adapted from Kern 2000b, 25–29.
70. Translation adapted from Dubs 1938, 263–264.
71. For "dawn to dusk never remiss" and its variants, see *Mao Shi* 234/3.4, 260/4.7, 261/1.8, and 300/3.9; for "rising early and going to bed late," see 58/5.3, 196/4.5, 256/4.4; for "anxious for and pities," see 257/5.3.
72. For the argument that this text isn't really a "self-narration," see Zhang 2018, 260–290; for a critique, see Nylan 2016b, 143, and Klein 2019, 41–47. For a complete translation, see Watson 1958, chapter 2.
73. The two exceptions are chapter 24, the "Treatise on Music" (Yue shu 樂書), and chapter 121, the "Collected Biographies of the Classicists" (Rulin liezhuan 儒林列傳).
74. Sima Ang's capture by Liu Bang in 205 (*Shiji* 8.359) goes unmentioned here.
75. On the importance of settling the mind, see, for example, *Guanzi* 49.938 (translation adapted from Rickett 1998, 50): "The spirit resides where it will. / Its going and coming / No one can contemplate. / Lose it, and the mind will be confused; / Grasp it, and the mind will be ordered. / Respectfully keep clean its abode / And its vital essence will naturally come. / Purify your thoughts to contemplate it. / Rest your mind to order it. / Maintain a dignified appearance and respectful attitude, / Then its vital essence will become settled. / Grasp it and never let it go" 有神自在身，一往一來，莫之能思。失之必亂，得之必治。敬除其舍，精將自來。精想思之，寧念治之，嚴容畏敬，精將至定。得之而勿舍.
76. For *li* 離, compare "Rain Without Limit" (Yu wu zheng 雨無正, 194/2.1–5): "The house of Zhou was destroyed, / There was no place to rest or reside. / The great officials left their homes, / No one knew how we toiled" 周宗既滅，靡所止戾．正大夫離居，莫知我勩.
77. This episode is recounted at *Shiji* 28.1397ff and translated in Watson 1961, 40–44.
78. See, for example, *Shiji* 31.1452, *Lunyu* 17/10, and *Hanshu* 81.3335 and 88.3589.
79. On the connection between Sima Qian, Kongzi, and the *Annals*, see especially Durrant 1995, chapters 1–2.
80. For the gloss of *you* 幽 as *you* 憂, see *Shiji* 50.1989.
81. For other examples of a "knotted" or "tied up" (*jie* 結) heart in the *Shi*, see 147/3.2 and 192/8.2.

82. See, for example, Li 2016 and Klein 2019, 88–91.
83. *Shiji* 63.2155
84. On the difficulty and significance of *jia* 家 in the *Shiji*, see especially Klein 2019, 15–17. In the context of the "Self-Narrtion," Klein insists on the "family" or "lineage" meaning of *jia* as opposed to "expert," the rendering endorsed by Csikszentmihalyi and Nylan 2003, 67–68.
85. Hansen 2017.
86. Nylan and Wilson 2010.
87. Bauer 1990, 79; quoted in Durrant 1995, 1.
88. Lewis 1999, 186.

4. THE *SHI* AND THE *VERSES OF CHU* (*CHUCI* 楚辭)

Hunter 2019 is an earlier version of this argument.
1. Kern 2011, 76; Owen 1996a, 155; Sukhu 2012, 1–3; Yu 1987, 84; Wang and Williams 2015, 2–7.
2. Yuan 2018, 37–38.
3. Hawkes 1985, 15, 26.
4. Exceptions include Zhu 1957, 368–71, and Waters 1985, 12–14.
5. *Shiji* 84.2482. For the identification of this passage as Liu An's commentary, see Ban Gu's 班固 (32–92) preface preserved at *Chuci buzhu* 1.49.
6. *Hanshu* 87a.3515–21.
7. *Chuci buzhu* 1.49.
8. Wang Yi includes two examples in a postface (*Chuci buzhu* 1.49) and a dozen more throughout his commentary, several of which are noted in this chapter.
9. For this debate, which I explore at greater length in this chapter, see especially Schimmelpfennig 2004.
10. This conclusion parallels Galal Walker's (1982, chapter 4) analysis of the use of *Shijing* rhyme categories in the earliest strata of the *Verses of Chu*. Walker nevertheless emphasized the differences between the *Shijing* and *Verses of Chu* more than the similarities (e.g., at page 116).
11. The one noteworthy exception is "Big Rat" (Shuo shu 碩鼠, #113).
12. For *juan gu* 睠顧 ("looked back"), see *Mao Shi* 203/1.7–8 and 207/2.9–12; for *fan fu* 反覆 ("reverse its fortunes"), see 207/3.9–12. Note that both phrases appear in "Minor Bright" (Xiao ming 小明, #207), which also features three instances of the line "How could I not long to return?" 豈不懷歸—a fitting question for Qu Yuan.
13. This biography is notoriously problematic; see Hawkes 1985, 51–60; Walker 1982, 75–108; and Kern 2003, 306–7.
14. This is not the first study to use the word *debate* in reference to disagreements about Qu Yuan; see Schimmelpfennig 2004, 111–112 (also n2).
15. See *Chuci buzhu* 15.274, 17.321; *Hou Hanshu* 40a.1332, 52.1726.
16. Readers will note that this analysis sidesteps two central topics within *Verses of Chu* scholarship: the relationship between "Parting's Sorrow" and the Qu Yuan biography, and the interpretation of "Parting's Sorrow" as a text inflected by shamanistic practices. For further discussion, see Hunter 2019, 6–7.
17. See *Mao Shi* 38/4.4–5 and 42/3.4.

18. This and all subsequent *Chuci* citations are from the *Chuci buzhu* edition. For "Parting's Sorrow," see *Chuci buzhu* 1.3–47.
19. The controversy over the interpretation of the coda is long and convoluted; see *Chuci jijiao jishi* 699–708. Wang Yi identifies "Peng Xian" as a single figure, a Shang grandee who drowned himself after failing to earn his ruler's trust (*Chuci buzhu* 1.13). However, this idea isn't attested prior to Wang Yi's commentary. In the *Lüshi chunqiu* (17.4/1088), Shaman Peng 巫彭 and Shaman Xian 巫咸 appear as two different figures. For this argument, see also Sukhu 2012, 103–4.
20. See also 204/7.1–2: "Would that I were an eagle or a falcon / That I might soar to Heaven" 匪鶉匪鳶，翰飛戾天.
21. See also "Dong jun" 東君 (2.74), "Zun jia" 尊嘉 (15.275) "Li shi" 離世 (16.288), "Xi xian" 惜賢 (16.296), and "You ku" 憂苦 (16.301).
22. For these connections, see the commentaries of Yu Yue 俞樾 and Shen Zumian 沈祖緜 at *Chuci jijiao jishi* 698, including Yu Yue's conclusion that "the verses of the *sao* poets were based on the *Shi*" (騷人之辭卽本之詩也).
23. See also *Chuci buzhu* 14.262 and 17.315.
24. *Chuci buzhu* 16.289, 292, 301, 306.
25. Hawkes 1974.
26. Hawkes 1974, 54.
27. Hawkes 1974, 62–63.
28. For this section of "Parting's Sorrow," see *Chuci buzhu* 1.3–7. This *Shi* appears in the "Yong feng" 鄘風 ("Airs of Yong"), an area eventually absorbed by the Wei 衛 state. The Mao commentary (3/232) identifies this Chu as Chuqiu 楚丘 in modern-day Henan. For my purposes, the name "Chu" need only have triggered an association with the Chu state. The other *Shi* to mention Chu is "Warriors of Yin" (Yin wu 殷武, 305/1.2,2.1), which celebrates a campaign against "Jing Chu" 荊楚.
29. Shen Zumian (*Chuci jijiao jishi* 698) also notes the connection between the *pufu* here and at the end of the poem.
30. See *Mao Shi* 197/7.1, 198/2.4, and 219/1.4.
31. See, for example, the "Hong fan" 洪範, "Da dao" 大誥, and "Kang gao" 康誥 chapters of the *Exalted Documents* (*Shangshu* 308, 346, 359) and also *Mengzi* 1B/5 (quoting "First Month").
32. For *long* ("Parting's Sorrow" ll. 337, 351, 359), see *Mao Shi* 128/2.5, 283/1.3, 300/3.7, 303/1.13; for *luan* (ll. 199, 344), see 127/3.3, 178/2.9, 260/7.6 and 8.2, 261/4.7, 291/1.6, 302/1.14.
33. *Mao Shi* 128/1–3, 167/5.6, 238/5.1–2.
34. *Qi* 旗 (ll. 347, 360) doesn't appear in the *Shijing* but *qi* 旂 (l. 349) is quite common: 168/3.4, 178/2.6, 182/3.5, 222/2.4–5, 262/2.7, 283/1.3, 299/1.4–5, 300/3.7, 303/1.13.
35. *Mao Shi* 54/1.1, 115/1.6, 163/2–5.3, 254/8.4.
36. *Mao Shi* 93/1.2–3, 104/1.4, 261/4.10.
37. For the varaint *yi* 貽 in the *Shi*, see *Mao Shi* 42/2.2 and 3.4, 74/3.4, 137/3.4, and 275/1.5.
38. See also *Mao Shi* 83/1.4 and 98/1–3.3 (for garnet pendants), and 82/3 (for the giving of pendants as gifts). On this connection between "Parting's Sorrow" and the *Shijing*, see Zhu Ji's 朱冀 commentary at *Chuci jijiao jishi* 473
39. *Chuci buzhu* 1.31–34.
40. For a close parallel, see "Axe-Handle" (Fa ke 伐柯, 158/1).
41. See, for example, *Mengzi* 3B/3, *Guanzi* 2.45 ("A woman who acts as her own matchmaker is ugly and faithless" 自媒之女，醜而不信) and 64.1188, and *Liji* 30.1656.

42. *Chuci buzhu* 1.37–38.
43. *Chuci jijiao jishi* 703–8.
44. This fragment is attributed to Liu An by Ban Gu in a preface to "Parting's Sorrow" (*Chuci buzhu* 1.51). It also appears unattributed within Qu Yuan's biography in the *Grand Scribe's Records* (84.2482). For the reference to Liu An's commentary, see *Hanshu* 44.2145; for a more complete discussion, see Schimmelpfennig 2004, 118–123.
45. Liu An's praise of Qu Yuan echoes a passage from another text submitted by Liu An to Emperor Wu, the *Huainanzi* (7.537).
46. *Shiji* 117.3056–3063.
47. See, for example, Slingerland 2019, which mentions the *Verses of Chu* only once in passing (on page 192).
48. Translation adapted from Hawkes 1985, 284–285.
49. Translation adapted from Hawkes 1985, 302.
50. For a useful introduction and survey, see Brindley 2013. For *gong* versus *si* in the *Shijing*, see 212/3.3–4: "Rains fall on the lord's fields / And then our private plots" 雨我公田．遂及我私.
51. For other explicit mentions of suicide, see also *Chuci buzhu* 4.146 and 16.292.
52. Knechtges 1982, 1–7.
53. *Hanshu* 87a.3515–21. See also Schimmelpfennig 2004, 126–133.
54. This is a departure from Knechtges's 1982 translation but a return to an earlier published translation; see pages 67–68, n31.
55. Translation adapted from Knechtges 1982, 16.
56. For a more complete discussion of this text, see Schimmelpfennig 2004, 114–118.
57. See the " 'Statutes on Abscondence' (Wang lü 亡律)" in Barbieri-Low and Yates 2015, volume 2, 574–593. For *wang* 亡 in "Parting's Sorrow," see *Chuci buzhu* 1.15 (where it follows *liu* 流, a legal term for refugees; see Barbieri-Low and Yates, 2015, 1411–1412) and 1.19. For other instances in the *Chuci*, see, for example, 3.110, 3.115, 4.132, 4.138, 4.150–51, and 4.158.
58. Falkenhausen 1999, 525; see also Falkenhausen 2006, 198–217, which discusses the modern institutional and political context for such views. For a parallel critique from a literary perspective, see Waters 1985, 12–13. A recent study with a parallel conclusion is Pines 2018, which searches in vain for evidence of local Chu identity in various looted manuscripts from the region. But even for Pines, those parts of the *Verses of Chu* that "display a strongly pronounced Chu identity" (Pines 2018, 24) stand in sharp contrast to the historical writings he considers in his study. On the difficulty of defining Chu, see Cook and Blakeley 1999, 5. See also Tian 2007, 313: "[T]he construction of the North and South as two large cultural terms fundamentally began in the Northern and Southern Dynasties."

5. COMPARING CANONS: THE *SHI* VERSUS THE MASTERS

1. A comprehensive survey of these efforts is beyond the scope of this book. A good introduction is Fischer 2008–2009.
2. See, for example, Brooks and Brooks 1998 and other accretion theories of the *Analects* (discussed at length in Hunter 2017b, 231–245), Pines 2002 (especially page

694 on his use of "traditional chronology"), and Goldin 2018 (which hinges on a timeline of "philosophical innovation[s]" [99] developed on the basis of the Masters Narrative).
3. For an overview, see van Els 2018.
4. Hunter 2017b.
5. On Mohist mottos, see Defoort 2014. After surveying the evidence for Mohist mottos within and outside the *Mozi*, Defoort concludes that there was "relatively little awareness of the ten dogmas in the book *Mozi* itself, and less still in other sources" (368). For a survey of Mozi references and quotations in pre-Han and Han sources, see also Zheng 2006.
6. *Xunzi* 20.381.
7. *Mozi* 3.11 and *Lüshi chunqiu* 2.4/96–97. Including "Suo ran," there are three episodes in the life of Mozi in sources dated to the Warring States and Western Han. The first is an anecdote at *Mozi* 49.480–481 about the crafting of a wooden bird; see *Han Feizi* 32.670 and *Huainanzi* 11.812. The second is the story at *Mozi* 50.482–489 of Mozi's persuasion of the King of Chu 楚王 to abandon his invasion of Song 宋, in the course of which he demonstrates his mastery of the defensive arts in a contest with Gongshu Pan 公輸般; see *Lüshi chunqiu* 21.5/1473 and *Huainanzi* 19.1324–1326. The third is another anecdote featuring Mozi and Master Gongshu 公輸子, with a parallel at *Mozi* 49.474–475; see *Lüshi chunqiu* 19.2/1255.
8. *Zhuangzi* 33.1077, *Shiji* 130.3290, and *Han Feizi* 49.1088.
9. Hunter 2014, 67–68.
10. *Xunzi* 6.94; for a discussion, see Csikszentmihalyi 2004, chapters 2–3.
11. Csikszentmihalyi 2004, 100.
12. *Shiji* 87.2547.
13. *Lüshi chunqiu* 14.8/835 and *Zhuangzi* 20.667–668; *Lüshi chunqiu* 13.3/694 and *Zhuangzi* 19.641–642.
14. *Shiji* 63.2143–44.
15. Klein 2011. See also the response from Liu Xiaogan 2015, 131–132, and the indispensable counter-response from Carine Defoort 2016.
16. Reviewed in Klein 2011, 349–351.
17. *Shiji* 63.2146–2155.
18. See, for example, Van Norden 2011; Nivison 1999, 746; and Li 2013, 206.
19. Ivanhoe and Van Norden 2001, viii.
20. De Bary, Bloom, and Chan 1999, 42.
21. Li 2000, 43: "Confucius and most other thinkers in the Warring States Period (483–221 BCE) were private teachers. Confucius has been considered the most respected private teacher. He left no permanent 'institutional' establishment. Similarly, many other thinkers influenced followers, and in this sense, they were founders of 'schools;' schools of thought, not institutions." For a review of scholarship on "disciples," see Weingarten 2015, 29–31.
22. Raphals 2017. For "schoolmen," see Lewis 1999, chapter 2 ("Writing the Masters").
23. Guo and Wu 2015.
24. Meyer 2015, 272; Goldin 2018, 105.
25. See, for example, Schiappa 1990 and 1999, Ford 1993, Nightingale 1996, and Mccoy 2008.

5. COMPARING CANONS

26. Denecke 2010, 22–24, also acknowledges this difficulty ("most of our contextual evidence about the identity and pursuits of the masters comes from Han times, so we are trapped again in anachronistic visions that postdate the genesis of the texts, sometimes by several centuries") yet still organizes her monograph around the Masters Narrative.
27. *Hanshu* 80.3324–3325.
28. See also Petersen 1995, 47–48: "The expression *zhuzi* appears to have been invented by the late Western Han court librarians ... It is abundantly evidenced from Eastern Han times on, but there exists only one example of the use of the term in Western Han sources, and this example is dubious." Petersen goes on to discuss the single mention in the *Shiji* biography of Jia Yi 賈誼 (201–169 BCE), a chapter of dubious authenticity (Kern 2003, 306–307). See *Shiji* 84.2491. Moreover, the *Hanshu* version of the same passage (47.2221) has *zhujia* 諸家 for *zhuzi* 諸子. An additional mention is at *Xinshu* 8.297; however, the authenticity of this text is also uncertain (see Nylan 1993).
29. In addition to the examples discussed below in this chapter, no figure listed within the intellectual taxonomies of *Xunzi* chapter 6, "Fei shi er zi" 非十二子 (Against the Twelve Men; 6.89–96), and *Zhuangzi* chapter 33, "Tian xia" 天下 (All Under Heaven), is identified with a—*zi* 子 with the exception of Mozi (33.1072–1078). The widely cited notion that use of the -*zi* suffix signaled a student's respect for a teacher doesn't stand up to scrutiny. See Hunter 2017b, 236–237, for a discussion of this assumption in relation to Zengzi's 曾子 supposed authorship of the *Analects*.
30. *Mengzi zhengyi* 1.3. For this reminder, and for the argument that *zi yue* in the *Analects* should be translated "he" or "the man said" instead of "The Master said," see Harbsmeier 1990, 139–140.
31. This is a violation of sinological convention. Durrant, Li, and Schaberg 2016, xxxvii, rightly criticize the conventional translation of *zi* as "count" on the grounds that feudal European terms "convey a sense of hierarchy and orderliness that was not always so clear in the world of early China." However, their translation ("Master") veers too far from the root meaning of *zi*, "son."
32. Summarized in Loewe 2000, 401.
33. *Hanshu* 30.1701.
34. For additional background, see Hunter 2018.
35. Not all entries include information tying a text to a particular historical context; thus, these numbers are very rough. For additional discussion, see Hunter 2018, 766.
36. *Fayan* 12.498. This line is prompted by a question about Mengzi, whom Yang Xiong exempts from *zhuzi* status. See also *Hanshu* 87b.3580.
37. See the preface to his *Fengsu tongyi* (1).
38. See, for example, *Lunheng* 39.610, 82.1160; for a discussion, see Denecke 2010, 78–88.
39. *Shiji* 32.1505; see also *Zuozhuan* Ai 5/1630–1631.
40. *Shiji* 85.2506.
41. The derisive comments attached to some titles suggest that this was a fairly low bar; see, for example, the comment at *Hanshu* 30.1744 describing a *Persuasions of the Yellow Emperor* (*Huangdi shuo* 黃帝說) text as a "blatant forgery" 迂誕依託.
42. For instance, the *Analects* and other sources of Kongzi material were listed after the classics within the more prestigious "Six Arts" (*liu yi* 六藝) division. A number of -*zi* texts dealing with technical topics were included in the divisions devoted to military

treatises, mantic arts, and materia medica. *Hanshu* 30.1756–1759. For a list of authors whose texts are listed within the "Masters" and other divisions of the "Yiwen zhi," and for the instability of *zhuzi*-related bibliographic labels more generally, see Gao 1934, 9–17.
43. Petersen 1995, 17ff.
44. Collins 1998, 137.
45. Collins 1998, 958, n1, and 890–892, also acknowledges this problem. However, he also expresses confidence that "the pattern of eminence in the network chart would not change" with new evidence about ancient intellectuals, and that "[w]ithin broad categories, . . . we already understand the stratification of creativity that actually existed" (892).
46. Collins 1998, 143, and Sivin 1995, 19–28.
47. Collins 1998, 950, n1. These include Feng 1952–1953, Needham 1956, Chan 1963, Schwartz 1985, Kuo 1986, and Graham 1989.
48. Ivanhoe and Van Norden 2001, xvi.
49. Ivanhoe and Van Norden 2001, xi. See also, for example, Graham 1989 on "disputers of the Tao;" Denecke 2010, 34–35 ("One can argue that Masters Literature was born with the first concerted attack of one master against another . . . The history of axial-age thought in China thus begins with ridicule and parody of the opponent."); and Goldin 2020 (who focuses on eight Master texts in part because that "they continually respond to each other's arguments" [1]).
50. Following Wang Xianqian (*Xunzi jijie* 23.436), adding e 惡 as suggested by Yang Liang.
51. For a recent overview, see Tang 2016, 165–166. Kanaya Osamu (1951, 31) and others have argued that the "human nature is bad" slogan in the *Xunzi* is a later interpolation.
52. Graham 1989, 250–251.
53. *Mengzi zhengyi* 15.
54. My thanks to Robert Ashmore (personal communication) for prompting this line of thought.
55. Beecroft (2010, introduction) writes of the panchoric nature of texts written by and for the literate elites of the Warring States period. If an authoritative text was one that spoke to "Panhuaxia" concerns, then elite authors had little incentive to preserve information about their own local contexts.

CONCLUSION: A CLASSIC OF N/ODES

1. Whitehead 1978, 39.
2. For these classic studies, see Caldarelli and Catanzaro 2012, chapters 1–2.
3. The concept of punctualization (or depunctualization) from actor-network theory, which "converts an entire network into a single point or node in another network" (Callon 1991, 153) is useful here. Some uses of the *Shi* might collapse it into a single node; others might connect with the *Shi* tradition at specific points (lines, couplets, poems, etc.).
4. Latour 1996, 5: "A network notion . . . has no a priori order relation; it is not tied to the axiological myth of a top and of a bottom of society; it makes absolutely no

CONCLUSION

assumption whether a specific locus is macro- or micro- and does not modify the tools to study the element 'a' or the element 'b.' "
5. For an overview of centrality concepts, see Newman 2010, chapter 7.
6. Borgatti and Everett 2006, 466.
7. *Zhuangzi* 26.927–928.
8. The lack of named authors in preimperial texts might be one such phenomenon. Given the tenuousness of first-personhood in the *Shi*, authors who tied their texts to the *Shi* might have been reticent to name themselves and speak in their own voices.

BIBLIOGRAPHY

PRIMARY SOURCES

Boshu Laozi jiaozhu 帛書老子校注. By Gao Ming 高明. Beijing: Zhonghua shuju, 1996.
Chuci buzhu 楚辭補註. By Hong Xingzu 洪興祖. Beijing: Zhonghua shuju, 1983.
Chuci jijiao jishi 楚辭集校集釋 (*Chucixue wenku* 楚辭學文庫, vol. 1), ed. Cui Fuzhang 崔富章 and Li Daming 李大明. Wuhan: Hubei jiaoyu, 2003.
Chunqiu Zuozhuan zhu 春秋左傳注. By Yang Bojun 楊伯峻. Beijing: Zhonghua shuju, 1990.
Da Dai Liji jiegu 大戴禮記解詁. By Wang Pinzhen 王聘珍. Beijing: Zhonghua shuju, 1983.
Fayan yishu 法言義疏. By Wang Rongbao 汪榮寶. Beijing: Zhonghua shuju, 1987.
Fengsu tongyi jiaozhu 風俗通義校注. By Wang Liqi 王利器. Beijing: Zhonghua shuju, 1981.
Guanzi jiaozhu 管子校注. By Li Xiangfeng 黎翔鳳. Beijing: Zhonghua shuju. 2004
Guodian chumu zhujian 郭店楚墓竹簡. Ed. Jingmen-shi bowuguan 荊門市博物館. Wenwu chubanshe, 1999.
Han Feizi xin jiaozhu 韓非子新校注. By Chen Qiyou 陳奇猷. Shanghai: Shanghai guji, 2000.
Hanshi waizhuan jishi 韓詩外傳集釋. By Xu Weiyu 許維遹. Beijing: Zhonghua shuju, 1980.
Hanshu 漢書. By Ban Gu 班固. Beijing: Zhonghua shuju, 1962.
Hou Hanshu 後漢書. By Fan Ye 范曄. Beijing: Zhonghua shuju, 1965.
Huainanzi jishi 淮南子集釋. By He Ning 何寧. Beijing: Zhonghua shuju, 1998.
Kongzi jiayu tongjie 孔子家語通解. By Yang Chaoming 楊朝明 and Song Lilin 宋立林. Jinan: Qi Lu shushe, 2009.
Laozi. See *Boshu Laozi jiaozhu.*
Liji zhengyi 禮記正義. Beijing: Beijing daxue, 2000.
Lunheng jiaoshi 論衡校釋. By Huang Hui 黃暉. Beijing: Zhonghua shuju, 1990.

Lunyu zhushu 論語注疏. Beijing: Beijing daxue, 2000.
Lunyu zhuzi suoyin 論語逐字索引. ICS Ancient Texts Concordance Series. Hong Kong: Shangwu yinshuguan, 1995.
Lüshi chunqiu xin jiaoshi 呂氏春秋新校釋. By Chen Qiyou 陳奇猷. Shanghai: Shanghai guji, 2002.
Mao Shi zhengyi 毛詩正義. Beijing: Beijing daxue, 2000.
Mao Shi zhuzi suoyin 毛詩逐字索引 (*A Concordance to the Mao Shi*), ed. Ho Che Wah 何志華. ICS Ancient Text Concordance Series, no. 10. Hong Kong: Shangwu yinshuguan.
Mengzi zhengyi 孟子正義. By Jiao Xun 焦循. Beijing: Zhonghua shuju, 1987.
Mozi jiangu 墨子閒詁. By Sun Yirang 孫詒讓. Beijing: Zhonghua shuju, 2001.
Quan Han Wen 全漢文. In *Quan Shanggu Sandai Qin Han Sanguo Liuchao wen* 全上古三代秦漢三國六朝文, compiled by Yan Kejun 嚴可均, pp. 125–470. Beijing: Zhonghua shuju. 1958.
Shangshu zhengyi 尚書正義. Beijing: Beijing daxue, 2000
Shiji 史記. Beijing: Zhonghua, 1959.
Shisan jing zhushu 十三經注疏. Ed. Ruan Yuan 阮元. Beijing: Zhonghua shuju, 1980.
Shuiyuan jiaozheng 說苑校證. By Xiang Zonglu 向宗魯. Beijing: Zhonghua shuju, 1987.
Wenxuan 文選. 6 vols. Compiled by Xiao Tong 蕭統, with commentary by Li Shan 李善. Shanghai: Shanghai guji, 1986.
Xunzi jijie 荀子集解. By Wang Xianqian 王先謙. Beijing: Zhonghua shuju, 1988.
Zhouli zhushu 周禮注疏. Beijing: Beijing daxue, 2000.
Zhouyi zhengyi 周易正義. Beijing: Beijing daxue. 2000.
Zhuangzi jishi 莊子集釋. By Guo Qingfan 郭慶藩. Beijing: Zhonghua shuju, 1961.
Zuozhuan. See *Chunqiu Zuozhuan zhu*.

SECONDARY SOURCES

Allan, Sarah. 1997. *The Way of Water and the Sprouts of Virtue*. Albany: SUNY Press.
———. 2003. "The Great One, Water, and the *Laozi*: New Light from Guodian." *T'oung Pao* 89: 237–285.
Allen, Joseph R. 1996. "Postface: A Literary History of the *Shi jing*." In Arthur Waley, *The Book of Songs*, edited by Joseph R. Allen, pp. 336–383. New York: Grove.
Assmann, Aleida. 1994. "Wholesome Knowledge: Concepts of Wisdom in a Historical and Cross-Cultural Perspective." In *Life-Span Development and Behavior*, vol. 12, edited by David L. Featherman, Richard M. Lerner, and Marion Perlmutter, pp. 187–224. Hillsdale, N.J.: Lawrence Erlbaum.
Assmann, Jan. 1992. *Das kulturelle Gedächtnis: Schrift, Erinnerung und politische Identität in frühen Hochkulturen*. Munich: C. H. Beck.
Barbieri-Low, Anthony J. 2017 (April 22). "The Context and Interpretation of Excavated and Unprovenanced Texts from Early China and Ancient Egypt," a paper presented at the conference "Methodological Perspectives for the Study of Ancient Texts" at Renmin University, Beijing.
Barbieri-Low, Anthony J., and Robin D. S. Yates. 2015. *Law, State, and Society in Early Imperial China: A Study with Critical Edition and Translation of the Legal Texts from Zhangjiashan Tomb no. 247*. 2 vols. Leiden: Brill.

BIBLIOGRAPHY

Bauer, Wolfgang. 1990. *Das Antlitz Chinas: Die Autobiographische Selbstdarstellung in Der Chinesischen Literatur Von Ihren Anfängen Bis Heute*. Munich: Hanser.

Beecroft, Alexander. 2010. *Authorship and Cultural Identity in Early Greece and China: Patterns of Literary Circulation*. Cambridge: Cambridge University Press.

Boltz, William G. 2015. "Binomes," in *Encyclopedia of Chinese Language and Linguistics*, ed. Rint Sybesma. Consulted online on August 13, 2019, http://dx.doi.org/10.1163/2210-7363_ecll_COM_00000036. Leiden: Brill.

Bo Mou, ed. 2009. *History of Chinese Philosophy*. Routledge History of World Philosophies, vol. 3. London: Routledge.

Borgatti, Stephen P., and Martin G. Everett. 2006. "A Graph-Theoretic Perspective on Centrality." *Social Networks* 28: 466–484.

Brindley, Erica. 2013. "The Polarization of the Concepts 'Si' (Private Interest) and 'Gong' (Public Interest) in Early Chinese Thought." *Asia Major* Third Series 26, no. 2: 1–31.

Brooks, E. Bruce, and A. Taeko Brooks. 1998. *The Original "Analects": Sayings of Confucius and His Successors, 0479–0249*. New York: Columbia University Press.

Caldarelli, Guido, and Michele Catanzaro. 2012. *Networks: A Very Short Introduction*. Oxford: Oxford University Press.

Callon, Michel. 1991. "Techno-Economic Networks and Irreversibility." In Law, John (ed.), *A Sociology of Monsters: Essays on Power, Technology and Domination*, pp. 132–164. London: Routledge.

Chan Hung Kan 陳雄根 and Ho Che Wah 何志華, eds. 2003. *Xian Qin Liang Han dianji yin "Shangshu" xiliao huibian* 先秦兩漢典籍引《尚書》資料彙編. Hong Kong: Chinese University Press.

Chan, Wing-Tsit. 1963. *A Sourcebook in Chinese Philosophy*. Princeton: Princeton University Press.

Chen Zhi. 2007. *The Shaping of the* Book of Songs: *From Ritualization to Secularization*. Sankt Augustin, Germany: Institut Monumenta Serica.

Chen Zhi and Nicholas M. Williams. 2018. "The *Shijing*: The Collection of Three Hundred." In *The Homeric Epics and the Chinese* Book of Songs, edited by Fritz-Heiner Mutschler, pp. 255–282. Newcastle upon Tyne: Cambridge Scholars Publishing.

Collins, Randall. 1998. *The Sociology of Philosophies: A Global Theory of Intellectual Change*. Cambridge, Mass.: The Belknap Press of Harvard University Press.

Cook, Constance A. 2009. "Ancestor Worship During the Eastern Zhou." In *Early Chinese Religion, Part One: Shang through Han (1250 BC–220 AD)*, edited by John Lagerwey and Marc Kalinowski, pp. 237–279. Leiden: Brill.

——. 2017. *Ancestors, Kings, and the Dao*. Cambridge, Mass.: Harvard University Asia Center.

Cook, Constance A., and Barry B. Blakeley. 1999. "Introduction." In *Defining Chu: Image and Reality in Ancient China*, edited by Constance A. Cook and John S. Major. Honolulu: University of Hawai'i Press.

Cook, Scott Bradley. 2002. "The Lüshi chunqiu and the Resolution of Philosophical Dissonance." *Harvard Journal of Asiatic Studies* 62, no. 2: 307–345.

——. 2012. *The Bamboo Texts of Guodian: A Study & Complete Translation*. 2 vols. Ithaca: Cornell University Press.

Cook, Scott Bradley (as Gu Shikao 顧史考). 2014. "Qinghua jian 'Zhou gong zhi qinwu' ji *Zhou song* zhi xingcheng shi-tan" 清華簡〈周公之琴舞〉及《周頌》之形成試

探, in *Disanjie Zhongguo gudian wen xianxue guoji xueshu yantaohui lunwenji* 第三屆中國古典文獻學國際學術研討會論文集, edited by Lin Boqian 林伯謙, pp. 83–99. Taipei: Dongwu daxue.

Csikszentmihalyi, Mark. 2004. *Material Virtue: Ethics and the Body in Early China*. Leiden: Brill.

Csikszentmihalyi, Mark, and Michael Nylan. 2003. "Constructing Lineages and Inventing Traditions Through Exemplary Figures in Early China." *T'oung Pao* 89: 59–99.

Culler, Jonathan D. 1997. *Literary Theory: A Very Short Introduction*. Oxford: Oxford University Press.

De Bary, William Theodore, Irene Bloom, and Wing-tsit Chan, ed. 1999. *Sources of Chinese Tradition*. 2nd ed. New York: Columbia University Press.

Defoort, Carine. 2014. "Do the Ten Mohist Theses Represent Mozi's Thought? Reading the Masters with a Focus on Mottos." *Bulletin of the School of Oriental and African Studies* 77, no. 2: 337–370.

———. 2016. "Mental Fasting in the Study of Chinese Philosophy: Liu Xiaogan Versus Esther Klein." *Problemos* supplemental issue (January): 9–23.

Deleuze, Gilles, and Felix Guattari (trans. Brian Massumi). 1987. *A Thousand Plateaus: Capitalism and Schizophrenia*. Minneapolis: University of Minnesota Press.

Denecke, Wiebke. 2010 *The Dynamics of Masters Literature: Early Chinese Thought from Confucius to Han Feizi*. Boston: Harvard University Asia Center.

Despres, C. 1991. 'The Meaning of Home: Literature Review and Directions for Future Research and Theoretical Development." *Journal of Architectural and Planning Research* 8, no. 2: 96–114.

Dirlik, Arif. 2009 (November 1–3). "Guoxue/National Learning in the Age of Global Modernity," a paper presented at the conference "Qinghua guoxue yanjiuyuan de jingshen" 清華國學研究院的精神 at Qinghua University, Beijing.

Dubs, Homer H. 1938. *The History of the Former Han Dynasty, by Pan Ku*. Vol. 1. Baltimore, Md.: Waverly Press.

Durrant, Stephen W. 1995. *The Cloudy Mirror: Tension and Conflict in the Writings of Sima Qian*. Albany: SUNY Press.

Durrant, Stephen W., Wai-yee Li, and David Schaberg. 2016. *Zuo Tradition / Zuozhuan* 左傳: *Commentary on the "Spring and Autumn Annals."* 3 vols. Seattle: University of Washington Press.

Falkenhausen, Lothar von. 1999. "The Waning of the Bronze Age: Material Culture and Social Developments, 770–481 B.C." In *The Cambridge History of Ancient China*, edited by Michael Loewe and Edward L. Shaughnessy, pp. 450–544. Cambridge: Cambridge University Press.

———. 2006. "The Regionalist Paradigm in Chinese Archaeology." In *Nationalism, Politics, and the Practice of Archaeology*, edited by Philip L. Kohl and Clare Fawcett, pp. 198–217. Cambridge: Cambridge University Press.

Feng Youlan. 1952–1953. *A History of Chinese Philosophy*. 2 vols. Princeton: Princeton University Press.

——— (trans. Derk Bodde). 1997 (rpt.). *A Short History of Chinese Philosophy*. New York: Free Press.

Fischer, Paul. 2008–2009. "Authentication Studies (辨偽學) Methodology and the Polymorphous Text Paradigm." *Early China* 32: 1–43.

Ford, Andrew. 1993. "Platonic Insults: Sophistic." *Common Knowledge* 2: 33–48.

BIBLIOGRAPHY

Fuller, Michael. 1993. "Pursuing the Complete Bamboo in the Breast." *Harvard Journal of Asiatic Studies* 53, no. 1: 5–23.
Fu Sinian 傅斯年. 2004 (rpt.). *Shijing jiangyi gao* 詩經講義稿. In *Zhongguo gudai wenxue shi jiangyi* 中國古代文學史講義, pp. 15–34. Beijing: Zhongguo renmin daxue.
Galambos, Imre. 2006. *Orthography of Early Chinese Writing*. Budapest: Department of East Asian Studies, ELTE, 2006.
Gao Weichang 高維昌. 1934. *Zhou-Qin zhuzi gailun* 周秦諸子概論. Shanghai: Shangwu yinshuguan.
Ge Zhaoguang. 2014. *An Intellectual History of China*. Translated by Michael S. Duke and Josephine Chiu-Duke. Leiden: Brill.
Gibson, John, ed. 2015. *The Philosophy of Poetry*. Oxford: Oxford University Press.
Giles, Herbert Allen. 1901. *A History of Chinese Literature*. London: Heinemann.
Goldin, Paul Rakita. 2011. *Confucianism*. Durham: Acumen.
——. 2013. "*Heng xian* and the Problem of Studying Looted Artifacts." *Dao* 12: 153–60.
——. 2018. "Confucius and His Disciples in the *Lunyu*: The Basis for the Traditional View." In *Confucius and the* Analects *Revisited: New Perspectives on Composition, Dating, and Authorship*, edited by Michael Hunter and Martin Kern, pp. 92–115. Leiden: Brill.
——. 2020. *The Art of Chinese Philosophy: Eight Classical Texts and How to Read Them*. Princeton, N.J.: Princeton University Press.
Graham, A. C. 1989. *Disputers of the Tao: Philosophical Argument in Ancient China*. La Salle, Ill.: Open Court.
Granet, Marcel (trans. E. D. Edwards). 1932. *Festivals and Songs of Ancient China*. London: George Routledge.
Gu Jiegang 顧頡剛. 1931. "Shijing zai Chunqiu Zhanguo jiande diwei" 《詩經》在春秋戰國間的地位. In *Gushi bian* 古史辨, vol. 3, edited by Gu Jiegang, Luo Genze 羅根澤, et al., pp. 309–367. Peiping: Peiping pushe.
——. 1977. *Shilin zashi chubian* 史林雜識初編. Beijing: Zhonghua shuju.
Guo Qiyong 郭齊勇 and Wu Genyou 吳根友. 2015. *Zhuzi xue tonglun* 諸子學通論. Beijing: Shangwu yinshuguan.
Hall, David L., and Roger T. Ames. 1987. *Thinking Through Confucius*. Albany: SUNY Press.
Hansen, Chad. 1992. *A Daoist Theory of Chinese Thought: A Philosophical Interpretation*. New York; Oxford: Oxford University Press.
——. 2017. "Daoism," in *The Stanford Encyclopedia of Philosophy* (Spring 2017 Edition), edited by Edward N. Zalta, https://plato.stanford.edu/archives/spr2017/entries/daoism/.
Harbsmeier, Christoph. 1990. "Confucius Ridens: Humor in the *Analects*." *Harvard Journal of Asiatic Studies* 50, no. 1:131–161.
Hawkes, David. 1974 "The Quest of the Goddess," reprinted in *Studies in Chinese Literary Genres*, edited by Cyril Birch, pp. 42–68. Berkeley: University of California Press.
——. 1985. *The Songs of the South*. Harmondsworth: Penguin Books.
Ho Che Wah 何志華 and Chan Hung Kan 陳雄根, eds. 2004. *Xian Qin Liang Han dianji yin "Shijing" xiliao huibian* 先秦兩漢典籍引《詩經》資料彙編. Hong Kong: Chinese University Press.
Hu Shih. 2013. *English Writings of Hu Shih, vol.2: Chinese Philosophy and Intellectual History*, edited by Chih-P'ing Chou. Berlin: Springer.

Hunter, Michael. 2014. "Did Mencius Know the *Analects*?" *T'oung Pao* 100: 33–79.
———. 2017a. "Against (Uninformed) Idleness: Situating the Didacticism of 'Wu yi' 無逸." In *Origins of Chinese Political Philosophy: Studies in the Composition and Thought of the* Shangshu, edited by Dirk Meyer and Martin Kern, pp. 393–415. Leiden: Brill.
———. 2017b. *Confucius Beyond the* Analects. Leiden: Brill.
———. 2018. "The "Yiwen zhi" 藝文志 (Treatise on Arts and Letters) Bibliography in its Own Context." *Journal of the American Oriental Society* 138, no. 4: 763–780.
———. 2019. "To Leave or Not to Leave: The *Chu ci* 楚辭 (*Verses of Chu*) as Response to the *Shi jing* 詩經 (*Classic of Odes*). *Early China* 2019: 1–36.
Ivanhoe, P. J., and Bryan W. Van Norden. 2001. *Readings in Classical Chinese Philosophy*. New York: Seven Bridges Press.
Jaspers, Karl (trans. Michael Bullock). 1953. *The Origin and Goal of History*. New Haven, Conn.: Yale University Press.
Jones, Nicholas. 2016. "Correlative Reasoning About Water in *Mengzi* 6A2." *Dao* 15:193–207.
Kanaya Osamu 金谷治. 1951. "*Junshi* no bunkenteki kenkyū" 荀子の文獻的研究. *Nihon Gakushiin Kiyō* 9.1: 9–33.
Karlgren, Bernhard. 1942. "Glosses on the Kuo feng Odes." *Bulletin of the Museum of Far Eastern Antiquities* 14: 71–247.
———. 1964. *Glosses on the Book of Odes*. Stockholm: Museum of Far Eastern Antiquities.
Kemp, Barry J. 1989. *Ancient Egypt: Anatomy of a Civilization*. London: Routledge.
Kern, Martin. 2000a. "*Shi jing* Songs as Performance Texts: A Case Study of 'Chu ci' ('Thorny Caltrop')." *Early China* 25: 49–111.
———. 2000b. *The Stele Inscriptions of Ch'in Shih-Huang: Text and Ritual in Early Chinese Imperial Representation*. New Haven, Conn.: American Oriental Society.
———. 2002. "Methodological Reflections on the Analysis of Textual Variants and the Modes of Manuscript Production in Early China." *Journal of East Asian Archaeology* 4, nos. 1–4: 143–181.
———. 2003. "The 'Biography of Sima Xiangru' and the Question of the Fu in Sima Qian's *Shiji*." *Journal of the American Oriental Society* 123, no. 2: 303–16.
———. 2005. "The *Odes* in Excavated Manuscripts." In *Text and Ritual in Early China*, edited by Martin Kern, pp. 149–193. Seattle: University of Washington Press.
———. 2007a. "Beyond the *Mao Odes*: *Shijing* Reception in Early Medieval China. *Journal of the American Oriental Society* 127, no. 2: 131–142.
———. 2007b. "Excavated Manuscripts and Their Socratic Pleasures: Newly Discovered Challenges in Reading the 'Airs of the States.'" *Asiatisches Studien/Études Asiatiques* 61, no. 3: 775–793.
———. 2009. "Bronze Inscriptions, the *Shijing* and the *Shangshu*: The Evolution of the Ancestral Sacrifice During the Western Zhou." In *Early Chinese Religion, Part One: Shang Through Han (1250 BC–220 AD)*, edited by John Lagerwey and Marc Kalinowski, pp. 143–200. Leiden: Brill.
———. 2010. "Lost in Tradition: The *Classic of Poetry* We Did Not Know." *Hsiang Lectures on Chinese Poetry*, vol. 5., edited by Grace S. Fong. Centre for East Asian Research, McGill University.
———. 2011. "Early Chinese Literature, Beginnings Through Western Han." In *Cambridge History of Chinese Literature*, vol. 1, edited by Stephen Owen, pp. 1–115. Cambridge: Cambridge University Press.

BIBLIOGRAPHY

———. 2018. "The Formation of the *Classic of Poetry*." In *The Homeric Epics and the Chinese* Book of Songs, edited by Fritz-Heiner Mutschler, pp. 39–71. Newcastle upon Tyne: Cambridge Scholars Publishing.
———. 2019. " 'Xi shuai' 蟋蟀 ('Cricket') and its Consequences: Issues in Early Chinese Poetry and Textual Studies." *Early China*: 1–36.
Klein, Esther. 2011. "Were There 'Inner Chapters' in the Warring States? A New Examination of Evidence About the *Zhuangzi*." *T'oung Pao* 96: 299–368.
———. 2019. *Reading Sima Qian from Han to Song: The Father of History in Pre-Modern China*. Leiden: Brill.
Knechtges, David R. 1982. "The *Han Shu* Biography of Yang Xiong (53 B.C.–A.D. 18)." Occasional Paper No. 14, Center for Asian Studies, Arizona State University.
———. 1987. *Wen xuan, or Selections of Refined Literature*, vol. 2. Princeton: Princeton University Press.
———. 1996. *Wen xuan, or Selections of Refined Literature*, vol. 3. Princeton: Princeton University Press.
Knechtges, David R., and Jerry Swanson. 1970–1971. "Seven Stimuli for the Prince: The *Ch'i-fa* of Mei Cheng." *Monumenta Serica* 29: 99–116.
Knoblock, John, and Jeffrey Riegel. 2000. *The Annals of Lü Buwei: A Complete Translation and Study*. Stanford: Stanford University Press.
Kuo, You-Yuh. 1986. "The Growth and Decline of Chinese Philosophical Genius." *Chinese Journal of Philosophy* 28: 81–91.
Lai, Karyn. 2008. *An Introduction to Chinese Philosophy*. New York: Cambridge University Press.
Latour, Bruno. 1996. "On Actor-Network Theory: A Few Clarifications." *Soziale Welt* 47: 369–381.
Lee, Haiyan. 2005. "Tears That Crumbled the Great Wall: The Archaeology of Feeling in the May Fourth Movement." *The Journal of Asian Studies* 64, no. 1: 35–65.
Lei Jinhao 雷晉豪. 2011. *Zhou dao: fengjian shidai de guandao* 周道：封建時代的官道. Beijing: Shehui kexue wenxian chubanshe.
Lewis, Mark Edward. 1999. *Writing and Authority in Early China*. Albany: SUNY Press.
Li Feng. 2013. *Early China: a Social and Cultural History*. Cambridge: Cambridge University Press.
Li Hongqi. 2000. *Education in Traditional China: A History*. Leiden: Brill.
Li Wai-yee. 2016. "The Letter to Ren An and Authorship in the Chinese Tradition." In *The Letter to Ren An and Sima Qian's Legacy*, edited by Stephen W. Durrant, Wai-yee Li, Michael Nylan, and Hans Van Ess, pp. 96–123. Seattle: University of Washington Press.
———. 2018. "Recurrent Concerns and Typical Scenes in the *Book of Songs*." In *The Homeric Epics and the Chinese* Book of Songs, edited by Fritz-Heiner Mutschler, pp. 329–358. Newcastle upon Tyne: Cambridge Scholars Publishing.
Li Xueqin 李學勤. 2008. "Comments on the Poetry (Shilun) and the Poetry (Shi)." *Contemporary Chinese Thought* 39, no. 4: 18–29.
Liu, JeeLoo. 2006. *An Introduction to Chinese Philosophy: From Ancient Philosophy to Chinese Buddhism*. Malden, Masss.; Oxford: Blackwell.
Liu Xiaogan. 2015. "Textual Issues in the *Zhuangzi*." In *Dao Companion to Chinese Philosophy*, edited by Liu Xiaogan, pp. 129–158. Springer: Dordrecht.
Loewe, Michael. 2000. *A Biographical Dictionary of the Qin, Former Han and Xin Periods (221 BC–AD 24)*. Leiden: Brill.

Ma Ruichen 馬瑞辰. 1989 (rpt.). *Mao shi zhuan jian tongshi* 毛詩傳箋通釋. Beijing: Zhonghua shuju.

Makeham, John. 2012. *Learning to Emulate the Wise: The Genesis of Chinese Philosophy As an Academic Discipline in Twentieth-Century China*. Hong Kong: Chinese University Press.

Matt, Susan J. 2011. *Homesickness: An American History*. New York: Oxford University Press.

Mattos, Gilbert L. 1988. *The Stone Drums of Chʻin*. Nettetal: Steyler.

Mccoy, Marina. 2008. *Plato on the Rhetoric of Philosophers and Sophists*. Cambridge: Cambridge University Press.

Meyer, Andrew. 2015. "What Made Mo Di a Master? Exploring the Construction of a Category in Warring States Sources." *T'oung Pao* 101, nos. 4–5: 271–297.

Miller, Paul Allen. 1994. *Lyric Texts and Lyric Consciousness: The Birth of a Genre from Archaic Greece to Augustan Rome*. London: Routledge.

Moretti, Franco. 2000. "Conjectures on World Literature." *New Left Review* 1 (January–February): 54–68.

——. 2005. *Graphs, Maps, Trees: Abstract Models for a Literary History*. London: Verso.

Mutschler, Fritz-Heiner, ed. 2018. *The Homeric Epics and the Chinese Book of Songs*. Newcastle upon Tyne: Cambridge Scholars Publishing.

Nagy, Gregory. 1990. *Pindar's Homer: The Lyric Possession of an Epic Past*. Baltimore, Md.: Johns Hopkins University Press.

Needham, Joseph. 1956. *Science and Civilization in China, Vol. 2: History of Scientific Thought*. Cambridge: Cambridge University Press.

Newman, Mark. 2010. *Networks: An Introduction*. Oxford: Oxford University Press.

Nightingale, Andrea Wilson. 1996. *Genres in Dialogue: Plato and the Construct of Philosophy*. Cambridge: Cambridge University Press.

Nivison, David Shepherd. 1999. "The Classical Philosophical Writings." In *The Cambridge History of Ancient China: From the Origins of Civilization to 221 B.C*, edited by Michael Loewe and Edward L Shaughnessy, pp. 745–812. Cambridge: Cambridge University Press.

Nugent, Christopher M. B. 2010. *Manifest in Words, Written on Paper: Producing and Circulating Poetry in Tang Dynasty China*. Boston: Harvard University Asia Center.

Nylan, Michael. 1993. "Hsin shu 新書." In *Early Chinese Texts: A Bibliographic Guide*, edited by Michael Loewe, pp. 166–168. The Society for the Study of Early China and The Institute of East Asian Studies, University of California, Berkeley.

——. 2001. *The Five "Confucian" Classics*. New Haven, Conn.: Yale University Press.

——. 2016a. "Academic Silos, or 'What I Wish Philosophers Knew about Early History in China.' " In *The Bloomsbury Research Handbook of Chinese Philosophy Methodologies*, edited by Sor-hoon Tan, pp. 91–114. London: Bloomsbury Academic.

——. 2016b. "Friendship and Other Tropes in the Letter to Ren An." In *The Letter to Ren An and Sima Qian's Legacy*, edited by Stephen W. Durrant, Wai-yee Li, Michael Nylan, and Hans Van Ess, pp. 71–95. Seattle: University of Washington Press.

Nylan, Michael, and Thomas A. Wilson. 2010. *Lives of Confucius: Civilization's Greatest Sage Through the Ages*. New York: London: Doubleday.

Owen, Stephen. 1981. *The Great Age of Chinese Poetry: The High T'Ang*. New Haven, Conn.: Yale University Press.

——. 1992. *Readings in Chinese Literary Thought*. Cambridge, Mass.: Council on East Asian Studies, Harvard University.

———. 1996a. *An Anthology of Chinese Literature: Beginnings to 1911*. New York: Norton.
———. 1996b. "Foreword." In Arthur Waley, *The Book of Songs*, edited by Joseph R. Allen, pp. xii–xxv. New York: Grove Press.
———. 2001. "Reproduction in the *Shijing* (*Classic of Poetry*)." *Harvard Journal of Asiatic Studies* 61, no. 2: 287–315.
———. 2006. *The Making of Early Chinese Classical Poetry*. Cambridge, Mass.: Harvard University Asia Center.
Pan Wuyun. 2015. "Xiéshēng 諧聲 (Phonetic Series)." In *Encyclopedia of Chinese Language and Linguistics*, General Editor Rint Sybesma. Consulted online on August 13, 2019, http://dx.doi.org/10.1163/2210-7363_ecll_COM_00000467. Leiden: Brill.
Petersen, Jens Østergard. 1995. "Which Books *Did* the First Emperor of Ch'in Burn? On the Meaning of *Pai Chia* in Early Chinese Sources." *Monumenta Serica* 43: 1–52.
Peterson, Willard J. 1988. "Squares and Circles: Mapping the History of Chinese Thought." *Journal of the History of Ideas* 49, no. 1: 47–60.
Pines, Yuri. 2002. "Lexical Changes in Zhanguo Texts." *Journal of the American Oriental Society* 122, no. 4: 691–705.
———. 2018. "Chu Identity As Seen from Its Manuscripts: A Reevaluation," *Journal of Chinese History* 2: 1–26.
Puett, Michael J. 2001. *The Ambivalence of Creation: Debates Concerning Innovation and Artifice in Early China*. Stanford, Calif.: Stanford University Press.
Puett, Michael J., and Christine Gross-Loh. 2016. *The Path: A New Way to Think About Everything*. New York: Simon & Schuster.
Qu Wanli 屈萬里. 1952. "*Shi* sanbai pian chengyu lingshi" 詩三百篇成語零釋. *Taiwan wenshi zhexue bao* 台灣文史哲學史 1952, no. 4: 2–4.
Raphals, Lisa. 2017. "Science and Chinese Philosophy." *The Stanford Encyclopedia of Philosophy* (Spring 2017 Edition), edited by Edward N. Zalta. https://plato.stanford.edu/archives/spr2017/entries/chinese-phil-science/.
Richardson, Joanna. 2019. *Place and Identity: The Performance of Home*. London: Routledge.
Richter, Matthias L. 2013. *The Embodied Text: Establishing Textual Identity in Early Chinese Manuscripts*. Leiden: Brill.
Rickett, W. Allyn. 1998. *Guanzi* 管子: *Political, Economic, and Philosophical Essays from Early China*, vol. 2. Princeton: Princeton University Press.
Riegel, Jeffrey. 1986. "Poetry and the Legend of Confucius' Exile." *Journal of the American Oriental Society* 106, 13–22.
Rusk, Bruce. 2012. *Critics and Commentators: The Book of Poems As Classic and Literature*. Boston: Harvard University Asia Center.
Saussy, Haun. 1993. *The Problem of a Chinese Aesthetic*. Stanford, Calif: Stanford University Press.
———. 1997a. "The Prestige of Writing: *Wen*, Letter, Picture, Image, Ideography." *Sino-Platonic Papers* 75, 1–40.
———. 1997b. "Repetition, Rhyme, and Exchange in the *Book of Odes*." *Harvard Journal of Asiatic Studies* 57, no. 2: 519–542.
———. 2016. *The Ethnography of Rhythm: Orality and Its Technologies*. New York: Fordham University Press.
Schaberg, David. 1999. "Song and the Historical Imagination in Early China." *Harvard Journal of Asiatic Studies* 59, no. 2: 305–361.

——. 2001. *A Patterned Past: Form and Thought in Early Chinese Historiography*. Cambridge, Mass.: Harvard University Asia Center.

——. 2018. "Cultural Roles of the *Book of Songs*: Inherited Language, Education, and the Problem of Composition." In *The Homeric Epics and the Chinese Book of Songs*, edited by Fritz-Heiner Mutschler, pp. 185–206.

Schiappa, Edward. 1990. "Did Plato Coin *Rhetorikē*?" *The American Journal of Philology* 111, 457–470.

——. 1999. *The Beginnings of Rhetorical Theory in Classical Greece*. New Haven, Conn.: Yale University Press.

Schimmelpfennig, Michael. 2004. "The Quest for a Classic: Wang Yi and the Exegetical Prehistory of his Commentary to the 'Songs of Chu.'" *Early China* 29, 111–62.

Schneider, Laurence A. 1971. *Ku Chieh-Kang and China's New History: Nationalism and the Quest for Alternative Traditions*. Berkeley: University of California Press.

Schuessler, Axel. 2009. *Minimal Old Chinese and Later Han Chinese: A Companion to Grammata Serica Recensa*. Honolulu: University of Hawai'i Press.

Schwartz, Benjamin I. 1985. *The World of Thought in Ancient China*. Cambridge, Mass.: The Belknap Press of the Harvard University Press.

Scott, James C. 2017. *Against the Grain: A Deep History of the Earliest States*. New Haven, Conn.: Yale University Press.

Shaughnessy, Edward L.
——. 2006. *Rewriting Early Chinese Texts*. Albany: SUNY Press.
——. 2015. "Unearthed Documents and the Question of the Oral Versus Written Nature of the *Classic of Poetry*." *Harvard Journal of Asiatic Studies* 75, no. 2: 331–375.

Shen, Vincent. 2013. "Wisdom and Hermeneutics of Poetry in Classical Confucianism." In *Dao Companion to Classical Confucian Philosophy*, edited by Shen Qingsong, pp. 245–262. Dordrecht: Springer.

Sivin, Nathan. 1995. "The Myth of the Naturalists." In *Medicine, Philosophy, and Religion in Ancient China: Researches and Reflections*, by Nathan Sivin, chap. 4, pp. 1–33. Aldershot: Variorum.

Slingerland, Edward G. 2003. *Effortless Action: Wu-Wei As Conceptual Metaphor and Spiritual Ideal in Early China*. New York: Oxford University Press.

——. 2019. *Mind and Body in Early China: Beyond Orientalism and the Myth of Holism*. Oxford: Oxford University Press.

Sukhu, Gopal. 2012. *The Shaman and the Heresiarch*. Albany: SUNY Press.

Sun, Cecile Chu-chin. 2011. *The Poetics of Repetition in English and Chinese Lyric Poetry*. Chicago, Ill.: University of Chicago Press.

Tang, Siufu. 2016. "*Xing* and Xunzi's Understanding of Our Nature." In *Dao Companion to Xunzi*, edited by Eric L. Hutton, pp. 165–166. Dordrecht: Springer.

Tian Xiaofei. 2007. *Beacon Fire and Shooting Star: The Literary Culture of the Liang (502–557)*. Cambridge, Mass.: Harvard University Asia Center.

van Els, Paul. 2018. "Confucius's Sayings Entombed: On Two Han Dynasty Bamboo *Lunyu* Manuscripts." In *Confucius and the* Analects *Revisited: New Perspectives on Composition, Dating, and Authorship*, edited by Michael Hunter and Martin Kern, pp. 152–186. Leiden: Brill.

Van Norden, Bryan W. 2011. *Introduction to Classical Chinese Philosophy*. Indianapolis, Ind.: Hackett.

Waley, Arthur. 1937. *The Book of Songs*. London: Allen & Unwin, Ltd.

———. *Three Ways of Thought in Ancient China*. Stanford, Calif.: Stanford University Press.

———. 1996. *The Book of Songs*, edited with additional translations by Joseph R. Allen. New York: Grove Press.

Walker, Galal. 1982. "Toward a Formal History of the *Chu ci*," Ph.D. dissertation, Cornell University.

Wang, C. H. 1988. *From Ritual to Allegory: Seven Essays in Early Chinese Poetry*. Hong Kong: Chinese University Press.

Wang, Ping, and Nicholas Williams (eds.). 2015. "Southland as Symbol." In *Southern Identity and Southern Estrangement in Medieval Chinese Poetry*. Hong Kong: Hong Kong University Press, 1–18.

Wang Xianqian 王先謙. 1987 (rpt.). *Shi sanjia yishu* 詩三家義集疏. Beijing: Zhonghua shuju.

Waters, Geoffrey. 1985. *Three Elegies of Ch'u: An Introduction to the Traditional Interpretation of the Ch'u Tz'u*. Madison: University of Wisconsin Press, 12–14.

Watson, Burton. 1958. *Ssu-ma Ch'ien, Grand Historian of China*. New York: Columbia University Press.

———. 1961. *Records of the Grand Historian of China*. New York: Columbia University Press.

Weingarten, Oliver. 2015. "What Did Disciples Do? *Dizi* 弟子 in Early Chinese Texts." *Harvard Journal of Asiatic Studies* 75, no. 1: 29–75.

Whitehead, Alfred North. 1978. *Process and Reality (Corrected Edition)*. New York: The Free Press.

Xie Jinqing 謝晉青. 1931. *Shijing zhi nüxing de yanjiu* 《詩經》之女性的研究. 4th ed. Shanghai: Shangwu yinshuguan.

Yang Shengnan 楊升南. 1984. "Shuo 'Zhou hang' 'Zhou dao'—Xi Zhou shiqi de jiaotong chutan" 說"周行""周道"—西周時期的交通初探. In *Xi Zhou shi yanjiu* 西周史研究, edited by Renwen zazhi bianji bu 人文雜誌編輯部, pp. 51–66. Xi'an: Shaanxi renmin chubanshe.

Yu, Pauline. 1987. *The Reading of Imagery in the Chinese Poetic Tradition*. Princeton, N.J.: Princeton University Press.

Yuan Xingpei 袁行霈 (trans. Paul White). 2018. *An Outline of Chinese Literature I*. New York: Routledge.

Yuan Xingpei 袁行霈, Xu Jianwei 徐建委, and Cheng Sudong 程蘇東. 2018. *Shijing guofeng xinzhu* 詩經國風新注. Beijing: Zhonghua shuju.

Zhang Fengqian 張丰乾. 2009. *Shijing yu Xian-Qin zhexue* 《詩經》與先秦哲學. Beijing: Beijing daxue chubanshe.

Zhang, Hanmo. 2018. *Authorship and Text-Making in Early China*. Boston: De Gruyter.

Zheng Jiewen 鄭傑文. 2006. *Zhongguo Moxue tongshi* 中國墨學通史 (2 vols.). Beijing: Renmin chubanshe.

Zhu Dongrun 朱東潤. 1957. "Lisao di zuozhe" 離騷底作者, in *Chuci yanjiu lunwen ji* 楚辭研究論文集, edited by Zuojia chubanshe bianjibu, 368–371. Beijing: Zuojia. (Madison: University of Wisconsin Press, 1985), 12–14.

INDEX

"Airs of the States" (Guo feng 國風), 2–3, 6, 24–27, 32–33, 42, 134, 140: difficulties reading, 9, 17–28, 195n33, 198n30; as folk poetry, 7–8; as journey, 36–38; offstage themes in, 38, 82

Allan, Sarah, 101, 105–106, 138

Ames, Roger, 79–80

Analects (*Lunyu* 論語): chronology of, 102, 108–109, 115, 170, 187, 191

—sections cited: 2/2, 35; 3/8, 17–18; 6/23, 103; 7/3, 126–127; 12/4, 127; 12/11, 97; 16/13, 114

ancestor worship, 13, 38–39, 51–52, 60–61, 113–114, 133–135, 139, 174

Annals (*Chunqiu* 春秋), 135, 137, 203n48

Annals of Lü Buwei (*Lüshi chunqiu* 呂氏春秋), 135–137, 170–171

—sections cited: 2.4, 174–175; 3.5, 91–93; 7.5, 99–101; 12.3, 85–88; 14.1, 91–93; postface, 96–97, 115

anxiety. *See you*

Assmann, Aleida, 77–78, 119

Axial Age, 10–11

Balanced Discussions (*Lunheng* 論衡), 177, 185–187

Ban Gu 班固, 140

Beecroft, Alexander, 5

bibliography, 173–179

centrality, 138, 172–179, 191–192

Changes (*Yi* 易), 17, 135, 137, 176, 195n40 : "Commentary to the Appended Phrases" (Xici zhuan 繫辭傳), 129, 132

Chong'er 重耳. *See* Lord Wen of Jin

Classic of Changes. *See* Changes

Classic of Documents. *See* Documents

Classic of Poetry. *See Shijing* or *Shi*

Collins, Randall, 179–182, 190

Commentaries and Sub-Commentaries to the Thirteen Classics (*Shisan jing zhuzhu* 十三經注疏), 29–31

Confucius. *See* Kongzi

connectivity, 84, 179–187, 191–192

Dao De Jing 道德經. *See* Laozi

dao 道 (the Way), 1, 14, 57, 88–94, 178, 192

digital texts, 12, 31

distant reading, 3, 28

Documents (*Shu* 書), 3, 11, 23, 29, 36, 119

—sections cited: "Canon of Shun" (Shun dian 舜典), 5, 36–38; "Great Plan" (Hong fan 洪範), 93–94; "Hounds of Lü" (Lü ao 旅獒), 89

du 獨 (alone, lonely), 57–60, 122–124, 157–158

INDEX

edicts, 84, 95, 129–131, 178
Elder Dai's Ritual Records (*Da Dai Liji* 大戴禮記), 102–103, 109
Exalted Documents. See *Documents*

Family Sayings of Kongzi (*Kongzi jiayu* 孔子家語), 102–103
"Father and mother to the people" (*min zhi fumu* 民之父母), 94–99
filial piety. See *xiao*
Five Classics, 3, 31, 114, 173, 190
Five Kinds of Conduct (*Wu xing* 五行), 27, 124–129, 171
folk literature, 7–8

Gaozi 告子
Garden of Persuasions (*Shuiyuan* 說苑), 102–103, 171
Giles, Herbert, 7
Golden Age, 1, 10–11
Graham, A. C., 185, 191
Grand Scribe's Records (*Shiji* 史記), 170–172
—sections cited: chap. 8, 85–88; chap. 10, 95, 129–131; chap. 32, 177–178; chap. 47, 109–110; chap. 75, 177–178; chap. 84, 141, 166–167; chap. 85, 177–178; chap. 130, 14, 131–138
Granet, Marcel, 7–8
"Great Unity Gives Birth to Water" (*Tai yi sheng shui* 太一生水), 101–102
"Greater Court Songs" (*Da ya* 大雅), 3, 6, 33, 38, 45, 65, 70, 97, 99, 117, 119
Gu Jiegang 顧頡剛, 7–8
Guanzi 管子
—sections cited: chap. 16, 97; chap. 20, 99–101; chap. 49, 127–128, 133; chap. 83, 95–96
gui 歸: and the Way, 88–94; familial versus political, 94–99; in Sima Qian's autobiography, 131–138; in the *Shi*, 13–14, 44–73, 81–82, 189; in the *Verses of Chu*, 141, 145, 157, 159, 164
Guodian 郭店, 101, 114, 171

Hall, David, 79–80
Han Emperor Cheng 漢成帝, 173, 175
Han Emperor Gaozu 漢高祖, 85–88
Han Emperor Jing 漢景帝, 115
Han Emperor Wen 漢文帝, 95, 115, 129–131
Han Emperor Wu 漢武帝, 129–131, 134, 158, 170
Han Feizi 韓非子, 10, 136–137, 170, 172, 182
—sections cited: chap. 49, 97; chaps. 20–21, 115
Han imperial archives, 175–179
Hanshu 漢書. See *History of the Han*
Hawkes, David, 140, 145–146
History of the Han (*Hanshu* 漢書), 6
—sections cited: biography of Yang Xiong 揚雄, 164–166; Liu Yu affair 劉宇, 173–174, 175; 122 BCE edict, 130–131; "Record of Arts and Letters" (Yiwen zhi 藝文志), 6, 175–179
Hu Shih 胡適, 12
Huainanzi 淮南子, 115

immanence, 80
individuation, 8, 13, 57–61, 80, 88, 129, 135, 157
inspection tours (*xun* 巡), 36–38, 89, 108, 133
Isocrates, 173
Ivanhoe, Philip J., 182

Jaspers, Karl, 11
Jia Yi 賈誼, 166–167
jia 家 (family), 133, 138
Jie Zhitui 介之推, 85–88, 137, 141

Karlgren, Bernhard, 8
Kern, Martin, 8–10, 12, 26–28
kineticism (in the *Shi*), 35–44
Kong Yingda 孔穎達, 31
Kongzi 孔子, 1, 10–11, 14, 17, 23, 92, 95, 105, 126–128, 170, 174–175, 182–183, 186, 187, 190–191: as compiler of the *Shi*, 4, 7; as projection of the *Shi*, 108–114; in the "Record of Arts and Letters" bibliography, 176–179; and Sima Qian, 134–138; versus Qu Yuan, 141, 165–166; and water, 102–103. See also *Analects*

Lament for Qu Yuan (*Diao Qu Yuan* 弔屈原), 166–167
Laozi 老子, 1, 10, 14, 83–84, 91, 132–133, 138, 174–175, 179, 182–183, 189, 192: as anti-*Shi*, 114–124; and anxiety, 124–129; chronology of, 114–115, 169–170, 172; and the *Verses of Chu*, 141, 157–158; and water, 101–102, 105
—sections cited: sect. 8, 101; sect. 12, 115–116; sect. 14, 115–116; sect. 16, 118–119; sect. 18, 120–121; sect. 19, 117–118; sect. 20, 121–124; sect. 25, 91; sect. 25, 119; sect. 28, 117; sect. 32, 118–119; sect. 38, 116–117; sect. 40, 117; sect. 47, 116; sect. 57, 116; sect. 65, 120; sect. 66, 101
"Lesser Court Songs" (*Xiao ya* 小雅), 3, 38, 42, 56, 70, 140

INDEX

Liang Qichao 梁啟超, 11
literature (as discipline), 2–8
Liu An 劉安, 140, 157
Liu Xiang 劉向, 145, 157, 159–161, 171, 175
Liu Xiaogan, 115
Liu Xiu 劉歆, 170
Liu Yu 劉宇, 173–174, 175
looted manuscripts, 16
Lord Huan of Qi 齊桓公, 95–96, 155
Lord Wen of Jin 晉文公, 85, 88
Lü Buwei 呂不韋, 135–137, 178
Lu Deming 陸德明, 31
Lu Ji 陸機, 31
lyric poetry, 13

Makeham, John, 11
Mao Shi 毛詩
Mao Shi 毛詩. See Shijing
Masters (zhuzi 諸子), 10–12, 115, 142: dearth of connections among, 179–187; Masters Narrative, 10–12, 15, 115, 168–169, 187–188, 189, 191; relative unimportance of, 172–179, 183; uncertain chronology of, 169–172
Mawangdui 馬王堆, 27, 114, 122, 124, 171
Mei Cheng 枚乘. See Seven Stimuli
Mengzi 孟子, 10, 103, 105, 115, 170, 171–172, 174–175, 179, 182–183, 188: in Xunzi versus for Wang Chong, 183–187
—sections cited: 6A/2, 105–106, 142, 191; 6B/15, 128–129; 6B/2, 93; 7A/2, 185–186
midrange reading, 12, 28–34
Model Sayings (Fayan 法言), 177
Mozi 墨子, 4, 10–11, 94, 105, 170–172, 174, 182–183, 187–188, 191

network theory, 189–192. See also connectivity, centrality
New Culture Movement, 7

Offices of Zhou (Zhou guan 周官), 72
ontology of events, 80
Owen, Stephen, 5–6, 8

philosophy, 2, 5, 9, 10–12, 79–80, 84, 138, 168, 172, 179–183, 187, 189–190
philosophy (as discipline), 2, 5, 10–12, 182–183, 189
Plato, 12, 173
poetics, 12–15, 28

Qin First Emperor 秦始皇, 87, 97, 137, 178–179, 188: stele inscriptions, 36–37, 129–131

Qu Yuan 屈原, 1, 88, 135–138, 139–142, 156–167

Ritual Records (Liji 禮記), 95
Ritual 禮 classic, 3
"Ritual Hymns" (Song 頌), 3, 38, 60–61, 97, 135
Ru 儒, 97, 170, 178,
Ruan Yuan 阮元, 29

Saussy, Haun, 8, 10
Schwartz, Benjamin, 11
Scott, James, 81–82
sedentism, 81–82
Seven Stimuli (Qi fa 七發), 103–106, 146, 175
Shi 詩: centrality within Zhou culture, 5; cultural authority of, 1–2, 5, 23–24, 29, 139–141, 167; introduced, 2–5; kineticism of, 13, 35–44; as multimedia performances, 4; as poetry of disclosure, 5–7; as repertoire, 3–4, 12, 27–34; transmission of, 3–4; variability of, 3–4, 9–10, 12, 17–28. See also Shijing
shi 詩 (as generic term), 4
Shijing 詩經: difficulties reading, 12, 17–31; as folk poetry, 7–8; "Great Preface" (Da xu 大序), 3, 24–25, 54, 79; Mao Shi 毛詩, 3, 18–28, 193–194n5, 196n3; versus Shi, 3
—"Airs of the States" cited: #1, 24–34, 41; #2, 38, 44–45; #3, 54–55, 144–145; #4, 19–20; #7, 33–34, 52–53; #8, 39–40; #9, 200n27; #11, 24; #12, 67; #13, 21, 38; #14, 41, 55–56, 110; #15, 21; #21, 38; #23, 38, 42–43; #26, 68–70, 141; #27, 21; #28, 66–67; #30, 21; #32, 21; #33, 89–90; #35, 21, 67–68; #36, 112; #37, 112; #39, 106–108; #40, 38, 63–64, 137, 141; #41, 21; #44, 39–40; #48, 41; #50, 147–148; #54, 22; #55, 106–108; #57, 18; #58, 67–68, 155; #59, 55–56; #68, 20–21, 54–55; #70, 200n28, 203n55; #71, 33–34, 68; #72, 21; #75, 21; #80, 197n13; #82, 38; #86, 58–59; #88, 44–45; #89, 21, 38; #92, 20–21; #93, 38, 58–59; #94, 38; #100, 38; #101, 21; #102, 204n65; #110, 63; #112, 21; #113, 201n9; #114, 16; #115, 41–42; #116, 20–21; #119, 57–58; #120, 197n13; #121, 98; #122, 21; #124, 54–55, 58–59; #125, 21; #129, 38, 42–43; #131, 65–66; #133, 21, 149; #134, 154; #137, 21; #137–141, 38; #139, 21; #140, 21; #143, 27; #145, 58–59; #146, 197n13; #149, 21; #150,

—"Airs of the States" cited (*continued*) 55–56; #154, 21, 47–48, 59–60; #156, 21, 64, 137, 141; #158, 21; #160, 195n37
—"Lesser Court Songs" cited: #162, 44–45, 89–90; #165, 21; #167, 21, 22; #168, 38, 62–63, 144–146; #171, 20; #172, 51, 202n19; #177, 21; #178, 21, 152–153; #181, 22, 63, 151; #188, 41; #189, 68; #191, 71–73, 111, 149–150; #191–200, 75; #192, 21, 57–58, 75–77, 131, 148–149, 151; #193, 21, 41, 57–58, 111, 122–123; #194, 70, 75–77, 201n15, 204n76; #195, 75–77, 90–91; #197, 41, 56–57, 90, 113–114, 122–123; #198, 72–73; #201, 21, 113–114; #202, 122–123; #204, 22, 71–72, 106–108, 122–123; #205, 21, 98; #206, 128; #207, 149–150; #209, 39, 51–52; #213, 51, 106–108; #218, 109–110; #222, 21; #223, 42–43; #225, 136–137, 197n15; #226, 21; #234, 65, 69, 98–98, 112
—"Greater Court Songs" cited: #235, 50–51, 74, 119; #236, 48–49; #237, 47, 88–89; #241, 48–49, 50–51, 58, 73–74, 119–120; #242, 45–47; #243, 45–47; #244, 45–47; #245, 39, 45, 47 ; #247, 85; #250, 108; #251, 45–47, 94–99; #252, 73, 166–167; #253–257, 75; #254, 71–73; #255, 34, 50; #256, 48–49, 74–75, 78–79; #257, 78–79; #260, 49, 51; #261, 89; #263, 52–53, 61–62, 65, 152–153
—"Ritual Hymns" cited: #270, 201n11; #273, 37–38; #285, 21; #286, 60–61, 111; #287, 60–61; #290, 52–53; #292, 21; #294, 21; #295, 21; #296, 37–38; #297, 35; #299, 106–108
Shun 舜, 5–6, 36–37, 91, 151, 184
Sima Qian 司馬遷
Sima Tan 司馬談, 132–137
Sima Xiangru 司馬相如, 158
Slingerland, Edward, 11
sound-symbolic binomes, 15, 26–27, 122
Spring and Autumn Annals. *See Annals*

Van Norden, Bryan W., 182
Verses of Chu (*Chuci* 楚辭), 14–15, 139–142
—sections cited: "Distant Roaming" (Yuan you 遠遊), 144, 156–157; "Lament for [a Broken] Oath" (Xi shi 惜誓), 156–157; "Lamenting My Lot" (Ai shi ming 哀時命), 145; "Mountain Spirit" (Shan gui 山鬼), 26–27; "Nine Changes" (Jiu bian 九變), 162; "Nine Laments" (Jiu tan 九歎), 145, 156–157, 159–161; "Nine Longings" (Jiu huai 九懷), 156–157, 163–164; "Nine Pieces" (Jiu zhang 九章), 145, 156–157, 161–162; "Nine Pinings" (Jiu si 九思), 156–157, 163–164; "Nine Songs" (Jiu ge 九歌), 145; "Parting's Sorrow" (Li sao 離騷), 139–156; "Seven Remonstrations" (Qi jian 七諫), 156–157, 163–164

Waley, Arthur, 8, 15, 43, 106
Wang Chong 王充, 177, 185–187
Wang Feng 王鳳, 173–175
Wang Guowei 王國維, 140
Wang Yi 王逸, 140–141, 150–151
Warring States, as Golden Age, 1, 10–12
water, 99–108, 142, 159–161, 185
Way. *See dao*
Western Zhou dynasty, 2–3, 36, 71, 81, 176
Whitehead, Alfred North, 189
wisdom: and anxiety (*you* 憂), 124–131; in the *Shi*, 73–79; and water, 99–108
wisdom, 77–78, 120

xiao 孝 (filial piety), 44, 60–61, 81, 92, 99–100, 135
xing 性 (human nature), 106–106, 171, 183–185
Xunzi 荀子, 10, 115, 142, 170–172, 182
—sections cited: chap. 6, 209n29; chap. 10, 100; chap. 23, 183–187; chap. 28, 103

Yang Xiong 揚雄, 140, 164–166, 177
Yao 堯, 91, 184
you 憂 (anxiety), 92, 98, 110, 113: controversy concerning, 121–131; in the *Shi*, 13–14, 44, 54–69, 82, 83; in Sima Qian's autobiography, 133–136; in the *Verses of Chu*, 145, 153–154, 157
Yu, Pauline, 6–7
Yuan Xingpei 袁行霈, 140

Zhao Qi 趙歧, 174, 185
Zheng Xuan 鄭玄, 18, 31, 43, 90
zheng 征 (campaign), 38, 61–63, 112–113, 134, 144–153
Zhuangzi 莊子, 10, 105, 115, 142, 170–172, 182, 192
—sections cited: chap. 1, 192; chap. 15, 127; chap. 33, 91–93, 209n29
zhuzi. *See Masters*
Zixia 子夏, 17–18, 95, 174, 186
Zuo Tradition (*Zuozhuan* 左傳)
—sections cited: Ai 5, 177–178; Ai 16, 110–111; Wen 13, 22–23; Xi 24, 85; Xiang 16, 23–24; Yin 1, 84–88; Zhao 3, 99–100

GPSR Authorized Representative: Easy Access System Europe, Mustamäe tee
50, 10621 Tallinn, Estonia, gpsr.requests@easproject.com

www.ingramcontent.com/pod-product-compliance
Lightning Source LLC
Chambersburg PA
CBHW021943290426
44108CB00012B/943